IMPROVING ORGANIZATIONAL SURVEYS

New Directions, Methods, and Applications

Paul Rosenfeld
Jack E. Edwards
Marie D. Thomas
editors

SAGE Publications
International Educational and Professional Publisher
Newbury Park   London   New Delhi

For information address:

 SAGE Publications, Inc.
2455 Teller Road
Newbury Park, California 91320

SAGE Publications Ltd.
6 Bonhill Street
London EC2A 4PU
United Kingdom

SAGE Publications India Pvt. Ltd.
M-32 Market
Greater Kailash I
New Delhi 110 048 India

Printed in the United States of America

Library of Congress Cataloging-in-Publication Data

Improving organizational surveys: new directions, methods, and
applications / edited by Paul Rosenfeld, Jack E. Edwards, Marie D.
Thomas.
    p.   cm.—(Sage focus editions; vol. 158)
    Includes bibliographical references and index.
    ISBN 0-8039-5193-0.—ISBN 0-8039-5194-9 (pbk.)
    1. Employee attitude surveys. I. Rosenfeld, Paul. II. Edwards,
Jack E. III. Thomas, Marie D.
    HF5549.5.A83I45   1993
    658.3′14—dc20   93-9488

93 94 95 96 10 9 8 7 6 5 4 3 2

Sage Production Editor: Tara S. Mead

Contents

Acknowledgments

In putting together *Improving Organizational Surveys*, we are indebted to a number of people for their professional and personal support. At Sage Publications, Harry Briggs has become a friend as well as an editor. At NPRDC, the support and encouragement of our supervisors Patricia Thomas and Richard Sorenson was greatly appreciated. Our NPRDC coworkers Stephanie Booth-Kewley, Carol Newell, and Dora Silva-Jalonen cheerfully put up with our grumblings and answered our pleas for assistance as deadlines approached. Also, we value the continued moral support and friendship of our current and former NPRDC colleagues: Catherine Riordan, Bob Giacalone, Elyse Kerce, Paul Magnusson, Danni Cranstoun, Walt Peterson, David Alderton, Brian Kewley, Jan Reynolds, Amy Culbertson, Ron Bearden, Linda Doherty, Zannette Perry, Darlene Davis, Dina Miyoshi, Thomas Trent, Darla Leithisher, John Kantor, Arneva Johnson, Bob Morrison, Sue Ryan, George Edward Seymour, and Ed Thomas. Finally, on a personal level, we would like to thank Mary Edwards, Harold Edwards, Jerry Larson, Barbara Rooney, Abraham and Judes Rosenfeld, the Shanskes, Mary Sellen, Edward Thomas, and Fred Thomas for their love, support, and encouragement.

Introduction

PAUL ROSENFELD
JACK E. EDWARDS
MARIE D. THOMAS

Surveys are part of our popular culture. From political polls predicting who the next president of the United States will be to consumer surveys to determine which new ice cream flavor is most popular, surveys reach out and touch everyone.

In fact, surveys are the most extensively used research method in the social sciences (Babbie, 1973). Although only one survey—the decennial census—is required by law (it is mentioned in the U.S. Constitution), it has been estimated that hundreds of thousands of surveys (and more than 30 million survey interviews) are conducted each year in the United States alone (Bradburn & Sudman, 1988). The popularity of surveys has also made them big business. In 1987, there were nearly 2,000 survey research firms in the United States earning about $2 billion (Stanton, 1989).

Although surveys are the most popular of social research techniques, they perhaps are also the most misunderstood. The explosion of daily polls of social attitudes and political preferences may make it seem that surveys only require writing questions and collecting answers. We and others who daily navigate the survey waters wish it were only so easy.

AUTHORS' NOTE: The opinions expressed are those of the authors. They are not official and do not represent the views of the Navy Department. The authors acknowledge the support of Patricia Thomas and Dr. Richard Sorenson. This chapter was written by government employees as part of official duties; therefore the material cannot be copyrighted and is in the public domain.

As is clear from the chapters in this book, surveys require much scientific knowledge and many practical skills—plus constant attention to updating and sharpening the survey researchers' "tool kit."

Organizational Surveys: The Power of the Few

Although surveys of voting preferences or social attitudes may receive the most popular attention, there has been a long history of survey use in organizational settings including private and public businesses, universities, and medical centers. Indeed, the federal government (for whom we work) is the single largest user of surveys (Bradburn & Sudman, 1988).

Surveys are popular in organizations because, when done properly, they can provide accurate information about major organizational issues. Often, answers affecting many personnel are solicited from the responses of relatively few people. One reason for the widespread use of organizational surveys stems from their adaptability. Because of this feature, organizational surveys can be used for such diverse purposes as measuring employee needs, obtaining consumers' opinions about the goods and services they receive, assessing employees' attitudes about the workplace, determining employee morale and motivation, assessing turnover intentions, and generating new ways of reducing costs and increasing profits (Nichols, 1989; Rosenfeld, Doherty, Vicino, Kantor, & Greaves, 1989; Schiemann, 1991). Organizational surveys also allow managers to monitor the effectiveness of new interventions (e.g., a Total Quality Management program; Miller, 1989-1990).

Organizational surveys appear to be gaining in popularity. Rosenfeld et al. (1989) noted, "The current emphasis in managerial training on employee involvement in decision making has led to a resurgence in the use of surveys, as managers need to better understand the attitudes, beliefs, and opinions of employees before making decisions that affect their working lives" (p. 146). One measure of this popularity comes from a Gallup (1988) survey conducted for *Personnel Journal*, which found that 70% of organizations had been involved in an employee attitude survey during the past decade. Almost 70% of companies surveyed indicated that they were likely to conduct another survey in the future.

In addition to providing organizations with useful information, organizational surveys can provide managers with a powerful motivational device. Surveys allow employees to feel part of the decision process—their views are important to management. This sense of empowerment may enhance employee motivation, organizational communication, and productivity (Guinn, 1990; Nichols, 1989; Schiemann, 1991).

Given the widespread role of organizational surveys, it is surprising that only a few treatises have addressed methodological concerns and practical applications—the science and the practice—of organizational surveys (see Howe & Gaeddert, 1991; Scarpello & Vandenberg, 1991; Schiemann, 1991). Improving the organizational survey process through linking the science and practice aspects is a goal of this book.

What Do We Do Now?

Although the three editors of this volume differ in many ways (e.g., task orientation, writing style, love of chocolate), we do share a common background. In previous lives, we all were academics. Now we are doing applied organizational research including organizational surveys. Our academic background gave us much that was essential to performing good research: statistics, sampling, data analysis, and an extreme fondness for long summer vacations. Despite our training in research methodology, however, when faced with the prospect of actually having to administer an organizational survey, our initial response was this: "What do we do now?!"

Given the complex nature of organizational surveys, certainly we were not the only ones asking, "What do we do now?" As the technology of surveys has rapidly advanced, there are many individuals who, despite their formal methodological training, need guidance about the new directions organizational surveys have taken. Similarly, because professionals in many academic and applied fields are contributing to improving survey methods, it is difficult for practitioners to know the latest advances in question writing (Edwards & Thomas, this volume), dealing with measurement errors (Dutka & Frankel, this volume), or asking sensitive questions (Hosseini & Armacost, this volume). Academics, on the other hand, may be unaware of government and military efforts to establish computer-based organizational survey systems (Booth-Kewley, Rosenfeld, & Edwards, this volume) or of civilian organization efforts to administer surveys through consortiums (Morris & LoVerde, this volume). As a result, the academic and practitioner approaches alone are not sufficient to successfully conduct organizational surveys. Through this edited book, we have attempted to bring together the methodology and practice of surveying in the hope that the organizational survey process will be improved.

This melding of method and practice in organizational surveys should provide information of interest to a diverse audience. In particular, *Improving Organizational Surveys* should be useful to (a) individuals charged with developing and administering organizational surveys, (b) managers and policymakers who use survey information, and (c) academics and graduate students who are interested in surveying in private and public sector organizations.

The chapters in this volume fall into three general categories. The chapters in Part I deal with method: how a survey is conducted, how to ask sensitive questions, and what to do about measurement error. The chapters in Part II consider new directions in organizational survey technology and practice. The final set, in Part III, deals with applications and practice: how organizational surveys are conducted in "real world" settings.

We start with the method—the nitty-gritty details that make up the survey process. Jack Edwards and Marie Thomas have provided a general step-by-step guide to conducting organizational surveys. Also, they give valuable pointers regarding the factors that must be considered at each step. Jamshid Hosseini and Robert Armacost consider issues related to asking sensitive and potentially embarrassing questions within surveys. They discuss the randomized response technique as one method of obtaining sensitive information. In the chapter by Solomon Dutka and Lester Frankel, the concept of measurement error is considered, particularly as it relates to marketing research.

We next turn to new directions in organizational surveys. The computer has revolutionized survey technology and two chapters discuss some of the changes computers have brought about. Stephanie Booth-Kewley, Paul Rosenfeld, and Jack Edwards compare and contrast computer and other organizational survey administration methods. While focusing on the advantages and disadvantages of computer administration of surveys, they provide a guide to alternative methods of survey administration and review the literature comparing computer-administered questionnaires to more traditional modes of administration. Richard Dunnington adds to the Booth-Kewley et al. and Edwards and Thomas chapters by providing information about and evaluations of the technology available for creating, analyzing, and administering surveys.

At times, it is not feasible for an organization to develop and conduct its own surveys on a regular basis. Gary Morris and Mark LoVerde discuss an alternative—the consortium—in which related organizations band together to create an instrument and survey process that the individual organizations would not be able to produce alone. Part III of *Improving Organizational Surveys* focuses on applications and practice. The first two chapters describe the application of organizational surveys to highly visible military issues: pregnancy, parenthood, and sexual harassment. Marie Thomas and Pat Thomas (no relation) review their multiyear survey program assessing pregnancy and parenthood among active-duty Navy personnel. Amy Culbertson and Paul Rosenfeld describe lessons they have learned from conducting several large-scale organizational surveys of sexual harassment.

As these two chapters indicate, issues relating to the overall quality of the work environment have become important organizational considerations. Elyse Kerce and Stephanie Booth-Kewley review the definitional, methodological, and practical aspects of conducting an organizational quality of work life survey. Because the quality of life at work may be affected by the cultural diversity of the work force, organizations may need to determine the equal opportunity climate perceived by their employees. Dan Landis, Mickey Dansby, and Robert Faley describe the development and implementation of the Military Equal Opportunity Climate Survey as an example of how organizations can assess the increasingly important diversity issues.

Appropriately, the final chapter addresses the exit survey—the last survey an employee is likely to complete. Bob Giacalone and Stephen Knouse's chapter on applications of exit surveying to security issues nobly serves this "last but not least" function.

Although conducting a well-written, well-administered organizational survey can be a difficult task, it is also very rewarding. Survey designers and administrators have the satisfaction of seeing a need for information turn into items; these items return as data and, after analysis and interpretation, they provide answers to the original questions. For respondents, organizational surveys provide a place to address their concerns and questions. It is our hope that the questions and concerns that organizational researchers and practitioners have will likewise be addressed by the chapters in *Improving Organizational Surveys*.

References

Babbie, E. R. (1973). *Survey research methods.* Belmont, CA: Wadsworth.

Bradburn, N., & Sudman, S. (1988). *Polls and surveys: Understanding what they tell us.* San Francisco: Jossey-Bass.

Gallup, G. (1988). Employee research: From nice to know to need to know. *Personnel Journal, 67,* 42-43.

Guinn, S. L. (1990). Surveys capture untold story. *HR Magazine, 35,* 64-66.

Howe, M. A., & Gaeddert, D. (1991). Customer survey research: Extending the partnership. In J. W. Jones, B. D. Steffy, & D. W. Bray (Eds.), *Applying psychology in business: The handbook for managers and human resource professionals* (pp. 640-652). Lexington, MA: Lexington.

Miller, R. E. (1989). The design and implementation of employee opinion surveys. *Employment Relations Today, 16,* 315-319.

Nichols, D. (1989). Bottom-up strategies: Asking the employees for advice. *Management Review, 78,* 44-49.

Rosenfeld, P., Doherty, L., Vicino, S. M., Kantor, J., & Greaves, J. (1989). Attitude assessment in organizations: Testing three microcomputer-based survey systems. *Journal of General Psychology, 116,* 145-154.

Scarpello, V., & Vandenberg, R. J. (1991). Some issues to consider when surveying employee opinions. In J. W. Jones, B. D. Steffy, & D. W. Bray (Eds.), *Applying psychology in business: The handbook for managers and human resource professionals* (pp. 611-622). Lexington, MA: Lexington.

Schiemann, W. A. (1991). Using employee surveys to increase organizational effectiveness. In J. W. Jones, B. D. Steffy, & D. W. Bray (Eds.), *Applying psychology in business: The handbook for managers and human resource professionals* (pp. 623-639). Lexington, MA: Lexington.

Stanton, M. (1989). Reporting what we think: The pollsters. *Occupational Outlook Quarterly, 33,* 12-19.

PART I

Methodological Issues

1

The Organizational Survey Process

General Steps and Practical Considerations

JACK E. EDWARDS
MARIE D. THOMAS

The reader of this book will quickly conclude that conducting an organizational survey efficiently and effectively requires detailed planning. To that end, this chapter provides an outline of the general steps common to most organizational surveys, whatever the purpose in conducting the survey. This chapter is written primarily for the person who has little experience conducting surveys and is faced with the need to learn quickly. This chapter, however, is not meant to be a guide for someone who has had *no* experience in conducting a survey. The complicated survey process cannot be explained in one short chapter.

Throughout the chapter, references are provided for additional information regarding issues in the survey process. In addition, the other chapters in this book cover specific aspects of the survey process in greater detail. The reader interested in learning more about the various aspects of the survey process is directed to books such as Rossi, Wright, and Anderson's (1983) *Handbook of Survey Research*, Alreck and Settle's (1985) *The Survey Research Handbook*, Converse and Presser's

AUTHORS' NOTE: The opinions expressed in this chapter are those of the authors. They are not official and do not represent the views of the Department of the Navy. This chapter was written by government employees as part of official duties; therefore the material cannot be copyrighted and is in the public domain.

(1986) *Survey Questions*, Fowler's (1988) *Survey Research Methods*, Bradburn and Sudman's (1988) *Polls and Surveys*, Fowler and Mangione's (1990) *Standardized Survey Interviewing*, Henry's (1990) *Practical Sampling*, and Devellis's (1991) *Scale Development.*

The survey process is complex, time-consuming, and expensive. There are several reasons for this conclusion. First, many survey steps require specialized knowledge and skills. Second, an urgent need for a particular type of information might suggest that an organization does not have adequate time for survey development. Third, the cost of developing a survey in-house may be prohibitive for small or medium-sized organizations.

Organizations have alternatives to developing and conducting a survey entirely in-house. One alternative is for organizations needing similar information to band together in a consortium and jointly underwrite the expense of developing a survey (see Morris & LoVerde, this volume). A second alternative would be to administer an off-the-shelf survey using in-house staff. With this alternative, an organization saves survey development time and avoids the cost of having external experts. A more expensive, but probably more immediate, alternative would be to hire an external consultant to administer the survey and provide feedback on the results.

Variations of these survey development and administration strategies provide additional options. Thus an organization can choose the strategy that fits its needs and budget. One major factor to be considered is the advantage of in-house versus off-the-shelf surveys. The survey developed specifically for use within a given organization can be tailored to meet the special needs of that organization. On the other hand, the psychometric characteristics (e.g., reliability and validity) of off-the-shelf instruments often exceed the characteristics found in home-grown organizational surveys. Also, off-the-shelf instruments are more likely to have norms. Norms allow an organization to compare itself against other organizations, possibly within the same industry.

Regardless of the approach taken, the steps in conducting a survey fall into five general phases. In the first phase, members of the organization identify the purpose(s) of the assessment, decide if a survey is the most effective method for accomplishing the organization's objective(s), and design a plan for conducting the survey (if a survey is deemed desirable). If a survey is desirable, a survey coordinator and/or survey team develops the survey during the second phase. (The term "survey team" will be used hereafter.) In the survey administration phase, the team identifies respondents and conducts the survey. In the fourth phase, data are entered into a computer, verified, and analyzed. The last stage involves feeding the results of the survey back to customers.

Phase 1: Presurvey Issues

Purpose of Survey

There are many reasons for administering an organizational survey. A few examples include diagnosing the sources of organizational problems (e.g., a high rate of absenteeism or turnover), obtaining frequency or importance information regarding an employee's duties (e.g., a task inventory), assessing potential customers' preferences for various goods and services (e.g., deciding what features to add to a new line of electronic testing equipment), or measuring key work-related attitudes on specific topics (e.g., potential incentive programs, alternative work schedules, recreational activities, and gender and race/ethnic issues related to a diverse work force). Different purposes suggest a need for organizational decision makers to determine whether a survey or another method is the optimum procedure for gathering the required information.

Is a Survey the Best Method for Gathering Data?

Although surveys are often the most effective and efficient means for gathering organizational information, the survey team should consider the relative advantages and disadvantages of all data-gathering methods before beginning instrument construction. For example, if few employees are to be the source of the data, it may be easier to interview each person. Similarly, providing an opinion box for anonymous suggestions might be a better means for gathering some information especially if the desired information is sensitive or rare. Once it has been decided (a) why data need to be gathered, (b) that a survey is the best vehicle for obtaining that information, and (c) whether the survey should be developed and conducted in-house, plans with deadlines can be developed for conducting the survey.

Planning a Survey

Figure 1.1 shows a 13-step strategy for conducting a survey totally in-house. If an organization decides to use consultants or external

Phase/Step	Nonpersonnel Cost ($)	1	2	3	4	5	6	7	8	9	10	11	12
Phase 1: Presurvey issues													
Phase 2: Survey construction													
Obtain content information													
Write items													
Pretest items													
Develop final survey instrument													
Obtain organizational approval of instrument													
Phase 3: Survey administration													
Select the respondents													
Prepare and distribute the surveys													
Await returns and mail return reminders													
Phase 4: Data entry and analysis													
Enter and verify the data													
Write and correct statistical analysis programs													
Run the analyses and interpret the results													
Phase 5: Presentation of findings													
Present the findings													
Write a report													

Month of the Survey Process

Figure 1.1. Five-Phase, 13-Step In-House Survey Procedure

6

materials for part of the survey process, the 13 steps offer reminders regarding the concerns and tasks to be considered at each point. Similarly, the steps can assist decision makers as they determine which steps to perform under contract.

Readers can use Figure 1.1 to plan an organizational survey and a time line for accomplishing each step. In several instances, the time lines for steps will overlap. For example, a survey team can write statistical analysis programs and portions of the report during the period between distribution and return of the surveys. Working simultaneously on several steps allows the survey process to be accomplished in the shortest possible time. Different survey purposes, organization sizes, administration methods, and so on prevent us from offering general time lines. Each survey will be somewhat different.

Phase 2: Survey Construction

Obtain Content Information

With each different purpose comes a different domain of potential organizational survey dimensions and items. Thus a first task for a survey team is to identify the full range of dimensions that will be used when writing the survey items. Interviews with subject matter experts or job incumbents, critical incidents documented in performance evaluations, job analyses, findings from earlier surveys in the same organization, and literature reviews are useful techniques for identifying the dimensions to be included in an organizational survey.

Write Items

The Items Themselves

Items are the basis of all surveys. As a result, the rigor that is required when developing items cannot be overemphasized. Any absence in rigor during item generation may result in later adverse consequences that will not be correctable. Therefore, the best prescription for developing an effective and efficient survey is to do it right the first time. Miller's (1991) and Fowler's (1988) books provide very good general guides to questionnaire construction.

Demographic items (i.e., items that provide descriptive information about each respondent) are needed for almost any survey. The survey team will determine which demographics to collect by examining what types of subgroup analyses are needed. For example, an organization doing a cultural diversity survey may be interested in the attitudes of subgroups broken down by gender, race, and level in the organizational hierarchy. Several authors (e.g., Frey, 1989; Miller, 1991) have recommended that demographic items be placed at the end of the survey.

A warning: If too much demographic data are requested, respondents may be suspicious about whether their answers are anonymous. Such suspicions can negatively affect return rates and respondent honesty and candidness, especially if the information requested is sensitive (e.g., substance abuse or sexual harassment).

Grammatical Issues in Item Writing

A method for ensuring that everyone will interpret the items as they are meant to be interpreted is to write in *short, simple, declarative sentences*. Another method is to write with *everyday language*, avoiding words that are not used in general speaking. One exception to this rule is that it is often advisable to use the jargon of the organization if all respondents are familiar with such terms. Fowler (1992) underscores the importance of writing clear, unambiguous items by demonstrating the bias in survey estimates that results when respondents are required to interpret unclear terminology. In addition, Schuman and Presser's (1981) book, *Questions and Answers in Attitude Scales: Experiments on Question Form, Wording, and Context*, provides other considerations for the item writer.

Readability Level

One such consideration is determining the readability level of the survey. Readability analyses determine the average grade level of schooling that someone will need to read and understand what is written. Among other things, such analyses might examine sentence and word length and the number of sentences per paragraph. Thus this type of analysis examines the words and how they are used together rather than how respondents answered the questions.

Until recently, readability analysis required special computer programs or hand scoring. Now, inexpensive programs that work with standard word processing software (e.g., Grammatik 5) include readability analyses. To illustrate, the readability level of this chapter is between the 11th and 13th grades. That is, someone with a reading level less than that of the average high school graduate would probably have difficulty reading this chapter.

When constructing Navy surveys, we attempt to keep the reading level low—around the level of seventh or eighth graders. This caution is used even though 99% of Navy enlisted personnel have at least a high school education and almost all Navy officers have at least a baccalaureate degree. Keeping the readability level low increases the likelihood that respondents will need to use little interpretation in answering the questions.

Rating Scales and Categorical Alternatives

The content of a survey determines the response format (i.e., the way in which items and answers are displayed). If suggestions are being sought or a survey team does not have firm ideas about what the answers will be, the answer format should be open-ended. That is, a respondent is asked to write a narrative answer. If a survey team has some ideas about the general answers that will be supplied, it will probably be useful to supply the respondent with a prespecified list of categorical alternatives (e.g., pay, vacation time, types of insurance, etc., might be alternatives for a question asking the respondent to identify what is the best incentive for working in the organization). All possible alternatives should be listed. If this cannot be done, a space for "other" answers should be included. The major advantage of a prespecified list is that the data will not need to be coded into categories later. Such postsurvey coding is often time consuming and costly and may add error if an assistant codes the information differently than the respondent would have.

If quantitative information is sought, the respondent can supply numbers or use any of a variety of rating scales. Although research has been performed to learn if one rating scale is better than another and how many points a rating scale should have, there is no consensus on this issue. Trite as it may sound, the best rule is to use the number of points and scale anchors that make sense.

One of the most commonly employed rating scales for attitude measurement uses five points. This Likert-format rating scale is anchored with adjectives that allow the respondent to describe how much he or she agrees or disagrees with an item. The points and anchors for such a rating scale are typically 1 = *strongly disagree*, 2 = *disagree*, 3 = *neither agree nor disagree*, 4 = *agree*, and 5 = *strongly agree*. Some organizations may want to force a respondent to agree or disagree. If this is the case, a rating scale with no midpoint or midpoint anchor would be used. Using a scale (i.e., continuum) without a midpoint can, however, also cause problems. A respondent may be forced to respond positively or negatively when the individual's attitude is really neutral regarding the issue being addressed. Sheatsley (1983) offers information about other rating scale formats for surveys.

Positively and Negatively Worded Items

One popular technique for minimizing response bias is to include both positively and negatively worded items when measuring a particular dimension. The respondent's answers to negatively worded items are then reverse scored. Underlying this procedure is an assumption that acquiescence or positive response bias (i.e., the tendency to agree with items) will be minimized by forcing a respondent to use both ends of a rating scale.

Although this process may avoid a *systematic* error, it may add *unsystematic* error. This unsystematic error may be caused by at least two problems. First, a negative answer to a negatively worded statement may not be equivalent to the positive answer to a positively worded statement. For example, disagreeing with the statement "My work is not meaningful" does not necessarily mean that the same individual would have agreed with the statement "My work is meaningful." Second, forcing a person to disagree with a negative statement may confuse respondents.

Reverse-scored items can cause an artificial "dimension" to appear (in a factor-analytic solution) when as few as 10% of the respondents fail to notice that a few of the items are opposite in meaning (i.e., negatively rather than positively worded) from the other items (Schmitt & Stults, 1985). Such an artificial "dimension" is less likely for respondents who have high levels of education and better reading ability (Fried & Ferris, 1986, as cited in Idaszak & Drasgow, 1987).

Other Item Issues

This chapter cannot go into depth about all of the decisions that must be made when writing items. Other considerations include whether questions should be direct or indirect, general or specific, and personal or impersonal. In addition, care must be taken to avoid writing biased or leading questions, or items that are unintentionally offensive to respondents. Miller (1991) has provided examples of appropriate and inappropriate items.

Survey Length

Each survey dimension should contain multiple items, but the length of the survey cannot be limitless. Often, it is very easy to add dimensions and items. Eventually, a survey would become so long that respondents would not complete it, even if they can do so on company time. If nonmembers of the organization (e.g., potential customers) are required to respond to the survey voluntarily on their own time, a long survey will almost surely have a lower response rate (i.e., the proportion of surveys returned) than a short survey.

Several factors determine the length of a survey. The time and cost for a respondent to complete the survey is an important consideration. Whenever we administer a Navy survey, we are required to compute the cost of respondents' time. Another issue influencing survey length is the nature and purpose of the survey. A survey measuring the prevalence of workplace sexual harassment might be contained on the front and back of a single page. If the purpose is defined more broadly as an assessment of equal opportunity, the survey might be 5-10 times as long and assess multiple dimensions. A few of the many other considerations are whether the survey (a) requires time for writing narrative answers, (b) is to be completed by organization members or external respondents, and (c) is influenced by situational concerns such as an immediate need for information on specific issues.

Pretest Items

Increasing the Reliability of Measurement

Reliability is a measurement property that shows how consistently a dimension is measured. There are three types of reliability. Internal consistency reliability indicates the degree to which all items in a given dimension measure a common factor. Test-retest reliability assesses the degree to which respondents could be expected to have the same dimension score from one time to another. The third type of reliability, alternate forms reliability, is probably of little interest to the survey developer as the organization will develop only one version of a survey. Alternate forms reliability indicates the degree to which respondents' scores would vary from, say, Form A to Form B of a survey. Murphy and Davidshofer's (1991) book is an excellent source for more information on reliability and its measurement.

There are three steps during the preadministration phase that will increase the reliability of dimension scores. These three steps are writing multiple items for each dimension, determining whether other organizational members would assign an item to the same dimension for which it was written, and grouping all items from a single dimension together.

For most surveys, *multiple items* should be used to measure each dimension. The multiple items allow the respondent to express different concerns about the various aspects of a single dimension. For example, the dimension "satisfaction with compensation" might include at least one item each to measure satisfaction with pay; annual, sick, and holiday leave policies; health and life insurance; and so on. If, however, a survey is to be completed by someone outside the organization (e.g., a customer at a hotel or restaurant), single-item dimensions would probably be more appropriate. Although single-item dimensions are not as good as multiple-item dimensions in terms of reliability, a short survey with several single-item dimensions is more likely to be completed than is a longer survey.

Once the items have been written, it is a good idea to determine whether the items measure the intended dimensions. This step could be accomplished by randomizing the items into a checklist format and preparing definitions of the dimensions. Two or three survey team members would then indicate (in the margin) to which dimension each item belonged. Later, the survey team would determine which items were inconsistently assigned to a given dimension. Those items would be eliminated or rewritten to fit the dimension better.

For attitude surveys, we generally advocate placing all of the items that measure a single dimension into a homogeneous module.[1] This grouping of items makes it easier for the respondent to determine what the survey is attempting to measure.

Experimental Administration of the Preliminary Survey

Preliminary to the actual survey administration is deciding how information will be obtained from the respondents. Surveys can be administered using any of five common methods: paper and pencil, scanner (bubble) sheets, computers, telephones, and personal interviews (see Booth-Kewley, Rosenfeld, & Edwards [this volume] for a description of these methods and a review of the relative advantages of each method). The experimental administration of the preliminary survey should use the administration method that will be used in the full-scale administration.

Accomplishment of all tasks to this point has resulted in a preliminary survey. The survey team now administers the organizational survey to a very small sample of people, perhaps 20 people who are representative of the respondents who will be surveyed later. This pretest has several goals. First, the respondents will be asked to tell how long the survey took to complete. This issue is often addressed when the survey team seeks final management approval for the survey. Second, the respondents are asked to comment about the content of the survey, the phrasing of the items, rating scales, instructions, the display of the information in the survey, and other concerns that came to mind when completing the survey. The survey team modifies the survey based on the comments and possibly the statistical findings of the responses to the items. Even the most well-designed organizational survey should be pretested. There are often unanticipated responses that may require changes.

Obtain Organizational Approval of Instrument

Although this step should be perfunctory, it can be long and torturous. It is assumed that the survey team has been providing intermittent updates to management and obtaining information from people to develop the survey items and dimensions. Such tasks require at least informal approval to be accomplished. Formal approval may be an entirely different matter. Sometimes, it appears as if everyone in the organization needs to approve the instrument formally. Furthermore, when one group makes changes, the survey may need to be rereviewed by others who approved an earlier version. Three types of players—top management, institutional review boards, and unions—are particularly important at this formal approval stage.

Top Management

Higher-level management decided that a survey was needed. Also, they have probably been given progress reports as tasks on the survey plan have been completed. These implicit approvals of early steps are not equivalent to approval for the final survey or the administration plan once they are presented in their "final" forms. Morris and LoVerde (this volume) discuss some of the problems that can occur when higher-level management seeks to change survey items.

Institutional Review Boards (IRBs)

IRBs exist to protect the rights (e.g., privacy) of the respondents or subjects in data-gathering exercises/experiments. Many organizations (e.g., universities and military personnel research centers) require that all experiments and formal data gathering be coordinated with their IRBs. If the items have no justification (e.g., a survey team member thinks that it might be useful for some future but unidentified project), permission to gather the data might not be granted. At such times, survey team members may view an IRB as a nuisance, but potential respondents might value the concern expressed by IRB members.

The following example illustrates how an IRB balances the needs of the surveyor and the respondent. One of the authors of this chapter sought IRB approval to gather data that would be used in a doctoral student's dissertation. A member of the university IRB wanted the student to leave selected items out of a widely used personality inventory. The IRB member thought some items would elicit bad memories for handicapped respondents. After explaining that (a) the instrument had been administered to tens of thousands of respondents, (b) leaving out items would preclude the use of the dimension norms, and (c) all of the dimensions were important to the study, the IRB permitted the use of the full instrument.

Unions

If at least some of the respondents are unionized, the survey coordinator may need to seek input from union representatives. The input may be required as part of the labor-management contract. Alternatively, an organization with a good working relationship with its union(s) may notify the union representative as a matter of courtesy.

One of the authors had a problem when conducting a survey at 30 sites located across the United States. Some unions approved the survey instrument whereas others did not. After many telephone conversations, all of the unions agreed to allow their members to participate. This incident highlights the fact that the objections of a single union may delay data gathering.

Develop the Final Survey Instrument

Survey revisions resulting from the experimental administration and approval steps are often minor. These revisions may, however, require time, especially when seeking high-level approval. During the slow periods in these stages, the survey team should have begun finalizing arrangements for the actual administration.

Phase 3: Survey Administration

For the survey administration section, many of the examples involve the most common administration method—standard paper and pencil. Our concentration on this administration method should not be a problem for survey teams that use other methods. Regardless of method, administration requires three general steps: selecting the respondents, preparing and distributing the survey, and awaiting returns and reminding the potential respondents to complete their surveys.

Select the Respondents

Among other concerns, the choice of respondents will depend on the purpose of the survey, the cost of obtaining data, and the availability of respondents. The general classes of survey participants might include one or more of the following groups: organization members, potential or actual customers, and recognized experts in a given occupational field. (In addition to the basic sampling issues presented below, the reader might wish to consult Kalton's [1983] *Introduction to Survey Sampling* or Henry's [1990] *Practical Sampling* for additional information on sampling.)

Sample Versus Population

Before administering a survey, the survey team must decide whether to survey everyone in or only a part (i.e., a sample) of a relevant population. If an organization is very small, a census would probably be desirable. In small organizations, the opinions of each individual have relatively more weight than the opinions of a single individual in a larger organization. Also, as sample sizes get progressively smaller, it becomes more likely that *sampling error* will influence the results. Sampling error is a measure of the degree to which a statistic from a sample can be expected to vary from the value that would have been obtained if data were gathered from the population.

If a sample is to be surveyed, a question arises as to which individuals to pick for the survey. If the sample is unrepresentative of the population, erroneous conclusions will probably be drawn (i.e., sampling error will be high). In the classic example of a biased sample, a 1936 political poll predicted that Franklin Roosevelt would lose a presidential election that he won by a landslide. In that instance, surveys were mailed to 10 million households that were listed in telephone directories or state automobile registries; of these, 2.4 million surveys were completed and returned (Bradburn & Sudman, 1988). In large part, the very different opinions of affluent potential voters (i.e., people who could afford telephones and automobiles during the Depression) versus the general U.S. population led to erroneous prediction.

One large U.S. firm has a unique method that uses sampling to obtain "census" information. The firm administers the same attitude survey every year, but in any given year, employees from only one third of its stores are surveyed. Thus information is obtained at each store every third year. This procedure maintains up-to-date information on every organizational unit, minimizes survey cost for conducting a census, and avoids the concerns that might arise if an organization administers a survey only when a problem is perceived.

Method of Sampling

Henry (1990) identified five types of sampling: simple random, systematic, stratified, cluster, and multistage. Simple random and systematic sampling are the easiest methods to use. With simple random, everyone in the survey population has the same probability to be chosen. The actual choices regarding who will be administered a survey can be accomplished with statistical packages that randomly assign a different number to everyone in the population and then select people based on their number. For the systematic sampling method, every nth person from a list is selected.

The stratified method is also frequently employed. To use this method, each individual is assigned to a group according to some set of relevant characteristics (e.g., organizational level, male versus female, type of job, and remote office versus headquarters). A specified number of people will then be selected randomly from each group. The variables used in the stratification will vary according to the organization, purpose of the survey, and so on. Sometimes, it is desirable to *oversample* members of some groups. For example, in Navy-wide surveys, black women are usually oversampled to decrease sampling error for this relatively small group. In other instances, it is desirable to oversample groups who are less likely to respond. For many surveys, individuals at lower organizational levels are less likely to respond to a survey. To offset this lower response rate (and higher probability of large sampling error), surveys can be distributed to more people at the lower levels to get back the same number of surveys for both the lower- and higher-level groups. Besides providing more accurate statistics for the subgroups, the data from the subgroups can be weighted to develop representative statistics for the entire sample.

The two other methods of sampling identified by Henry (1990) are variations of the three methods just reviewed. For cluster sampling, individuals are assigned to a group or cluster. All members of a cluster are then either selected or not selected randomly. Finally, multistage sampling requires the formation of clusters and the random sampling of individuals from the clusters. The clustering in the multistage sampling can be done at more than one level of grouping.

Prepare and Distribute the Survey

Most of the tasks in this step should have been arranged during an earlier step in the survey process. These tasks often require coordination with people in other departments or external organizations. The tasks included below are basic to most surveys; other tasks might be included, depending on the specific situation:

1. Logistical arrangements must be made. Conducting a large-scale survey might require special orders of supplies and a place to store them.
2. The survey must be duplicated. The method of copying will determine the amount of lead time necessary. For example, customized scanner sheets may require several weeks for production, whereas plain photocopying would probably require much less time.
3. Survey packets must be assembled. If the survey is to be administered by mail, each packet should include a mailing envelope, the survey, and a preaddressed return envelope. Furthermore, address labels may need to be

printed for each envelope, and postage must be affixed to (or printed on) each mail-out and return envelope (especially for surveys going to respondents outside the organization).

4. The organization mailroom may desire to save money by presorting and bundling the surveys by ZIP code. Much of the personnel time here can be saved by sorting the addresses with a computer before printing them (if the addresses are computerized).

Await Returns and Mail Follow-Up Notices

Approximately 3 weeks to 1 month after a mail-out survey, follow-up notices should be sent to all potential respondents if the survey was to be completed anonymously. These reminders increase the return rate.

Alternatives to Survey Distribution Methods

If the survey is being conducted in-house, company mail can be used for distribution, especially if all organization members are in a single location. Alternatively, surveys could be administered to groups of respondents who assemble in a single room. This method would probably result in a higher response rate than would mail-out surveying. A potential disadvantage of this method could be a perceived lack of anonymity if a "boss" or his or her designate is the one overseeing the organizational survey administration.

If the organization has multiple locations, a point of contact could administer the survey to members in groups or distribute and collect surveys at each group. Another alternative is to administer the survey with computers. This method can use personal computers (a) stored in a location that has to be visited by respondents or (b) connected to a central computer or bulletin board (see Booth-Kewley et al., this volume).

Phase 4: Data Entry and Analysis

Enter and Verify Data

During the early survey planning process, the survey team should have decided who will be responsible for data entry and verification. This issue is avoided with some survey administration methods such as computers and scanner sheets (see Booth-Kewley et al., this volume). If data must be entered following the survey administration, the people involved will likely include members of the survey team and their clerical assistants, employees from the organization's data processing department, or external contractors. It is seldom cost-beneficial to use the survey team for data entry as they probably do not possess the clerical skills required to enter data quickly. Also, their skills and organizational levels are probably such that the organization should be expecting more than data entry for their salaries.

Early planning will increase the likelihood that an organization's own data processing department can arrange to enter the data. If the data are personal and the respondents can be identified from answers to the questions, external contractors might be a better alternative. It must be made clear to whomever is responsible for data entry that 100% verification of data is required. Even with the most careful data entry personnel, occasional errors can be expected.

A data entry horror story highlights what can go wrong at this step. A federal agency once asked for bids for data entry. Because of a federal law, the contract was to be completed by inmates at a prison in the same state. Despite a contract specification of 99% accuracy, more than 50% of the data from the initial forms was entered incorrectly. The completion of the project was delayed as a result of canceling that contract and issuing a new one.

Coding and Entering Open-Ended Data

The information given in this section thus far has assumed that all of the data were categorical, rating scale based, or simple counts. Entering and coding narrative information, such as comments, is much more labor intensive (Geer, 1991). However, narrative information mixed with items containing precoded answers often compensates the company for the added costs of coding and entering the data. Narrative information adds flesh to the sometimes sterile numbers and deductions that are drawn from precoded qualitative information or quantitative data. Numbers alone often do not tell the whole story (Geer, 1991). Narrative data provide suggestions for management and material for future surveys.

The first step in analyzing narrative information is to sort the comments using any of several criteria. For some questions, the comments might be sorted along a favorableness-unfavorableness continuum. In other cases, the comments might be sorted according to the content of the comments. Frequently, such sorting would be done on a subset of the returned surveys. A coding scheme would then be designed for each question eliciting narrative information. All of the comments from all the surveys would be coded before the narrative and quantitative data are entered into the computer.

Dealing With Missing Data

Whenever respondents leave selected items unanswered, they cause analysis problems. The problems involve questions about why the items were not answered and how the items should be scored. An item might be left blank for several reasons:

- The respondent simply forgot to answer the question.
- The question was not relevant for the respondent.
- The question was of such a personal nature that the respondent did not wish to share the information.
- The respondent was concerned about the retribution that might occur if his or her answer and name were linked.
- Responding to the question would have required a long answer that the respondent did not have the time to provide.

This partial list of reasons highlights the fact that very different motives may cause a respondent to leave an item unanswered. Survey planning can provide ways to minimize the number of nonresponses. Some ways in which nonresponding can be minimized are by allowing the respondent to answer the items anonymously, keeping the survey length to a minimum, providing a precoded categorical response of "not applicable/don't know," and providing precoded response categories so that a respondent can answer an item with a single mark rather than with a narrative answer.

A data analyst will rarely be able to learn why an item has been left blank. As a result, all nonresponses for a given item will probably be assigned the same missing value code. Items that have a larger number of nonresponses than do other items should be examined for potential nonresponse reasons. If very sensitive questions have a higher nonresponse rate, such a finding may suggest that respondents have fears about what the organization will do to them if they answer honestly.

Missing data are especially a problem when dimension scores are computed. For instance, a respondent answers each of the 10 satisfaction-with-supervision dimension items with a "1" (*strongly disagree*) on a 5-point scale. Another respondent answers only 2 of the same 10 questions, for which the respondent assigns a "5" (*strongly agree*). If a dimension mean or total score were taken without regard for the number of items answered, both respondents would have the same mean score of 1.0. It is, however, very unlikely that the two respondents would be describing the same degree of (dis)satisfaction with supervision. There is no single right answer on how to treat missing data. This section was written only as a caution to analysts.

Write and Correct the Statistical Analysis Programs

In many cases, the statistical analyses can probably be performed on a personal computer. Common data base management programs (e.g., Excel and Lotus 1-2-3) have subroutines that compute most, if not all, of the statistics that are required to analyze survey information. If more complex analyses (e.g., reliabilities) are required, special statistical programs (e.g., SPSS-X and SAS) can be used. In either case, an analyst is no longer faced with the intimidating task of writing computer programs in specialized language, such as FORTRAN or COBOL.

To use time optimally, the analysis programs can be written, tested, and corrected in the period between the survey's finalization and the time at which data are entered into the computer. This efficient use of time can speed the survey process to its end more quickly than if the programs are written after the data are entered.

Run the Analyses and Interpret the Results

Overall and Subgroup Analyses

As was suggested in the section on sampling, organizations usually want information on their various subgroups in addition to findings pertaining to the full organization. When these subgroup analyses are conducted, care must be exercised to protect the respondent. If the subgroup analyses are broken into very small groups, it might be possible for the answers given by an individual respondent to be identified. To avoid retribution and other problems, many surveying firms have a general rule that they will not provide analyses that result in less than eight respondents per subgroup. Providing this degree of anonymity should enhance the probability that respondents will give honest answers. Another reason for not computing statistics on small groups is that the estimates from the sample can be

negative feedback to respondents, providing quick and accurate feedback is one way to reinforce future survey efforts. Respondents who spend time completing surveys they never hear about again might be reluctant when called on to complete a later survey.

Presenting the Findings

Survey findings are generally presented orally and/or as a written report. Whatever the form of feedback, the following format, which is based on the style developed by the American Psychological Association (1983) might be followed. The degree of detail within each category will depend on the audience to whom the findings are being presented. In our Navy work, we often write detailed reports of our survey findings. Our briefings to sponsors are generally less "dense," focusing only on the highlights of the survey process—more a "management report" than a research paper.

Background/Introduction

This section should discuss why the survey was conducted. Details might include such topics as conditions, problems, or questions that led to the decision to conduct the survey, who requested the survey, and information about previous findings in the survey subject area. Also, the objectives of the project should be stated explicitly.

Method

The method section should describe who was surveyed, the development of the survey, and the procedure used to conduct it.[2] The sample section will include a description of how people were selected to receive the survey (e.g., census, random sample, stratified sample), how many surveys were administered, and how many were returned (response rate). In addition, important demographic characteristics of the survey respondents should be summarized (e.g., numbers of men and women, mean age, frequency count of personnel in different work centers), if these demographics are important for interpretation of the results.

The development of the survey should then be described. If standardized scales were used, it may be useful to discuss why the particular scales were chosen and to present reliabilities. If the survey was developed in-house, a presentation of the findings should include definitions of the dimensions, a description of why particular dimensions were chosen, how items were written (e.g., Did the survey team write all the items? Did they solicit items from different departments?), and how the survey was pretested.

Finally, the procedures used to administer the survey (e.g., paper and pencil, computers, etc.) should be discussed.

For most oral presentations, the method section will be brief because the focus will be on results. In written reports, the method section is more important. The method section in the written report should be detailed to the extent that someone reading the report could replicate the survey using only the information from the report.

Results

This section consists of a presentation of findings from the obtained data. The format and depth of the presentation will depend on the audience and purpose. In our Navy briefings, the focus is usually on answering the questions that prompted the original research (e.g., what percentage of Navy women are pregnant at a given point in time?). Our analyses are generally simple; for example, we might present the percentages of people falling into different categories, such as marital status. We often use tables and figures to illustrate the results. For much of our work, statistics and significance tests are not appropriate and might not be understood fully by some of our audience. Morris and LoVerde (this volume) note that their consortium uses a similar level of simplicity when reporting findings. So, know your audience! Tailor your presentation to their interests, needs, and level of sophistication.

Discussion, Conclusions, and Recommendations

The final section of any presentation or report should discuss how the obtained results relate to the original purpose of the survey. If the results suggest a course of action, such conclusions would be discussed at this time. Some general topics to cover might include the following: What overall conclusions can be drawn from the survey results? What questions remain unanswered? Were there problems in the survey process, and how might they be avoided in the future? What is the next step to take?

The organizational policymakers who authorized the survey will expect more than just numbers—they will expect answers to the organizational concerns that originally led to the administration of the survey.

Although some survey teams are hesitant to make recommendations, stating clear, action-oriented recommendations is one of the most important functions of a survey team. The team should know more about what the survey findings mean than anyone else in the organization. After all, the survey team wrote the items and spent much time analyzing the data. In making recommendations, the survey team should, however, be careful to base their recommendations firmly on the data.

Again, it is important to remember that these are general guidelines for presentations or reports. The actual form that any presentation or report takes will be guided by the organization, the purpose of the survey and presentation, and the time and resources available.

Summary and Conclusions

Planning a survey takes time and effort. Such planning is required to ensure that the process runs as smoothly as possible. Allow adequate time and resources to accomplish the survey. A proper survey cannot be constructed, administered, and analyzed overnight.

Follow-through is crucial. If the goal of a survey is to determine what areas in the organization require change, it is important that the results of the survey be used to highlight these areas. Feedback to respondents (and, of course, visible changes as the result of the survey) will increase the chances that the next survey will be taken seriously. If personnel are surveyed regularly but see no tangible results, they will begin to question the need for their participation.

Finally, it is extremely important to have organization-wide involvement in the survey. Use personnel at different levels of the organization as "subject matter experts" when writing survey items. Try to obtain a commitment from all who have a stake in the organization—from upper management to unionized employees. Organization-wide cooperation will help to ensure that the survey results will accurately reflect respondents' opinions and attitudes.

The purpose of this chapter was to give the reader a glimpse of the complexities involved in the survey process. Despite these complexities, the organizational survey is a powerful tool to gather information about vital organizational issues.

Notes

1. Many surveys mix items from different dimensions in order to "hide" the measured dimensions. The logic for hiding attitude survey dimensions is probably similar to the logic for hiding the dimensions in performance-evaluation rating formats. Landy (1989) noted, "The logic for the mixed standard format is derived from some early findings indicating that halo errors [an inability to distinguish among dimensions] are smaller when ratings are not made on an obvious scale. The random arrangement of performance statements is thought to make it difficult for the rater to determine the exact nature of the performance scale" (p. 139). An equally strong case can be put forth for making the dimensions overt. The positive side of halo is that it results in greater internal consistency of measurement (Bartlett, 1982). Also, survey respondents might give more accurate, well-thought-out answers if they know precisely what dimensions the survey is assessing. Basic to surveying are assumptions that people have opinions that they wish to express and that the organization believes that these opinions are important to gather. Items grouped into dimensions might provide a better opportunity for respondents to formulate and report their opinions.

Although hiding dimensions may be desirable in tests/inventories that measure social deviancy, use of this procedure for attitude surveys may have undesirable order effects (e.g., see Schuman & Presser, 1981). A question-order effect occurs when the answer to an item is influenced by previous items and answers. Thus, if (a) a survey instrument is constructed using dimensions that were embedded in previously published instruments and (b) an order effect is operating, item and dimension means might differ from those obtained in other organizations even if the attitudes/opinions in the two organizations are similar.

2. A copy of the survey should be included in an appendix.

References

Alreck, P. L., & Settle, R. B. (1985). *The survey research handbook*. Homewood, IL: Irwin.

American Psychological Association. (1983). *Publication manual of the American Psychological Association* (3rd ed). Washington, DC: Author.

Bartlett, C. J. (1982, August). *What's the difference between valid and invalid halo? Forced-choice measurement without forcing a choice*. Paper presented at the annual meeting of the Academy of Management, New York.

Bradburn, N. M., & Sudman, S. (1988). *Polls and surveys: Understanding what they tell us*. San Francisco: Jossey-Bass.

Converse, J. M., & Presser, S. (1986). *Survey questions: Handcrafting the standardized questionnaire*. Beverly Hills, CA: Sage.

Devellis, R. F. (1991). *Scale development: Theory and applications*. Newbury Park, CA: Sage.

Fowler, F. J., Jr. (1988). *Survey research methods*. Newbury Park, CA: Sage.

Fowler, F. J., Jr. (1992). How unclear terms affect survey data. *Public Opinion Quarterly*, *56*, 218-231.

Fowler, F. J., Jr., & Mangione, T. W. (1990). *Standardized survey interviewing: Minimizing interviewer-related error*. Newbury Park, CA: Sage.

Frey, J. H. (1989). *Survey research by telephone* (2nd ed.). Newbury Park, CA: Sage.

Fried, Y., & Ferris, G. R. (1986). *The dimensionality of job characteristics: Some neglected issues*. Manuscript submitted for publication.

Geer, J. G. (1991). Do open-ended questions measure "salient" issues? *Public Opinion Quarterly, 55*, 360-370.

Henry, G. T. (1990). *Practical sampling*. Newbury Park, CA: Sage.

Idaszak, J. R., & Drasgow, F. (1987). A revision of the Job Diagnostic Survey: Elimination of a measurement artifact. *Journal of Applied Psychology, 72*, 69-74.

Kalton, G. (1983). *Introduction to survey sampling*. Beverly Hills, CA: Sage.

Landy, F. J. (1989). *Psychology of work behavior* (4th ed.). Belmont, CA: Wadsworth.

Miller, D. C. (1991). *Handbook of research design and social measurement* (5th ed.). Newbury, CA: Sage.

Murphy, K. R., & Davidshofer, C. O. (1991). *Psychological testing: Principles and applications* (2nd ed.). Englewood Cliffs, NJ: Prentice-Hall.

Rossi, P. H., Wright, J. D., & Anderson, A. B. (Eds.). (1983). *Handbook of survey research*. Orlando, FL: Academic Press.

Schmitt, N., & Stults, D. M. (1985). Factors defined by negatively keyed items: The result of careless respondents? *Applied Psychological Measurement, 9*, 367-373.

Schuman, H., & Presser, S. (1981). *Questions and answers in attitude scales: Experiments on question form, wording, and context*. New York: Academic Press.

Sheatsley, P. B. (1983). Questionnaire construction and item writing. In P. H. Rossi, J. D. Wright, & A. B. Anderson (Eds.), *Handbook of survey research* (pp. 195-230). Orlando, FL: Academic Press.

2

Gathering Sensitive Data in Organizations

JAMSHID C. HOSSEINI
ROBERT L. ARMACOST

In organizational surveys, the need for gathering information of a sensitive nature arises in several different contexts. Organizations have an ongoing need to gather data about internal affairs (e.g., surveys of employees, managers, or executives), and external issues (e.g., data collection involving competitors, consumers, and the community at large). With respect to employees, for instance, companies may need to gather information about drug and alcohol use/abuse, embezzlement, sexual harassment, racial attitudes and practices, compliance with regulations, and other illegal or socially deviant behavior affecting employees' job performance.

Managerial practices are even more prone to sensitivity as they relate to the company's strategic and tactical conduct in its dealings with its owners (or shareholders), employees, competitors, consumers, government, community, and other stakeholders. Using surveys, organizations often attempt to gather data regarding product/service usage and/or preferences of the actual and potential consumers. Questions such as degree of usage of alcoholic beverages, smoking substances, readership of certain publications, hobbies, and the like would be considered sensitive.

Finally, many organizations need to gather information about general trends of behavior, changes in the culture, and social norms to better understand the environment in which they are operating. These types

Modes of Data Collection

With regard to collecting sensitive data, the mode of data collection should be chosen so that both response and nonresponse biases are as low as possible. Methods that are more technically sophisticated and involved may require personal interviews to permit the interviewer to explain the process in detail. However, the very presence of an interviewer may lead to intensified social desirability effects as well as increased nonresponse and response errors. In general, if the complexity of the survey is kept at a manageable level and anonymity is provided, self-administered mail surveys are the best approach for collecting sensitive data (Sudman & Bradburn, 1974). For more intricate instruments and situations where self-administered methods are not feasible, personal interviews are preferred to telephone surveys.

Response Bias Due to Question Sensitivity

Sensitive data may be regarded as the extreme case of data that is prone to socially desirable responding. In most cases, possessing (or lacking) the characteristic is viewed as deviant, unacceptable, or undesirable based on social norms and standards. Because of the stigma or the threat perceived by the respondent, not only are such questions prone to response error (e.g., giving the expected or favorable answer) but also there is usually an increased possibility for nonresponse.

Numerous ways have been developed for detecting the presence of social desirability that is presumed to be evidence of a response bias. A number of different techniques have been developed to reduce the perceived sensitivity of the questions and thereby reduce response bias.

The most obvious approach is to try to pose the question in a neutral way, often by a prefatory comment. This is often difficult to do for very sensitive issues. Another approach is using forced-choice items where the respondent must choose between two items, both of which are sensitive. When interviews are involved, careful selection of interviewers who can establish rapport with the respondent may reduce socially desirable responding. Finally, using proxy subjects (in lieu of the actual respondent) may be effective when behavior rather than attitudes or perceptions are being evaluated.

The primary focus of this chapter is on another method for reducing response and nonresponse bias due to question sensitivity, namely, the

RRT. In the following section, we develop the rationale for RRT, provide several models that have been used successfully, and discuss the advantages and disadvantages of using RRT for obtaining sensitive data in organizations.

Randomized Response Technique (RRT)

The RRT represents a family of statistical randomization techniques that is useful for reducing both response and nonresponse bias in organizational surveys. Fox and Tracy (1986) provided a thorough exposition of RRT. Hosseini and Armacost (1990) described several of these techniques in the context of organizational surveys. Statisticians and social science researchers have devoted much attention to investigating the potential advantages of RRT due to its perceived superiority in eliciting sensitive information:

1. RRT offers the respondents more security regarding anonymity of their responses.
2. RRT enables researchers to reduce nonresponse, which is considered a sampling error, and decrease false responses, which is a nonsampling error.
3. RRT provides researchers with appropriate data to estimate the population parameters, make inferences about the population of interest with respect to the sensitive characteristic(s), and conduct other exploratory or descriptive analyses.

In this section, we describe RRT, present several commonly used RRT designs, and provide several simple numerical examples of their application.

General Description of RRT

The most common forms of RRT mix the sensitive questions (e.g., "Have you ever shoplifted?") with innocuous questions (e.g., "Is your birthday in February?") in a way that the responses can be attributed to the respondents on a probability basis only. For example, the respondent may be told to flip a coin. If it lands "heads," the respondent answers the sensitive question; if it lands "tails," the respondent answers the innocuous question. Note that the recorder does not know the outcome of the coin flip. If a respondent answered "yes," the researcher would not know which question was answered but could determine the probability—.5—that it was the sensitive question. Because the question that the respondent answered is not known with certainty, the privacy of the respondent is maintained. Thus survey respondents could provide truthful responses to sensitive questions while maintaining legal protection to them in cases where admission of "sensitive" behavior could be incriminating (e.g., fraud, drug use, or tax evasion). Furthermore, RRT provides legal protection to the researcher and the involved organizations because the respondents cannot be associated with specific questions.

The RRT is theoretically well-grounded. During the past three decades, sound statistical foundations have been established for numerous RRT models (Boruch, 1972; Greenberg et al., 1969; Horvitz, Greenberg, & Abernathy, 1975; Warner, 1965, 1971). Moreover, comparative studies have shown that randomizing responses enable the researcher to obtain sensitive information better than (or at least as well as) the use of conventional methods.

The RRT is considered a general approach. A number of different designs or models for implementing RRT have been developed and tested. These models are grouped into two categories: qualitative and quantitative. Qualitative designs aim to obtain information on categorical responses. Therefore, the questions are stated in a dichotomous or multichotomous format (e.g., "Have you had an induced abortion during the past 3 years?"). Quantitative designs, on the other hand, attempt to measure discrete or continuous variables with respect to their frequency, intensity, or amount (e.g., "How many abortions have you had during the past 5 years?"; "How much is your net income?"). All randomized response designs assume large sample sizes and yield estimates of the sample mean (or proportion) and variance of the individuals with the sensitive characteristic. Therefore, all inferences, such as confidence intervals and test statistics for hypothesis testing, can be obtained. Table 2.1 provides the symbols and their corresponding definitions used in various qualitative and quantitative RRT designs presented in this chapter.

Qualitative Response Models

Four different qualitative models are used to illustrate the diversity of the types of RRT designs. These are Warner's design, unrelated question design, Morton's design, and the contamination design. The basic premise of these models is to obtain information on whether the

Table 2.1 Mathematical Symbols and Their Definitions for Various RRT
Designs

λ	=	Probability of "yes" responses
P_A	=	Probability of selecting (sensitive) Question A
P_B	=	Probability of selecting (innocuous) Question B
π_A	=	Sample proportion of "yes" responses to the sensitive question
π_B	=	Sample proportion of "yes" responses to the innocuous question
μ	=	Mean quantity reported for both sensitive and innocuous questions
σ^2	=	Variance of the quantity reported for both sensitive and innocuous questions
μ_A	=	Mean value of the quantity reported for the sensitive question
μ_B	=	Mean value of the quantity reported for the innocuous question
μ_R	=	Mean value of the random (integer) value used as "contamination factor" in quantitative RRT designs
σ_R^2	=	Variance of the random (integer) value used as "contamination factor" in quantitative RRT designs
N	=	Population size
n	=	Sample size
φ_N	=	Proportion of false negative responses
φ_P	=	Proportion of false positive responses

NOTE: The symbol "^" is used to indicate sample estimates of each population parameter.

respondents possess one or several sensitive characteristics. The models
yield estimates of the population proportions (e.g., $\hat{\pi}$) with respect to
the sensitive characteristic(s) as well as estimates of their variances,
that is, $\text{Var}(\hat{\pi})$. This information is then used to make inferences about
the sensitive characteristics in the relevant population.

Warner's Design

Warner (1965) proposed the first method for randomizing responses.
He developed a design in which the respondent is provided with two
related (complementary) statements, such as the following:

A: I have taken something of value from my employer since I started working
for this company.

B: I have not taken something of value from my employer since I started
working for this company.

The respondent is also given a randomizing device. For example, the
respondent might be given a spinner that can point to A with probability

(P_A), or to B with probability $(1 - P_A)$.[2] Without revealing to the researcher which statement was selected (A or B), the respondent responds ("yes" or "no") based on the chosen question and his or her status with respect to the question.

The maximum likelihood estimates of the proportion, $\hat{\pi}_A$, and variance, $\text{Var}(\hat{\pi}_A)$, of individuals whose responses to Question A were "true," in a random sample of n respondents is then obtained by

$$\hat{\pi}_A = \frac{\hat{\lambda} - (1 - P_A)}{2P_A - 1}, \quad P_A \neq \frac{1}{2} \tag{1}$$

where $\hat{\lambda}$ is the sample proportion of "yes" responses in the sample of size n:

$$\text{Var}(\hat{\pi}_A) = \frac{\pi_A(1 - \pi_A)}{n} = \frac{P_A(1 - P_A)}{n(2P_A - 1)^2} \tag{2}$$

Warner (1965) showed that $\hat{\pi}_A$ is an unbiased estimate of the proportion of "true" responses to A, π_A. The variance of the estimate is the sum of the variance due to sampling and the variance due to the randomization device.

To illustrate the method, suppose the respondent was given a spinner that directed the respondent to answer Question A above with probability $P = .8$ (80% of the time it landed on A). As indicated above, the RRT requires a group of respondents. Suppose the questions were posed to 30 employees and 10 of them responded "yes." At this point, the researcher does not know which question each individual answered, thereby guaranteeing the respondent's privacy. Substituting in Equation 1, the estimated proportion of persons who have taken something of value from the company is

$$\hat{\pi}_A = \frac{(10/30) - (1 - .8)}{2(.8) - 1} = .2217$$

Suppose further that the company believed that approximately 25% of its employees had taken something of value ($\pi_A = .25$). Then, the variance of the estimated proportion using Equation 2 is

$$\text{Var}(\hat{\pi}_A) = \frac{(.25)(1 - .25)}{30} = \frac{.8(1 - .8)}{30[2(.8) - 1]^2}$$

$$= .00625 + .01481 = .02106$$

and the standard deviation of $\hat{\pi}_A$ is .145.

Obviously, this is a relatively large variance, two thirds of which is due to the randomization device. Increasing the sample size will decrease the variance but will not affect the relative contributions. Note that if there were no prior estimate of π_A, the variance could be estimated by substituting $\hat{\pi}_A$ in Equation 2.

Unrelated Question Design

Instead of using two related questions, Greenberg et al. (1969) suggested that respondents can be given two unrelated statements. One of the two statements is sensitive and the other unrelated and innocuous. For example:

A: I have been under the influence of alcohol, while at work, at least once during the past 4 weeks.

B: My birthday is in January.

The basic form of this design assumes that the probability of having the innocuous characteristic is known a priori (e.g., the census data reveals the probability of having been born in January). The relevant maximum likelihood estimates of the proportion of the population possessing the sensitive characteristic given the proportion possessing the innocuous characteristic, $\hat{\pi}_A | \pi_B$, and its corresponding variance, $\text{Var}(\hat{\pi}_A | \pi_B)$, are then obtained by

$$\hat{\pi}_A \mid \pi_B = \frac{\hat{\lambda} - (1 - P_A)\pi_B}{P_A} \qquad [3]$$

and

$$\text{Var}(\hat{\pi}_A \mid \pi_B) = \frac{\lambda(1 - \lambda)}{nP_A^2} \qquad [4]$$

where

$$\lambda = P_A \pi_A + (1 - P_A) \pi_B .$$ [5]

If the probability of the innocuous characteristic is unknown, two samples are required (Greenberg et al., 1969; Moors, 1971). One sample is used as a control group to elicit the proportion of the innocuous characteristic directly. The second sample is used as a design group that would answer the sensitive/innocuous pair of questions. Reinmuth and Geurts (1975) extended this design to a two-stage model, collecting both qualitative (proportion) and quantitative (frequency) responses to sensitive questions.

Again, to illustrate the unrelated question model, assume that respondents use a spinner that directs answering Question A 80% of the time ($P_A = .8$). For simplicity, assume that the probability of being born in January is one twelfth (= .0833). Assume that, here also, 10 of 30 respondents answer "yes" to the questionnaire. Then the estimated proportion is given by Equation 3 as

$$\hat{\pi}_A \mid \pi_B = \frac{(10/30) - (1 - .8)(.0833)}{.8}$$

$$= .3958 .$$

Similar to the previous example, if the company believed that 25% of its employees used alcohol at work during the previous week ($\pi_A = .25$), the sample probability of a "yes" response would be $\lambda = (.8)(.25) + (1 - .8)(.0833) = .2167$. The resulting variance would be obtained by Equation 4 as

$$\mathrm{Var}(\hat{\pi}_A \mid \pi_B) = \frac{(.2167)(1 - .2167)}{30(.8)^2} = .00884$$

In comparison with Warner's design, the total variance for the unrelated question design is significantly reduced (58% reduction).

Morton's Design

Horvitz et al. (1975) reported on a design suggested by Richard Morton of the University of Sheffield in England. This design extends the unrelated question design by eliminating the need for the knowledge of the probability of the innocuous question. The randomizing device in this method selects one of three statements A, B, or C (with probabilities P_A, P_B, or P_C, respectively). One of the three statements is sensitive (A); the other two are innocuous (B and C). One of the innocuous statements is always "true," and the other is always "false." For example:

A: I have used the company's confidential information for personal gain at least once during the past 6 months.
B: There are 7 days in a week.
C: There are 9 days in a week.

The estimator and variance for this design are the same as those in the unrelated question design as follows:

$$\hat{\pi}_A = \frac{\hat{\lambda} - P_B}{P_A} \qquad [6]$$

and

$$\text{Var}(\hat{\pi}_A) = \frac{\lambda(1 - \lambda)}{nP_A^2} \qquad [7]$$

where

$$\lambda = P_A\pi_A + P_B. \qquad [8]$$

To continue the illustration, suppose that the spinner lands on A 80% of the time and on B and C each 10% of the time ($P_A = .8$, $P_B = .1$, $P_C = .1$). Assume that 10 of 30 respondents mark "yes." Then, the estimated proportion responding yes to the sensitive question (from Equation 6) is

$$\hat{\pi}_A = \frac{(10/30) - .1}{.8} = .2917$$

If the hypothesized proportion of individuals possessing the sensitive characteristic were .25, then the probability of "yes" responses would be $\lambda = (.8)(.25) + .1 = .3$ and the variance (from Equation 7) would be

$$\text{Var}(\hat{\pi}_A) = \frac{(.3)(1-.3)}{30(.8)^2} = .01094$$

Clearly, the two unrelated questions design is more efficient (lower variance) than Warner's method but not as efficient as the one unrelated question method when π_B is known. The advantage of Morton's method is that there is no requirement to determine the probability associated with the innocuous question.

Contamination Design

The contamination design (Boruch, 1972) requires only the sensitive question. Error, however, is introduced by instructing the respondents to lie or tell the truth depending on the outcome of a randomizing device. For example, the respondent is given the following question: "Have you ever used the company's vehicle for personal use?" The respondent is then asked to tell the truth if he or she draws a "white" bead but to tell the opposite to the truth if a "red" bead is drawn. If the randomization device indicates that the respondent should tell the truth with probability P, and lie (either false negative or false positive) with probability $1 - P$, then the proportion and its variance are given by Equations 1 and 2 with $P_A = P$. Thus when the probability of a false positive, φ_P, and the probability of a false negative, φ_N, are both equal to the probability of lying, the contamination method is equivalent to Warner's original approach. If a randomization device is used that provides different probabilities for lying if the true answer is yes, φ_N, and for lying if the true answer is no, φ_P, then the proportion estimate and its variance are given by

$$\hat{\pi}_A = \frac{(\lambda - \varphi_P)}{1 - (\varphi_P + \varphi_N)} \qquad [9]$$

and

$$\text{Var}(\hat{\pi}_A) = \frac{\hat{\pi}_A(1 - \hat{\pi}_A)}{n} + \frac{\hat{\pi}_A[\varphi_N(1 - \varphi_N) - \varphi_P(1 - \varphi_P)] + \varphi_P(1 - \varphi_P)}{n(1 - \varphi_P - \varphi_N)^2} \qquad [10]$$

where $\varphi_P + \varphi_N < 1$.
For space considerations, we leave the construction of a simple numerical example with $\varphi_P \neq \varphi_N$ to the reader.

Quantitative Response Models

RRT does not need to be restricted to qualitative data. It can also be employed to assess the frequency, intensity, or amount of a sensitive characteristic possessed by the respondents. The following designs demonstrate how RRT can be used to gather quantitative (both continuous and discrete) data.

Greenberg's Design

Greenberg, Kuebler, Abernathy, and Horvitz (1971) developed this design and its estimation procedures by extending the unrelated question randomized response design. In its simplest form, the sensitive question and the innocuous question have similar types and levels of quantitative responses, such as "How many times?" or "How much?" As in the unrelated question design, a randomization device is used to direct the respondent to truthfully answer the sensitive question or the innocuous question. With the unrelated question design for qualitative data, it was assumed that the distribution (probability) of a yes to the innocuous question was known. If not, a two-sample approach was required. The same situation applies for quantitative data.

Suppose we were interested in evaluating abuse of sick leave among employees. When administering the questionnaire, a card with a number on it (0, 1, or 2) is given to the respondent. Using a randomization device, the respondent is asked to answer one of the following two questions:

A: How many times during the past 3 months have you used sick time when you really were not sick?

B: What number was on the card that you received with this questionnaire?

Note that the same type of responses are needed for both the sensitive and the innocuous question to Ensure the respondent's anonymity. The distribution for the responses to the innocuous question needs to be known. Here, assume that cards with numbers 0, 1, and 2 are equally distributed, in which case, $\mu_B = 1$. The mean and variance of the distribution of the days of sick leave used fraudulently are given by

$$\hat{\mu}_A = [\hat{\mu} - (1 - P_A)\mu_B]/P_A \qquad [11]$$

and

Multiplicative Design

Warner (1971) also suggested this design. Poole (1974) used this model to estimate the distribution function for a continuous variable. In this model, the respondent is instructed to multiply the true response by a random number (e.g., by using a random number table). Because the distribution of the multiplicative factor is known in advance, population parameter estimates can be calculated by

$$\hat{\mu}_A = \hat{\mu}/\mu_R \qquad [17]$$

and

$$\text{Var}(\hat{\mu}_A) = \sigma^2/n\mu_R^2 , \qquad [18]$$

where

$$\sigma^2 = \mu_R^2\sigma_A^2 + \mu_A^2\sigma_R^2 + \sigma_A^2\sigma_R^2. \qquad [19]$$

The spinner used in the additive constants model could be used for the multiplicative model as well.

Comparative Evaluations, Applications, and Practical Considerations

Since Warner's (1965) introduction of the RRT and subsequent extension of it to include quantitative variables (Warner, 1971), over 100 articles in various journals have addressed this topic. These studies have included minor modifications to the initial design as well as radically different designs. All of this research shares the common characteristic of trying to guarantee that a given respondent cannot be associated with his or her response to a sensitive question.

Comparative and/or Validational Studies

Much of the methodological research has involved developing and testing RRT models. A number of articles have focused on the relative efficiency (as measured by the variance of the estimator) of the alternative designs. For example, Dowling and Shachtman (1975) showed that the unrelated question design is always more efficient than Warner's design when the probability of selecting the sensitive question is at least $1/3$. Horvitz et al. (1975) showed that the one unrelated question design will always be more efficient than the two unrelated questions design when the probabilities for the innocuous questions are known.

When Pollock and Bek (1976) compared the three quantitative RRT designs, they concluded that the additive constants model is more efficient than Greenberg's model when the probability of selecting the sensitive question is less than (or equal to) 0.7. The multiplicative design was found to be more efficient than the additive constants design when $\mu_B > (\mu_A^2 + \sigma_A^2)^{1/2}$. Edgell, Himmelfarb, and Cira (1986) empirically compared the Greenberg design and the additive constants design and reported that the latter model is more efficient.

Many articles have applied various RRT models to empirically test their effectiveness against results obtained from direct questioning (DQ). Lamb and Stem (1978), Buchman and Tracy (1982), and Himmelfarb and Lickteig (1982) provided good overviews of comparisons of qualitative RRT versus other methods. Many of the application-oriented articles have asserted superiority of RRT over DQ because of the generally higher percentage of "yes" responses to the sensitive question.

Locander et al. (1976) tested a set of questions with different degrees of sensitivity using several data-gathering methods, including telephone interviews, self-administered questionnaires, personal interviews, and an unrelated-question RRT model. The proportion of "yes" responses was used to conclude that RRT outperformed the other methods; however, the differences in methods were not statistically significant.

Several validational studies compared RRT and DQ when there were known records. Lamb and Stem (1978) used both DQ and RRT to determine (a) whether the students had failed a course and (b) the number of courses they had failed. They compared these results with individual student records and found no difference between the methods with respect to the first question, but RRT performed significantly better than DQ with respect to the number of course failures. The authors concluded that RRT is the preferred method in situations of heightened sensitivity.

In comparing DQ and RRT—using the Greenberg et al. (1971) design for quantitative data—Tracy and Fox (1981) obtained both self-reported criminal behaviors and data from respondents' criminal records. For both techniques, arrests were underreported. RRT did, however, reduce error by 15% as compared to DQ. Although not definitive, these studies do suggest that gathering sensitive data with RRT procedures may produce more reliable data than using DQ.

Zdep, Rhodes, Schwarz, and Kilkenny (1979), Stem and Lamb (1981), Orwin and Boruch (1982), and Armacost, Hosseini, Morris, and Rehbein (1991) have summarized other recent RRT research. Their research addressed comparative and/or validational issues in using RRT.

Applications of RRT to Organizational Surveys

Most of the published applications of RRT have involved social issues or have been health related. For example, many of the early applications of RRT addressed the incidence and frequency of induced abortion (Abernathy, Greenberg, & Horvitz, 1970), illegitimate births (Greenberg, Abernathy, & Horvitz, 1970), sexual practices (Fidler & Kleinknecht, 1977), and drug abuse (Greenberg et al., 1971). More recent applications have dealt with such issues as rape (Soeken & Damrosh, 1986).

Applications of RRT to organizations, while not as extensive, have covered a diverse set of topics. Perhaps the greatest interest has been in the consumer/employee behavior and the retailing areas. Buchman and Tracy (1982) used a modified unrelated question RRT design (directed "yes") in an accounting application. They attempted to identify the extent to which various audit procedures were susceptible to false sign-offs (e.g., indicating that an audit procedure had been completed when, in fact, it had not been completed). Buchman and Tracy (1982) found a significantly higher proportion of "yes" responses to the sensitive questions when using RRT than were found in their comparison DQ survey. In another accounting application, Schneider and Wilner (1990) used a two-sample version of Greenberg's quantitative design to estimate the dollar level where having an audit would act as a deterrent to financial reporting irregularities. In particular, they examined the effect of having no auditing, an internal auditing group, and an external auditing group. They concluded that both internal and external auditing did have a deterrent effect. Reinmuth and Geurts (1975) developed a two-stage qualitative/quantitative RRT model to identify the incidence and prevalence of shoplifting. They reported that use of the RRT approach did significantly reduce nonresponse bias. Stem and Steinhorst (1984), in comparing mail and telephone RRT (unrelated-question) surveys, examined the frequency of illegal connections to telephone lines (when separate connection charges were still required for each telephone set) and also examined automobile selling practices. They pointed out several important practical considerations in using RRT in either mail or telephone surveys. Soeken and Macready (1986) proposed a setwise randomized response procedure to apply RRT to estimating the occurrence of a set of sensitive behaviors. The specific application involved the behavior of nurses in a hospital environment. They found that the proportion of positive responses was higher using RRT than was found in the comparable DQ survey. Soeken (1987) reported another organizational application involving the question of whether nurses have "consciously given less than quality care to a patient for personal reasons." Again, affirmative responses were significantly higher using the RRT than were those obtained by a companion DQ survey. Finally, Armacost et al. (1991) used a two unrelated-question RRT design to estimate the prevalence of unethical corporate intelligence gathering. They found that RRT performed better than DQ.

Many of the social issue applications are relevant for organizational applications, particularly as they might apply to human resource management questions. The above organizational applications illustrate the diversity of the applications. Some of the applications had a comparison or validation issue as the study focus, whereas others simply used RRT to try to provide estimates of the occurrence of sensitive behaviors. Lamb and Stem (1978) provided numerous suggestions in the marketing and consumer behavior areas, Soeken (1987) suggested numerous applications in health areas, and Tracy and Fox (1981) suggested criminal justice system applications.

Practical Considerations for Implementation of RRT in Organizations

Generally, implementation of RRT is more involved than DQ methods, but as discussed above, RRT may offer improved performance for eliciting sensitive information. To successfully implement RRT, several considerations and issues must be addressed. These considerations include all aspects of research design, such as research method, sampling, instrumentation, and administration. Furthermore, care must be taken to ensure that the respondents understand the process sufficiently.

Identifying What Is Really Sensitive

In designing the survey it is important to determine which questions, if any, will be considered sensitive by the respondents. For example, in

Lamb and Stem's (1978) study, the incidence of failing a course was not considered sensitive by the students. When there is no logical difference between DQ and RRT with respect to the likelihood of eliciting truthful responses, DQ should be preferred because of its reduced administration time and smaller required sample size.

Method of Administration

In a survey, data collection is generally performed using personal interviews, telephone interviews, or self-administered (e.g., mail-out) instruments. RRT can be used with any of these methods, but in each case, certain issues must be addressed. The most common difficulty is describing the process to the respondent. This description can most easily be given in personal interviews; however, care must be taken to ensure privacy in the process of data collection. Explaining the process is most difficult in a telephone interview. A self-administered design conducted via a mail survey might be more successful in convincing the respondent of anonymity and preservation of privacy. (The appendix presents a portion of one questionnaire and its instructions as an example of this type of survey.)

Choice of an RRT Design

Among the qualitative techniques, the unrelated-question design is superior to the Warner design under most circumstances (Dowling & Shachtman, 1975). The choice of an innocuous question, however, entails some potential difficulties. If a single sample is to be used, the probability of any respondent possessing the innocuous characteristic must be known (or estimated with accuracy). Often, unrelated questions are based on known respondent characteristics (e.g., see Orwin & Boruch, 1982).

The contamination method is promising because of its lack of dependence on an innocuous question. However, this design has the feature of confronting the respondent with the sensitive question directly. This may invoke more "no" (or "false") responses than designs with at least one innocuous question.

Morton's design appears to offer remedies to the difficulties of the Warner, unrelated question, and contamination designs:

1. It does not provide the respondents with two related (complementary) sensitive questions.
2. It offers the respondents the possibility of answering innocuous questions as well as the sensitive question.

3. The responses to the innocuous questions are always known with certainty and need not be estimated.

In addition, the researcher may be interested in either the incidence of the sensitive behavior or its intensity (frequency). This consideration would determine whether a qualitative or quantitative design should be used. When a quantitative design is required, the issue of whether it is necessary to include an innocuous question (Greenberg's design) or if respondents will respond truthfully with contamination must be resolved.

Sampling Considerations

Generally, RRT requires larger sample sizes than the DQ methods to achieve comparable variances. The reduced bias of the results may, however, compensate for the larger sample size. The required sample sizes may range from 2 to 10 times that required with DQ, with the single-sample unrelated question design generally requiring smaller samples than the other RRT designs.

Selecting Probabilities

As the probability of selecting the sensitive question increases, the accuracy increases while the perceived privacy of the respondents decreases. For most designs, this probability should be more than .5, with .7 being the most commonly used probability. Due to calculation difficulties, this probability must not equal .5 for most RRT designs.

Randomization Device

Various devices have been developed for randomizing responses. These variations include simple devices, such as flipping several coins or using a random number table, as well as more complex devices, such as urns and spinners. If the RRT design allows simple devices, the more complex ones should not be used. For quantitative designs, the randomizing devices will generally be more complex in order to represent an appropriate probability distribution.

Education of Participants

All of the RRT designs provide complete privacy for the respondents. Convincing the respondents of this fact is a key factor in successful

One important area of research that is required to facilitate the use of RRT in organizations is a simple compilation of RRT methods and guidelines for their use. Simple examples, including sample questionnaires, sample randomization devices, and example statistical analyses, would be extremely useful. Hopefully, this chapter has begun that first step.

Summary and Conclusions

Organizations often need to gather information, some of which may be sensitive in nature, about their employees, managers, competitors, customers, and other stakeholders. Reliance on published information or archival records does not always satisfy this need. Certain kinds of information are not available through secondary data sources. For example, undetected crime (e.g., insider trading), unreported victimization (e.g., sexual harassment), and questionable intelligence-gathering practices are usually not available through published sources. In addition, due to privacy and security issues, certain sensitive data are inaccessible to researchers and to the public (e.g., criminal history of specific individuals). Finally, logistical problems (e.g., geographic disparity or levels of aggregation) may prevent access or usability of certain public data (Fox & Tracy, 1986). Therefore, surveys are often necessary to obtain information charged with social desirability and question sensitivity.

Organizational surveys involving sensitive data are not only susceptible to response error but also to nonresponse bias. The randomized response techniques provide an effective approach to reduce both response and nonresponse errors. The RRT literature indicates that this approach enables the researcher to elicit better responses to sensitive questions than is possible with other questioning methods. RRT is well-established as a viable technique. Its successful applications in general social science areas and organizations suggest the potential for useful application in other areas in organizational surveys where sensitive issues are involved.

Among the qualitative designs, Morton's method appears to be superior both in terms of efficiency and ease of use. Among quantitative designs, the additive constants design appears to be favored by researchers and statisticians.

In conclusion, RRT offers a valuable approach for eliciting responses to sensitive questions. This approach facilitates the researcher's and management's understanding of certain behaviors of potential consumers, competitors, individuals in the society, managers, and/or employees that affect the operation and performance of an organization.

Appendix: A Partial RRT Mail Survey Instrument

INTRODUCTION AND QUESTIONNAIRE INSTRUCTIONS

This questionnaire contains a number of items that some executives might consider sensitive. In order to obtain reliable responses to the questions, it is crucial that anonymity be maintained. The approach used here, called Randomized Response, guarantees the anonymity of the person completing the questionnaire. In short, you provide an answer, but it is never known whether you answered the sensitive question. A simple example illustrates this procedure.

EXAMPLE: Suppose we are interested in whether people are cheating on their tax returns. The following procedure could be used to estimate the answer.

Pick a number between 0 and 9.   □ Usually/
If the number equals 2, mark usually/always and go to the next question.   Always
If it equals 3 or 4, mark rarely/never and go to the next question.   □ Rarely/
If it equals any other number, answer the following question: Never

Do you cheat on your Federal Income Tax Return?

Note that because of the number used, a person may be responding in a way that would actually be a false answer to the question. Even so, it is important that the instructions be followed exactly. Using this approach, we can estimate the probability that a "usually/always" answer is associated with the sensitive question for the group of respondents, but there is no way to know whether or not the sensitive question was answered by an individual respondent. This absolutely guarantees the privacy of the respondent. The questionnaire includes 13 items that require the use of single-digit random numbers. The following simple procedure should be used for completing the questionnaire.

RANDOM NUMBER INSTRUCTIONS

We would like you to use the following procedure to obtain the random numbers. You will need four residential telephone numbers. These can be phone numbers with which you are familiar, or they can be selected at random from any convenient White Pages.

The last four digits of each phone number will serve as the single-digit random numbers, the first phone number for questions 1-4, and so on. The following example illustrates how to use the worksheet below.

EXAMPLE: Telephone listing: 555-1248

Write:

555-1248 Question 1._1_   Question 2._2_   Question 3._4_   Question 4._8_

Repeat the process three times to fill in spaces for questions 5-8, 9-12, and 13 with random numbers. Always use the LAST four digits of the telephone listing. (Use the last digit of the last phone number of question 13.) List four telephone numbers in the first column below and complete the worksheet, assigning single digits to each of the thirteen questions. Use these numbers when completing the questionnaire.

Random Number Worksheet

Phone Numbers

_____ Question 1.___   Question 2.___   Question 3.___   Question 4.___
_____ Question 5.___   Question 6.___   Question 7.___   Question 8.___
_____ Question 9.___   Question 10.___   Question 11.___   Question 12.___
_____ Question 13.___

To preserve your complete anonymity, we must not know the numbers you chose. Please use these numbers when completing the questionnaire, but DO NOT MAIL THIS SHEET BACK to us with the questionnaire.

BUSINESS PRACTICES QUESTIONNAIRE

Please mark the appropriate response to each item.

Questions on Intelligence Gathering Tactics

Responses

1. Refer to the random number for question 1.
   If the number equals 0, mark yes and go to question 2.   ☐ Yes
   If it equals 1 or 2, mark no and go to question 2.
   If it equals any other number, answer the following question: ☐ No

Has your firm ever made a payment or other compensation to an employee of another company to obtain information of a proprietary nature?

2. Refer to the random number for question 2.   ☐ Usually/
   If the number equals 2, mark usually/always and go to question 3.   Always
   If it equals 3 or 4, mark rarely/never and go to question 3.   ☐ Rarely/
   If it equals any other number, answer the following question: Never

A CEO learns that a competitor has made a scientific breakthrough that may result in a significant technological innovation at some point in the future. In these situations, would you try to hire one of the competitor's employees who knows the details of the discovery?

3. Refer to the random number for question 3.   ☐ Usually/
   If the number equals 4, mark usually/always and go to question 4.   Always
   If it equals 5 or 6, mark rarely/never and go to question 4.   ☐ Rarely/
   If it equals any other number, answer the following question: Never

Does your firm ask buyers for information about competitors on the pretext of needing to know this information in order to better serve the buyer?

4. Refer to the random number for question 4.   ☐ Usually/
   If the number equals 6, mark usually/always and go to question 5.   Always
   If it equals 7 or 8, mark rarely/never and go to question 5.   ☐ Rarely/
   If it equals any other number, answer the following question: Never

Because engineers and scientists often brag about how they overcame technical challenges, many firms instruct their employees to be alert at conferences and professional meetings, listening carefully and divulging nothing. After hearing such a warning, a young scientist takes advantage of numerous social occasions to solicit proprietary information from conferees. In these situations, if the young scientist were your employee, would you support him, either explicitly or implicitly?

5. Refer to the random number for question 5.   ☐ Usually/
   If the number equals 8, mark usually/always and go to question 6.   Always
   If it equals 9 or 0, mark rarely/never and go to question 6.   ☐ Rarely/
   If it equals any other number, answer the following question: Never

A personnel director hears a rumor that two high-level managers in a competitor's company are disgruntled because they feel they aren't getting promoted fast enough. The personnel director suggests that his firm conduct phony job interviews in the hope that they will apply and then volunteer some useful information while trying to impress the interviewers. If your personnel director came up with plans like this, would you allow the interviews?

Notes

1. Issues related to ethics, legality, and right to privacy are not discussed here. The researcher interested in such issues is referred to the work sponsored by the National Academy of Sciences (e.g., 1979, 1991) in which, among other related topics, issues related to privacy, confidentiality, disclosure limitation approaches, and data access are discussed.
2. Fox and Tracy (1986) provide descriptions for several commonly used randomizing devices.

References

Abernathy, J. R., Greenberg, B. G., & Horvitz, D. G. (1970). Estimates of induced abortion in urban North Carolina. *Demography, 7*, 19-29.

Armacost, R. L., Hosseini, J. C., Morris, S. A., & Rehbein, K. A. (1991). An empirical comparison of direct questioning, scenario, and randomized response methods for obtaining sensitive business information, *Decision Sciences, 22*, 1073-1087.

Boruch, R. F. (1972). Relations among statistical methods for assuring confidentiality of social research data. *Social Science Research, 1*, 403-414.

Buchman, T. A., & Tracy, J. A. (1982). Obtaining responses to sensitive questions: Conventional questionnaire versus randomized response technique. *Journal of Accounting Research, 20*, 263-271.

Burstin, K., Doughtie, E. B., & Raphaeli, A. (1980). Contrastive vignette technique: An indirect methodology designed to address reactive social attitude measurement. *Journal of Applied Social Psychology, 10*, 147-165.

Cavanagh, G. F., & Fritzsche, D. J. (1985). Using vignettes in business ethics research. *Research in Corporate Social Performance and Policy, 7*, 279-293.

Crowne, D. P., & Marlowe, D. (1964). *The approval motive: Studies in evaluative dependence.* New York: John Wiley.

Dowling, T. A., & Shachtman, R. H. (1975). On the relative efficiency of randomized response models. *Journal of the American Statistical Association, 70*, 84-87.

Edgell, S. E., Himmelfarb, S., & Cira, D. J. (1986). Statistical efficiency of using two quantitative randomized response techniques to estimate correlation. *Psychological Bulletin, 100*, 251-256.

Edwards, A. L. (1953). The relationship between the judged desirability of a trait and the probability that the trait will be endorsed. *Journal of Applied Psychology, 37*, 90-93.

Fidler, D. S., & Kleinknecht, R. E. (1977). Randomized response versus direct questioning: Two data collection methods for sensitive information. *Psychological Bulletin, 84*, 1045-1049.

Fox, J. A., & Tracy, P. E. (1986). *Randomized response: A method for sensitive surveys* (Quantitative Applications in the Social Sciences, No. 58). Beverly Hills, CA: Sage.

Ganster, D. C., Hennessey, H. W., & Luthans, F. (1983). Social desirability response effects: Three alternative models. *Academy of Management Journal, 26*, 321-331.

Greenberg, B. G., Abernathy, J. R., & Horvitz, D. G. (1970). A new survey technique and its application in the field of public health. *Milbank Memorial Fund Quarterly, 48*, 39-55.

3

Measurement Errors in Organizational Surveys

SOLOMON DUTKA
LESTER R. FRANKEL

The term *organizational surveys,* as used in this chapter, includes all surveys where information is obtained from organizations. In some cases, the unit of information is the organization itself, such as hospitals, libraries, business establishments, retail stores, and so on. The purpose of the survey may be to describe the characteristics of groups. In other cases, individuals within the organizations provide the relevant personal information, such as the owner, manager, receptionist, head nurse, computer operator, and others. Administrative records within organizations serve as a source of survey information. For example, hospital admission and discharge records provide important resources for obtaining public health information.

Organizational surveys are used extensively in many diverse areas of investigation, such as personnel management, employee attitudes, use of manpower, studies of the environment, and energy use. Information derived from organizational surveys is generally in the form of quantitative estimates. These data are often not exact and are subject to various types of errors. This chapter is concerned with defining and exploring such errors. It should be emphasized that while measurement at the source is but one part of a survey operation it also interacts with the other operations that are involved in obtaining the estimates.

The approach taken in this chapter is to (a) summarize the different measurement techniques that are used, (b) discuss in general the concept

Table 3.1 Measurement Techniques in Organizational Surveys

Interviewing methods:
  Face-to-face interviews
  Telephone interviews
  Use of self-administered questionnaires delivered by mail or by person
  Combination of the above
Record retrieval procedures:
  Hand transcription (i.e., invoices, purchase orders, sales, prescriptions written
    and filled, etc.)
  Scanner devices in retail outlets, libraries, and so on
  Data banks maintained by hospitals, wholesalers, and other types of organizations
Observation methods:
  Static phenomena
    Distribution of brands in retail outlets and service operations, such as hotels,
      theaters, and sporting arenas
    Shelf facings in supermarkets
    Incidence of specific outdoor and indoor advertising
  Dynamic phenomena (all measurements made within samples of time durations)
    Counts of people entering and leaving specific sites, certain types of
      establishments, or localities such as retail stores, museum exhibits, sporting
      events, and so on
    Movement of objects, such as sales of perishable foods in stores, soft drink
      sales from vending machines, and number of times that specific issues of
      magazines are picked up in waiting rooms
    Traffic counts to determine use of different car makes
    Behavior of sales and other service personnel

---

and role of measurement error in sample surveys, and (c) give a few illustrations of how measurement errors are detected and controlled.

Measurement Techniques

The measurement techniques used in organizational surveys are outlined in Table 3.1. They fall into three classes: interviewing methods, record retrieval procedures, and observation methods.

Interviewing Methods

Interviewing methods are often major sources of obtaining organizational survey data. The personal, or face-to-face, interview method is recommended for obtaining valid data on attitudes, likes, dislikes, personal satisfaction with job, awareness of health and dietary hazards, top-of-the-mind awareness of advertised brands, ease of use of equipment, and other subjective phenomena. Personal interviewing is also used to obtain factual and behavioral information. In organizational surveys, interviewing is usually done on location. However, in certain situations that involve matters of convenience, privacy, or confidentiality, interviewing is sometimes done at the respondent's home.

The telephone is often the only practical method of gathering information. It is especially useful when potential respondents are at different locations. It is also useful when a minimum amount of information from a single respondent is called for, although many respondents within the same organization are required.

Self-administered, printed questionnaires are also employed to obtain detailed information. Computer input by respondents is currently being used in a number of surveys. The computers are generally located at a central location, or, in some cases, portable computers are carried by interviewers. The various methods of survey administration have been described in detail earlier in this book.

Record Retrieval

In the course of their operations, organizations maintain administrative records for operational, fiscal, and tax purposes. These records contain information about the characteristics of each organization, such as size, employee turnover, raw material used, the products made, and those shipped. Records of individual employees, including each person's characteristics and job behavior, are also kept.

Many establishments function as conduits in the flow of information and the usefulness of these data extend beyond the organization itself. Records of prescriptions filled in pharmacies provide information on the use of prescribed drugs. Because consumer packaged goods flow from the producer to the household through wholesalers, distributors, and retailers, the records kept by these organizations give market researchers indications of the ultimate consumption of these products.

Record retrieval is the procedure used to obtain such data. Information is obtained from computerized data banks. For example, a number of wholesale organizations have realized the value of such information beyond their own needs and sell parts of it to market researchers.

Observation Methods

Observation methods involving the measurement of static phenomena have always had important uses in the analysis of organizational data. The number and location of employee rest areas and eating facilities are factors contributing to employees' satisfaction with their jobs. In marketing, the distribution and availability of brands at various retail outlets and personal service facilities are vital factors in the sales of soft drinks. In advertising, the location and sizes of outdoor posters are determinants of the fees paid for their use. Systematic survey procedures are used for the measurement of the incidence.

Quantitative behavioral observation techniques have also emerged as important measurement procedures. In the 1920s, to improve the efficiency and to reduce the obtrusiveness of direct observation, behavioral scientists developed techniques for sampling time-related phenomena (Suen & Ary, 1988). Thus surveys of traffic involving the use of passenger vehicles by commuters or the use of interstate highways by different-sized commercial vehicles are determined by observation methods. In museum research, quantitative behavior observation techniques are used to determine the attendance at various exhibits as well as by gender and broad age groupings. This method was introduced in marketing research in 1960 (Dutka & Frankel, 1960; Houseman & Lipstein, 1960) as a means of measuring the sales of perishable foods in supermarkets.

Role of Measurement Error in Sample Surveys

Measurement error was first recognized on a formal basis in the physical sciences. When certain phenomena were measured (e.g., the weight of a cubic centimeter of a specific metal through the use of a balance scale), repeated weighing yielded different values. The standard deviation of the measurements defined the precision of the measuring instrument. When the average of several hundred measurements was obtained and compared with the established value of the specific gravity of the metal, the difference specified the accuracy of the instrument. These two terms, *precision* and *accuracy*, have known meanings in statistics and the physical sciences.

In the social sciences, the terms *reliability* and *validity* have parallel meanings. Tests used for the determination of educational achievement are characterized by these terms. Formal scaling techniques, before being accepted, have to specify these two criteria.

The terms *measurement variation* and *measurement bias* have similar meanings in sample surveys. Measurement variation occurs when the measurement or response to a question of the same unit varies when the measurement is repeated. Bias occurs when the measurement or response to a question is incorrect. *Measurement error* occurs when one or both of these are present.

In sample surveys, there is another type of error in addition to measurement error. Known as *sampling error,* it is the error that occurs because not all units in a population are measured. Sampling error in sample surveys can be controlled and reduced by increasing the size of the sample as well as through the use of stratification and estimation procedures. The total error of a survey is composed of the measurement error and the statistical sampling error. This is known among survey statisticians as the *mean square error.* In designing a sample survey, the statistician attempts to minimize the mean square error through such procedures as increasing the sample size, stratification, allocation, estimating procedures, and employing precise measuring devices. In doing so, he or she has to take into account the costs of these efforts (Dutka & Frankel, 1975; Frankel, 1970).

Control of Measurement Errors

Interviewing Methods

Unintended Response Bias

Many measurement errors occur because of the inability of respondents in a verbal interview to furnish accurate information (O'Muircheartaigh, 1991). When this inability is detected and quantified, then alternative and sometimes more expensive information gathering procedures may be used.

In a particular telephone survey, interviews were conducted with the owners or managers of small restaurants to determine what kinds of appliances they had on the premises as well as the brand names of those appliances. The items of interest were ovens, microwaves, grills, refrigerators, freezers, dishwashers, toasters, and blenders.

A pretest was conducted to determine the accuracy of the telephone response. A sample of 100 interviews was conducted by telephone and incidence and brand data for all of the appliances were recorded. Follow-up personal visits were completed with 92 restaurants, and incidence and brand information was obtained by personal observation for 580 appliances. Of these, 552, or 95.2%, of the brands coincided with information obtained from the telephone interviews. The overall disagreement rate was 4.8%, and the rate varied by type of appliance. For an appliance with a 50% brand share reported by phone, the bias is 50 × (.048), or 2.4%. If the reported share is 80%, then the bias is 80 × (.048), or 3.84%.

The implication of this finding is that when telephone interviews are used there is a measurable bias to the response. Such a measurement bias can be reduced through the use of personal observation.

How do such considerations affect the overall survey design? Using hypothetical data, suppose that for the survey a budget of $2,500 is allocated for data collection. Assume that a telephone interview costs $5 per interview, whereas a personal observation costs $12.50.

Some consideration in the overall survey design might proceed as follows: Suppose that only personal observations are used. Then 200 observations are possible. There is no measurement error, and the total error is determined by the standard statistical formula for the sampling variance. The size of the total error varies by the incidence of ownership of the different appliances (see Table 3.2, column 2).

If observations are all made by telephone interviewing instead of making 200 personal observations, 500 telephone interviews are possible at the same total cost. Because all information obtained is dependent on the statement of the respondent, each is subject to response error. The size of the total error, which takes into account both measurement and sampling error, is shown in the fourth column of Table 3.2.

Suppose now that half of the interviews are made by telephone and half are obtained through observation. The budget provides for 286 total interviews: 143 by telephone and 143 by observation. Both procedures are subject to sampling error, but the telephone interviews have, in addition, a response error. The total error of this mixed mode design is shown in the third column of Table 3.2.

When the three survey designs are examined in Table 3.2, it is seen that the survey error varies, depending on the incidence of ownership of the appliance (see Table 3.2, column 1). For those appliances that have a low incidence of ownership, say, 30% or less, it is more efficient to conduct telephone interviewing with its attendant response error than to make personal observations, which have little response error. On the

Table 3.2 Total Survey Error of Brand Share for Estimated Incidence of Appliance Ownership Using Mixed Mode Measurement

Total budget		$2,500.00	
Per telephone interview cost		$5.00	
Per unit of observation cost		$12.50	
Relative bias of telephone response		0.048	
Percentage observation interviews	100	50	0
Percentage telephone interviews	0	50	100
Sample size	500	286	200

Percentage Incidence	Percentage Error of Brand Share		
0	0.0	0.0	0.0
10	2.1	1.8	1.4
20	2.8	2.4	2.0
30	3.2	2.8	2.5
40	3.5	3.1	2.9
50	3.5	3.2	3.3
60	3.5	3.6	3.6
70	3.2	3.2	3.9
80	2.8	3.0	4.2
90	2.1	2.8	4.5
100	0.0	2.4	4.8

other hand, personal observation is desirable when there is a high incidence of ownership of an appliance.

Deliberate Response Bias

In organizational surveys, biases are sometimes deliberately introduced by the respondent for fear that any detrimental statement concerning attitudes or past histories will be entered into personnel records or come to the attention of peers or supervisors. It is not unusual for a respondent to engage in role-playing and provide a socially desirable response.

This phenomenon has been apparent for many years. Hence a number of statistical techniques such as *randomized response* (Hosseini & Armacost, this volume; Warner, 1965) and the *unrelated questions method* (Greenberg, Abul-Ela, Simmons, & Horvitz, 1969) have been used to circumvent the problem when response to a question calls for a "yes-no" answer. In using randomized response, the respondent resorts to a randomizing device that determines whether to respond with the truthful answer or the untruthful one. For example, he or she may be instructed by the interviewer to roll a die. If the outcome, unseen by the interviewer, is 1 or 2, the respondent gives the true answer. Otherwise, he or she gives the false answer. Knowing the probabilities of selection, it is possible when the results are summarized to estimate the true proportions of agreement and disagreement with the question. In a similar manner, with the unrelated questions method two separate statements are presented and the respondent is asked to state whether he or she agrees or disagrees. The statement that he or she responds to is determined by the rolling of a die, the outcome of which is seen only by the respondent.

Although these two methods are theoretically sound, in actual practice they are very difficult to use and have been subject to criticism because they require the respondent to perform complex tasks, require interviewers to give long explanations, cause confusion, and sometimes induce suspicion among respondents (Shimizu & Bonham, 1978; Wiseman, Moriarty, & Schafer, 1975-1976).

To avoid many of these problems, another form of indirect questioning called the *item count technique* was introduced by Miller (1984). In its simplest form, a sample is randomly split into two halves. The first half is presented with a list of four behaviors, of which three are socially acceptable and one socially deviant. The other half is shown only the three behaviors that are socially acceptable. Both groups are asked to state how many of the activities shown they had engaged in. Averages are then computed for each of the two halves. The difference between the two averages provides an estimate of the proportion that had engaged in the deviant behavior.

In 1990, the method was perfected so it could be used in the National Household Seroprevalence Survey to estimate the prevalence of AIDS in certain population groups. An extensive pretest has been successfully completed and reported on (Droitcour et al., 1991).

The techniques of indirect questioning described above require the use of large samples and are applicable in obtaining statistical summaries for groups of the population. They are not effective when individual data are needed, for example, to compute correlation coefficients.

Even when these techniques are used, if there is a strong fear that a truthful response may be detrimental to a respondent's interest, the respondent will often not cooperate in the survey. This is especially true when the respondent is suspicious of the sponsor's motivations. Even though he or she consents to an interview, the credibility of the responses is doubtful.

This situation was confronted in a study conducted for a women's magazine to determine the influence of women in the purchase of a new car. The survey was conducted among automobile dealers to determine the features and car characteristics that are important to a woman in the showroom (a) when she is shopping alone and (b) when she is with a male companion. Interviews were made with the owner, manager, or head salesman of the dealership.

When pretests were conducted by highly experienced interviewers, they sensed that some respondents were evasive. Apparently, many suspected that the survey was sponsored by a competitive dealer or that the study was being conducted for the dealer's own car manufacturer.

Subsequently, the cooperation of the National Association of Automotive Dealers (NAAD) was gained by offering the Association a chance to add questions on behalf of its membership. By announcing the NAAD's sponsorship through an advance letter, excellent respondent cooperation and more candid responses were obtained.

Record Retrieval Methods

Throughout organizations, records are maintained for various administrative, internal financial accounting, and tax purposes. Other records are kept to comply with funding requirements. It is often believed that measurements obtained from such records are devoid of measurement error. As indicated in examples below, such may not be the case.

Out-of-Scope Data

One commercial method for obtaining detailed sales of branded merchandise to consumers through retail outlets over time is by measuring the flow of such goods from warehouses to retailers. This procedure appears to be very efficient for measuring consumption of grocery items, with their wide variety of brands and package sizes, because these data are generally already on computer tapes.

A bias may exist, however, by assuming that all of the shipments from wholesalers go to retail outlets to be purchased by consumers. However, some of the items are "out of scope," that is, those shipped by wholesalers to restaurants, hotels, steamship companies, schools, army bases, and other institutions. The consumer purchase market may therefore be overstated.

Misleading Records

It is believed that manufacturer shipments provide an impeccable source of estimates of consumer sales over an extended period of time. Because record-keeping practices vary among manufacturers, it is difficult to use such shipment data to reflect brand shares or units sold in the domestic market.

Some shipments of goods, such as toasters or detergents, go to commercial users. Other shipments are exported. Some manufacturers franchise the use of their brand names in other countries. These brands are manufactured abroad, and, in some instances, where foreign labor costs are low, manufactured articles are shipped back to this country to be sold by retailers. The impact of the "gray" market will not be accounted for in the manufacturers' records.

Hospital records also might be misleading. For example, when these are used for a census of current patients the data are usually obtained from admission records. These records indicate the diagnosis at admission. When the initial diagnosis changes, records that are supposed to be corrected at discharge showing additional diagnoses often are not.

Contamination

In many organizations, whether records are maintained in the form of a computer data base or on paper listings or card files, the possibility of contamination nevertheless exists. A data base or file is contaminated when it contains records inconsistent with the purpose(s) of the survey.

The use of such files leads to biases when the records are required for statistical summaries. For example, if magazine subscription lists are not purged periodically, summary statistics for current subscribers (critical for advertising revenues) may be misleading. When health records and records of educational achievement are kept, the information may be obsolete by the time the data are summarized.

Often, contamination occurs because of misclassification. This occurs when the file or data base is set up for one purpose and used for another. For example, if a study is designed to obtain wage rates for semiskilled workers in a particular group of establishments, a bias will be introduced if some establishments include office or clerical workers in their files.

Observation Methods

When observation methods are used and executed by well-trained and conscientious interviewers, the principal source of measurement error is due to statistical variation.

Static Phenomena

When the observation method is used to measure a static phenomenon, a sample of sites is selected and at each site the number or the incidence of the variable to be estimated is observed. For all of the sites in the sample, the average number or average incidence is computed. The total number, or the overall incidence for the population, is obtained by multiplying sample averages by the number of sites from which the sample was selected. In general, the more sites selected for the sample and the smaller the variability from site to site, the more reliable is the estimate. The variability of the average or incidence is determined by standard statistical methods.

This procedure can be employed by a city that has contracted a company to place posters at heavy traffic locations advertising the use of condoms for "safe sex." The number actually placed by the contractor can be determined with measurable precision.

Dynamic Phenomena

The measurement of dynamic phenomena involves observing the movement of people or objects within a fixed time interval. To measure the number of people who view a certain exhibit at a museum, an observer is stationed at one corner of the room where the exhibit is located and counts the number who enter at certain time periods. The frequencies obtained are usually expressed in terms of an hourly rate and then projected to the total "open to the public" hours for the location. This technique is sometimes referred to as time interval sampling.

Assuming that the reporting of movement is accurate, the only source of error is sampling variation. There are two components of variation: the reliability of the measurement at the individual site during the selected time periods and the sampling variation introduced through the use of a sample of time periods.

The reliability of the measurement at a single site is determined by two factors: the length of the time interval used for observation and the rate of the movement. The longer the interval of observation and the greater the movement, the more reliable is the estimate. The sampling distribution, which takes into account these two factors, is described by the *Poisson distribution* (Deming, 1950). From this, the reliability of the estimate can be determined. For example, if the average number of visitors to a museum exhibit is 10 per hour and the observation period is 1 hour, then any estimate of the number of viewers for any time period is subject to a relative error of 32%. If the observation period is 3 hours, then the relative error is 18%. For a more popular exhibit where the average can be expected to be 40 visitors per hour, then the relative error of the estimate based on a 1-hour observation period is 16%.

In the design of an observation, the number of sites and the number and length of the time intervals is specified. These affect sampling reliability. Budget and operational costs factors have to be taken into account. These involve the cost of travel and establishing operations at a site and the hourly direct interviewing cost for the observations. From these two factors, costs and statistical error, the survey designer determines the optimum sample design, that is, obtaining the most reliable information for a fixed cost or, conversely, achieving a fixed or predetermined total survey error at a minimum cost.

Summary and Conclusions

In organizational surveys, a wide variety of measurement techniques are used. They fall into three classes: interviewing methods, record retrieval procedures, and observation methods. All three are subject to errors, whether they be caused by biases or statistical variability of the measuring instrument.

Measurement errors that occur in the interviewing process may arise from the inability of respondents to recall certain events or facts during the interviewing process or through deliberate misstatements. In the former case, an illustration was presented to show how it was possible to use one interviewing procedure in conjunction with an alternative information-gathering procedure to derive the most cost- and statistically efficient estimate.

Although record retrieval methods make use of data banks, errors of measurement still occur because information in these banks may not be adequate for the purposes of the survey. Illustrations were also given of the occurrence of measurement error because of out-of-scope data, misleading records, or data contamination.

Observation methods are often used to measure dynamic phenomena, such as the movement of traffic by car occupancy on highways at certain times of day, visitors to museum exhibits, sales of brands of soft drinks through vending machines in shopping malls, sales of perishable fruits and vegetables at retail outlets, and so on. The principal source of error for these methods is due to statistical variability. An example was given showing how the variability is controlled.

Throughout this chapter it was emphasized that although measurement error can be defined and controlled for there are other factors in the design of an organization survey that should be taken into account.

References

Deming, W. E. (1950). *Some theory of sampling*. New York: John Wiley.

Droitcour, J., Caspar, R. A., Hubbard, M. I., Parsley, T. L., Visscher, W., & Ezzati, T. M. (1991). The item count technique as a method of indirect questioning: A review of its development and a case study application. In P. R. Biemar, R. M. Groves, L. E. Lyberg, N. A. Mathiowetz, & S. Sudman (Eds.), *Measurement errors in surveys* (pp. 185-210). New York: John Wiley.

Dutka, S., & Frankel, L. R. (1960). Observation techniques in store auditing. *Agricultural Economics Research, 12*(3), 11-12.

Dutka, S., & Frankel, L. R. (1975). *Let's not forget about response error* (Modern Marketing Series, No. 12). New York: Audits & Surveys.

Frankel, L. R. (1970). *The role of accuracy and precision in sampling surveys* (Modern Marketing Series, No. 7). New York: Audits & Surveys.

Greenberg, B., Abul-Ela, A. A., Simmons, W. R., & Horvitz, D. G. (1969). The unrelated questions randomized response model: Theoretical framework. *Journal of the American Statistical Association, 64*, 520-539.

Houseman, E. E., & Lipstein, B. (1960). Observation and audit techniques for measuring retail sales. *Agricultural Economics Research, 12*(3), 12-22.

Johnson N. L., & Smith, H., Jr. (1969). *New developments in survey sampling*. New York: John Wiley

Miller, J. (1984). *A new survey technique for studying deviant behavior*. Unpublished doctoral dissertation, George Washington University.

O'Muircheartaigh, C. (1991). Simple response: estimation and determinants. In P. R. Biemar, R. M. Groves, L. E. Lyberg, N. A. Mathiowetz, & S. Sudman (Eds.), *Measurement errors in surveys* (pp. 551-574). New York: John Wiley.

Shimizu, I., & Bonham, G. (1978). Randomized response in a national study. *Journal of the American Statistical Association, 73*, 35-39.

Suen, H. K., & Ary, D. (1988). *Analyzing quantitative behavioral observation data*. Hillsdale, NJ: Lawrence Erlbaum.

Warner, S. (1965). Randomized response: A survey technique for eliminating evasive answer bias. *Journal of the American Statistical Association, 60*, 63-69.

Wiseman, F., Moriarty, M., & Schafer, M. (1975-1976). Estimating public opinion with the randomized response model. *Public Opinion Quarterly, 39*, 507-513.

PART II

New Directions in Practice

4

Computer-Administered Surveys in Organizational Settings

Alternatives, Advantages, and Applications

STEPHANIE BOOTH-KEWLEY
PAUL ROSENFELD
JACK E. EDWARDS

Like the advertising campaign for a well-known high-tech firm, computer-administered surveys had, for many years, a "what if?" quality. Although theoretically possible, computer-administered surveys were not practical for most organizations. Until recently, the use of computers for administering surveys required specialized computer skills and hard-to-get or expensive equipment. With the increasing availability of computers has come specialized software for transferring surveys from paper to computer. Also, the availability of relatively inexpensive but increasingly sophisticated personal computers has made computer administration of surveys in organizational settings more feasible. Now the "what if?" question has been replaced by issues relating to applications, advantages, and alternatives. How does one do a computerized organizational survey? Under

AUTHORS' NOTE: The opinions expressed herein are those of the authors. They are not official and do not represent the views of the Department of the Navy. The authors acknowledge the assistance of Monica Aguirre, Dora Silva, and Carol Newell. This chapter was written by government employees as part of official duties; therefore it cannot be copyrighted and is in the public domain.

open-ended questions can be used; and (g) response rates tend to be high. Face-to-face interviews appear to the best choice for lengthy, in-depth surveys requiring an hour or more to complete (Fowler, 1988). Face-to-face interview surveys also have a number of disadvantages relative to paper and computer surveys. They are expensive to conduct, both because of the costs of training interviewers and because it takes many more hours to gather data using interviews than using paper surveys. If interviewers are not trained or are poorly trained, the quality of data may be variable (Miller, 1991). Because the interviewer represents a status figure and it is difficult for respondents in face-to-face interviews to feel completely anonymous, individuals may give more socially desirable responses than they would on paper or a computer (Martin & Nagao, 1989).

Telephone Surveys/Interviews

Telephones are frequently used to conduct surveys or interviews (see Lavrakas, 1987). With virtually all residences in the United States having telephones, a nonbiased, cross-sectional sample can be obtained in a telephone survey (Miller, 1991). In telephone polls of the general population, variations of *random-digit dialing* can be used to precisely select random samples that represent various populations or subgroups of interest. Common examples of such telephone surveys are political polls, television-viewing surveys, and marketing surveys.

Telephone surveys or interviews have a number of advantages over other survey methods. One major advantage is that they can be administered more efficiently and much less expensively than in-person interviews (Fowler, 1988). In many cases, telephone surveys can be done for about half the cost of in-person interviews (Miller, 1991). Furthermore, rising crime rates have resulted in people becoming more hesitant about letting strangers into their homes for in-person interviews. No one wants to be interviewed by the next Jeffrey Dahmer! As a result, many face-to-face interview surveys are now conducted in shopping malls, with telephone surveys used as an alternative.

There are disadvantages to telephone surveys as well. One problem is that respondents' nonverbal behaviors (e.g., frowns, grimaces, smiles) cannot be assessed. Also, compared with face-to-face interviews, rapport is more difficult to establish in a telephone survey. Thus it is not surprising that individuals are more likely to resist answering sensitive questions in a telephone interview than in person (Groves & Kahn,

1979). In addition, the nature of a telephone interaction limits the type and number of questions (Lavrakas, 1987), precluding, for example, the use of visual materials (e.g., cards, scales). Finally, as answering machines become more prevalent, it may be harder to contact individuals who regularly "screen" their calls (Tuckel & Feinberg, 1991).

Compared to a mail-out paper survey, a telephone survey may be less expensive, particularly if the survey is brief. It may be cheaper to administer brief surveys by telephone than to pay the costs (outgoing and return postage, envelopes, printed labels, etc.) of mailing the surveys. It should be noted, however, that, like face-to-face interviews, telephone surveys are expensive relative to nonmailed paper surveys (e.g., surveys conducted within a single branch of an organization). Also, unlike telephone surveys of the general population, when an organizational survey is administered by telephone the employees may doubt the confidentiality and anonymity of their responses, especially if the telephone call is placed to their homes. To our knowledge, most organizations do not conduct surveys of their employees at their homes because there is concern about the employees' right to privacy.

As telephone surveys have become more complex, they have become increasingly susceptible to interviewer error, especially when filtering or branching questions are asked. This problem has led to attempts to automate the telephone survey process through the development of computer-assisted telephone interviewing (CATI) systems. In a CATI system, the telephone interview is controlled by a computer. The computer presents questions to the interviewee in the correct order, branches to other questions if required, issues error messages when responses are "out of range," and stores responses in a data base for subsequent analysis. U.S. government agencies such as the Census Bureau and the Air Force have used CATI systems for telephone surveys (Frey, 1989).

By automating much of the survey process, CATI provides the gains in efficiency and error reduction offered by computer surveys. CATI systems also facilitate precise sampling while minimizing interviewer error. However, installation of a fully-networked CATI system may be expensive. As Frey (1989) noted, "Installing the hardware for a CATI system of 12-15 stations usually calls for an outlay of approximately $100,000, a sum not available to many survey operations" (p. 211). The cost per stand-alone CATI station has been estimated at between $1,500 and $5,000 (Frey, 1989), although as PC-based CATI systems continue to be developed by firms such as Sawtooth Software, the costs should drop.

With the proliferation of sophisticated software for administering surveys, the distinctions between CATI and computer surveys are being blurred. Currently, CATI-like systems can automatically select respondents, dial the telephone numbers, ask a set of prerecorded questions, and record the responses through voice-mail or by directing the respondent to hit a key on the phone corresponding to the desired response (Frey, 1989). Organizations that presently use telephone surveys and wish to capitalize on the advantages of computer technology might consider the CATI approach, whereas those who presently use standard paper surveys may want to consider using computer surveys.

Scannable Surveys

A major advantage of computer-administered over paper surveys is that the computer automates the data entry phase, thereby increasing the accuracy of data entry and saving the time and costs associated with it. This advantage has been translated to paper surveys through the use of scannable surveys. In scannable surveys, a respondent completes a specially designed form by filling in a circle, oval, or square to show his or her answer. Some scannable forms allow a respondent to print a letter or number in each of a series of blocks. An optical scanner then typically reads the responses by either sending light through the survey form and reading the intensity (transoptic scanning) or bouncing light off one side of the form and measuring the intensity of the reflected light (reflective scanning). Although form scanning has been around for a long time for psychological and aptitude tests (e.g., Scholastic Aptitude Test, or SAT), greater sophistication of scanning equipment and software and reduced hardware and software costs have made it an increasingly popular mode of survey administration.

Scannable surveys come in many sizes and shapes. Some surveys use a generic machine-scorable sheet, with the questions presented on an answer form that is separate from the survey questions. Although these are less costly and require less time to develop than actually having the survey items on the scanner sheet, they have disadvantages. One potential problem is that a generic scanner sheet typically requires that all questions be answered using a standard number of alternatives. This restriction could cause problems if items requiring a dichotomous yes or no response (2-point scale) are needed in addition to those requiring a rating scale with multiple scale steps (e.g., a 7-point scale). Even though costs are saved through generic sheets, they are more cumbersome for the respondents, who must read the questions on one page and then record their responses on another. Although this process may also lead to errors if respondents incorrectly record their responses on the answer sheets, research (Veit & Scruggs, 1986; Wise, Plake, Eastman, & Novak, 1987) has shown this to be a minor issue. When the achievement test scores of students using traditional test booklets and separate machine-scorable answer sheets were compared, only minimal differences were obtained. The differences were minimal even when test takers were in early elementary school or had learning disabilities.

On customized scannable surveys, the questions and response options are printed directly on the scannable form. This format is much less cumbersome for the respondent and minimizes errors that occur when respondents record responses on a separate sheet. Customized scannable surveys, however, take time to design and entail development and reproduction expenses. Some of our colleagues have had success designing their own customized scannable organizational surveys using a PC-based software program called *Survey Design*. For small-scale organizational surveys ($N < 3,000$), the system produces a professional-looking and accurately scorable product. The main disadvantage of the system is that it is slow and initially difficult to use. Alternatively, the *Compose Right* system by National Computer Systems (NCS) of Owatonna, Minnesota is available for Macintosh computers (and soon for IBM-based machines). The user develops the form with the special *Compose Right* software and then either electronically sends the form or mails the diskette overnight to NCS, where it is printed, collated, bound, and returned to the customer (usually in 5 days or less). Having an outside company such as NCS perform these tasks may be too expensive for some organizations. However, as scanner technology has become more commonplace, it has also become cheaper. Booker (1990) reported that features such as double-sided scanning and scanning of bar codes, which several years ago were available only in $50,000 scanner systems, now could be purchased for $6,000.

If these trends continue, scanner surveys may soon become as commonplace as paper ones. The ability of scannable surveys to eliminate the tedious task of data entry is an advantage over paper surveys, which probably explains their increasing popularity as vehicles for administering organizational surveys. For example, customized scannable forms have recently been used in large-sample federal government personnel surveys to gather data on sexual harassment (U.S. Merit Systems Protection Board, 1988), employee turnover (U.S. Merit Systems Protection

Board, 1989), and employees' perceptions of pay and working conditions (U.S. Merit Systems Protection Board, 1990).

Factors Determining Whether Computer-Administered Survey Administration Should Be Used

Given that each method of administering organizational surveys has advantages and disadvantages, it cannot unequivocally be stated that computers are *the* best way to administer an organizational survey. The choice of administration method depends on a number of factors: cost, time factors, number of people to be surveyed, type of data needed, sensitivity of information requested, number of data-gathering sites, frequency of administration, availability of special equipment and computers, characteristics of the respondents, respondents' attitudes toward computer administration, and response characteristics needed. Each of these topics is reviewed below.

Cost

Traditional paper surveys are generally the least expensive method of administration, even if mailing costs are involved. They require no special equipment, no interviewers, and usually no travel. At this time, scannable surveys are generally more expensive than traditional paper surveys, especially if complex forms must be designed or purchased and/or scanning equipment must be purchased or contracted. The savings in data entry time afforded by scannable surveys may make them an economical choice in the long run if the survey is to be administered on a large-scale or ongoing basis. Customized scannable surveys also look "professional," which may increase response rates or the degree to which respondents take the survey seriously. Face-to-face interviews are generally the most expensive administration mode for organizational surveys; telephone surveys offer a cheaper alternative if the task involves a limited number of questions. The cost of computer-administered surveys varies widely, depending on the circumstances. If, for example, an ample number of personal computers are already available to an organization and respondents can be easily brought to the site of the computers, administration of a computer survey would be about as expensive as a paper survey (and possibly cheaper in the long run because of the elimination of data entry). On the other hand, if a large number of computers and software must be purchased or rented for the sole purpose of the survey and/or respondents are located at diverse sites, a computer survey can quickly become more expensive than other administration methods. Similarly, if a computer bulletin board is used to administer a survey, maintenance and the need for a point of contact to answer questions may make it prohibitively expensive unless it will be used frequently. If an organization is linked to an existing e-mail network such as BITNET or INTERNET, it may be possible to conduct a low-cost electronic survey using these computer networks. However, particular e-mail groups may have policies that limit such activities.

Time Factors

As in other businesses, time is money with surveys. Thus the ability of computer administration to speed data collection and analysis is one of its biggest selling points. The vast majority of studies that have examined speed of responding (all using the Minnesota Multiphasic Personality Inventory, or MMPI) found that questionnaire completion time was significantly less on the computer than on paper (Dunn, Lushene, & O'Neil, 1972; Honaker, 1988; Russell, Peace, & Mellsop, 1986; Watson et al., 1990; White, Clements, & Fowler, 1985). Only one study (Bresolin, 1984) found no difference between computer and paper conditions in completion time; however, the sample in this study differed from the other studies in that it included psychotic individuals.

In addition to producing faster responding, computer-administered surveys can usually be analyzed more quickly than paper ones. Similarly, telephone interviews, especially in conjunction with a CATI system, save considerable time over face-to-face interview surveys. It has been our experience that computer surveys involving several hundred respondents can be administered, analyzed, and the results presented within a week's time. Although scannable surveys can be processed faster than paper ones, someone still needs to run the surveys through the scanner, leaving open the possibility that the scanner (and the person running it!) might experience a breakdown.

Number of People to Be Surveyed

For complex, large-scale surveys of several thousand individuals or more, most organizations are best served with a paper survey or, if sufficient funds are available, a scannable survey. Although telephone surveys can be done with large sample sizes, many organizational surveys are simply too complicated to administer by phone. Similarly, face-to-face interviews for long organizational surveys administered to large samples are very time-consuming and expensive. Our own experience recommends computer surveys as a preferred mode for sample sizes of 500 or less. In surveys of small organizations or for surveys of select subgroups (e.g., managers), computers are a viable option.

Type of Data Needed

Paper, scannable, and computer-administered surveys are excellent means for gathering quantitative data (i.e., numbers), especially when standard psychological scales are used. If most of the questions are closed-ended (e.g., agree-disagree, true-false, etc.), paper, scannable, and computer-administered surveys are much more cost-effective than interviews. These methods are often less efficient for gathering an extensive amount of qualitative data (e.g., answers to open-ended questions and comments). Although open-ended items can be included in paper, scannable, or computer-administered surveys, the interview (either by telephone or in person) is generally a better method for gathering primarily qualitative information. Finally, because a computer can be programmed to allow for question branching (i.e., modification of subsequent questions based on answers to previous items) in a manner that is transparent to the user, an organizational survey using many branching items (e.g., marital status—married individuals get different follow-up questions than single people) is easier to complete on computer than on paper. Branching can also be efficiently done using face-to-face or telephone interviews (especially using CATI systems).

Sensitivity of Information Requested

Sensitivity of information requested is an important aspect of organizational surveys (see Hosseini & Armacost, this volume). If the survey addresses sensitive or highly personal topics, such as sexual harassment or drug and alcohol abuse, guarantees of anonymity and confidentiality are crucial. It may be easier to establish confidentiality and anonymity with paper (especially mail-out), scannable, or computer-administered surveys than with face-to-face interviews or telephone surveys.

Number of Data-Gathering Sites

Although computers can be linked through networks or electronic mail sites (and organizational surveys have been administered in this fashion) (see Tyburski, Petrey, Wilson, & Kewley, 1989), they are easier and cheaper if one central testing area is used. When respondents are at multiple sites, the chances of equipment failure and a "survey meltdown" increase. Also, there is a need for a full- or part-time troubleshooter to answer questions from remote sites. In a multisite computer bulletin board survey of civilian Navy personnel (see Tyburski, 1992), contact personnel had to be trained at each location. Problems occurred when these individuals were unavailable during the survey administration period (due to illness or vacation) or were replaced by untrained individuals. Contact personnel may also be necessary when organizational surveys contained on self-administered floppy diskettes are mailed to remote survey sites. For a civilian Navy project, respondents were to complete an organizational survey (contained on a floppy diskette) on their office PC and mail it back to a central location (Tyburski, 1992). Although the system was user friendly (and seemingly "idiot proof"), some respondents could not use it without extensive help; others tried to "crack" the software. Thus the survey administrators found themselves answering numerous telephone calls from respondents having difficulty accessing or completing the survey. With remote computer surveys we have found that Murphy's Law reigns supreme: If something can go wrong, it will! Thus, if multiple sites are essential, mail-out paper or scanner surveys may provide a better alternative than computer administration. If the survey is short, telephones can "reach out and touch everyone" more efficiently than computers can.

Frequency of Administration

Some organizational surveys are "one-shot wonders" focusing on the specific issue of the day (e.g., where the company's holiday party should be held), whereas others may be institutionalized and part of a recurring process (e.g., the Navy's biennial survey of equal opportunity issues). In general, as the frequency of administration of a survey goes up, the benefits of using automated methods (scannable and computer-administrated surveys) increase. If an organization plans to administer a survey on a routine basis, it may be cost-effective to purchase scanning equipment or personal computers and survey software. However, if an organization is administering a survey on a one-shot basis and will have no future use for the specialized equipment and software, a paper survey may be a better choice.

Availability of Special Equipment and Computers

If specialized scanning equipment is already available, then a scannable survey would likely be preferable to a paper one. Also, if an ample number of personal computers are already available to an organization, administration of a computer survey may be more cost-effective when the savings in data entry are factored in. In addition, relatively inexpensive software for designing and administering surveys is now available.

Characteristics of the Respondents

Even though computers have become commonplace in work settings, they are not always accepted by employees. Lack of satisfaction with and anxiety toward computers can undermine their successful integration in the workplace (Davis, Bagozzi, & Warshaw, 1992). It might be thought that individuals with little previous exposure or negative attitudes toward computers would respond differently on computer than on paper survey measures. However, in our own studies (e.g., Edwards, Booth-Kewley, & Rosenfeld, 1991) individuals who had relatively higher computer anxiety did not answer computer-administered surveys any differently from the way they answered paper surveys. Meier (1988), however, found that individuals high on computer aversion demonstrated lower performance on cognitive tests administered on the computer than they did in a paper format. Also, George, Lankford, and Wilson (1992) found that individuals high in computer anxiety had higher depression scores in a computer condition than in a paper one. Thus caution may be warranted when administering computer surveys to respondents with little or no computer experience or showing high computer anxiety.

Respondents' Attitudes Toward Computer Administration

A substantial number of studies have found that respondents react more positively to surveys and other instruments presented on computer than in a paper format. This tendency has been found for personality instruments (Harrell & Lombardo, 1984; Lukin, Dowd, Plake, & Kraft, 1985; Rozensky, Honor, Rasinski, Tovian, & Herz, 1986; Russell et al., 1986; Watson et al., 1990; White et al., 1985), organizational surveys (Booth-Kewley et al., 1992; Rosenfeld, Doherty, Carroll, Kantor, & Thomas, 1986; Rosenfeld, Giacalone, et al., 1991), and substance use surveys (Erdman, Klein, & Greist, 1983; Skinner & Allen, 1983).

However, two studies (Llabre, Clements, Fitzhugh, & Lancelotta, 1987; Lushene, O'Neil, & Dunn, 1974) found that computer administration elicited more anxiety in respondents than did paper assessment, and two studies (Kantor, 1991; Katz & Dalby, 1981) found respondents' liking for computer and paper administration formats to be equal. Also, Martin and Nagao (1989) found that respondents for a high-status position (management trainee) had greater resentment of computer and paper interviews than for a similar face-to-face interview. No difference in degree of resentment between computer and paper interviews was found.

Why do respondents generally prefer the computer to the paper format? A number of studies (Booth-Kewley et al., 1992; Erdman et al., 1983; Skinner & Allen, 1983; Watson et al., 1990) have shown that respondents find the computer format more interesting. Two studies (Booth-Kewley et al., 1992; Matheson & Zanna, 1988) suggest that responding on the computer may lead to higher levels of self-awareness. Other studies (Lukin et al., 1985; Rozensky et al., 1986; Skinner & Allen, 1983) have found that respondents using the computer condition perceive computer administration as "faster"—that is, time appears to pass more quickly—than when responding on paper. Other research has shown that respondents completing measures on the computer perceive the assessment as more useful (Davis & Cowles, 1989) and regard the experience as more relevant (Rozensky et al., 1986).

Tracking of Response Characteristics

One capability of computer-administered surveys is their ability to track and record response characteristics. This information has a variety of possible applications. Space (1981) suggested that response latency and key pressure could be used as validity checks for random responding or fatigue. One recent study (Temple & Geisinger, 1990) found that response latencies for emotionally arousing questionnaire items were longer than for nonarousing items. This finding suggests the possibility of using response latency as an indicator of arousal. However, as Ben-Porath and Butcher (1986) noted, "As it now stands, computers can measure many more variables than we actually know how to interpret" (p. 175). More work is clearly needed on how to interpret variables such as response latency and key pressure before they will become useful to researchers and practitioners.

In sum, whether or not an organization chooses to administer a computer survey will depend on many factors. It is recommended that an organization administer a computer survey if the majority of the following conditions exist: (a) Ample computer equipment exists or funds are available for renting; (b) the survey is to be administered on a routine or ongoing basis, (c) the data to be gathered are primarily closed-ended and quantitative rather than open-ended or qualitative, (d) results are needed quickly, (e) most of the potential respondents have had some previous experience with computers, (f) respondents can be easily brought to a single location (g) tailored assessment (i.e., branching items) will be used, and (h) the number of respondents to be surveyed is 500 or less.

A Review of Research Findings

Although we have reviewed the major modes of organizational survey administration, the overwhelming number of comparisons in the research literature have been between computer and paper surveys and questionnaires.[2] Because paper administration has been the standard, we focus here on research that has sought to determine if computer administration is better, worse, or equivalent to its paper counterpart.

Nonaptitude Psychological Measures

Although many organizational surveys consist only of job- and organization-related items, organizational researchers are increasingly recognizing the impact of personality variables on organizational behavior (Hogan & Hogan, 1989; Staw, Bell, & Clausen, 1986). Thus the research that has evaluated the effects of computer and paper administration modes on personality measures has applicability for the organizational arena. Much of this research has evaluated the Minnesota Multiphasic Personality Inventory (MMPI).

Research Using the MMPI

Research comparing computer versus traditional administration of the MMPI has been equivocal (see Honaker, 1988, for a review). Some studies (e.g., Rozensky et al., 1986; Russell et al., 1986; Watson et al., 1990; White et al., 1985) found no mean differences on any of the MMPI clinical scales. Several other studies (e.g., Biskin & Kolotkin, 1977; Bresolin, 1984) found differences on one or more of the MMPI scales, and, in most cases, means in the computer condition were *lower* than in the paper condition, indicating less psychopathology. However, there has not been consistency regarding the scales on which the administration-based differences occurred.

As pointed out by Honaker (1988), studies that reported few or no mean MMPI score differences across administration conditions were more likely to have used computer programs that provided roughly the same response options as are available in the paper MMPI format. Conversely, studies finding more pronounced MMPI score differences were more likely to have used computer programs that provided response options that differed from the traditional paper format (e.g., by not allowing the respondent to skip items or give "?" responses). These findings suggest that responses to the computer-administered and paper MMPI would probably be similar or equivalent if response options were held constant and underscore the importance of keeping all aspects of the testing session as similar as possible when instruments are adapted for computer administration.

Other Personality Measures

The effects of computer administration on personality measures other than the MMPI have been less widely studied. Katz and Dalby (1981) compared computer and paper administration of the Eysenck Personality Inventory (EPI). Respondents were administered the EPI in both formats on two different occasions, with the order of administration counterbalanced. No difference was found on any of the three scales— Extraversion, Neuroticism, and Lie. Another study (Davis & Cowles, 1989) compared responses to paper-and-pencil and computer-administered versions of the EPI and Anxiety and Locus of Control scales. No difference in mean scores was found on any measure.

Harrell and Lombardo (1984) compared computer and paper modes of administration on the 16PF, a widely used personality inventory. The 16PF and the State Scale of the State-Trait Anxiety Inventory were administered twice in either computer-computer, computer-paper, paper-computer, or computer-paper administration conditions. No significant difference in scale score means was found on any of the measures.

Scissons (1976) compared computer and paper modes of administration for the California Psychological Inventory (CPI). Respondents completed the CPI using paper, or, in a computer-administered mode, using a light pen. Significant scale mean differences were found on eight of the personality scales for males but on only one of the scales for females. For all of the personality scales in which a difference was found, means in the computer condition were *lower* than those on paper, with a lower scale mean usually connoting less socially desirable responses. It appeared that the mean scale differences occurred because respondents in the computer condition omitted significantly more questions. This, in turn, was likely due to differences between the two conditions in item presentation. On the computer, the "omit" option was presented on the screen next to each item. In the paper condition, "omit" was not presented as a choice next to each item, although respondents were told (once) that they could omit responses. As was true for much of the MMPI research, procedural differences between the two administration modes probably caused the scale mean differences.

Substance Use and Personal Problem Behaviors

Given the sensitive nature of questions about drug/alcohol use and personal problem behaviors, researchers have tried to determine if computer rather than paper surveys can elicit more candid responses. Thus several studies have compared computer and paper-and-pencil assessments of substance use. Erdman et al. (1983) compared computer and paper assessments of cigarette, alcohol, and drug use among high school students. Results were comparable for the two methods on most items, although subjects admitted to significantly more alcohol use on paper than they did on the computer. Similarly, Skinner and Allen (1983) evaluated computer and paper assessments of alcohol, caffeine, tobacco, and drug use. No difference across administration conditions was found for overall usage, but respondents in the paper condition admitted eating more chocolate than did those in the computer condition. Millstein (1987) compared responses of female adolescents to a substance use questionnaire given either on computer or on paper and found no difference across administration conditions. Davis and Morse (1991) similarly compared responses to an alcoholism screening test given either on computer or on paper. No differences in mean scores or in percentages classified as alcoholics were found across conditions.

In a recent study, Hinkle, Sampson, and Radonsky (1991) compared computer and paper assessments of personal problems. Mental health clinic outpatients responded to paper-and-pencil and computer versions of the Personal Problem Checklist (PPC), which assesses life problems in job, family, finances, and so on. A significantly greater number of problems were reported on the computer than on paper, but no difference was found for severity of problems.

Overall, studies of computer and paper administration of nonaptitude psychological measures have generally found that the two modes of administration yield similar responses. However, for both the MMPI and the CPI, scores in the computer conditions tended to be lower than those obtained on paper, probably due to respondents' greater tendency to omit responses or give "?" responses on the computer. We conclude that it is very important that instructions, instrument presentation, and response formatting be kept as similar as possible across computer and paper conditions. Although, under some conditions, respondents on the computer appear more willing to report negative emotions, problems, or socially undesirable behaviors than they do on paper, the conditions under which this tendency can be reliably expected to occur need to be more precisely determined.

Computer Surveys in Organizational Settings

Organizations have not ignored the potential benefits of computer-administered surveys. However, in both the private and government sectors, organizational goals and the need to protect sensitive and proprietary information have often limited the documenting of computer-based organizational systems in the research and professional literatures. Recently, several articles have been published (e.g., Read's, 1991, description of on-line surveying at IBM) that detail computer survey systems in academic, private, and public sector organizations.

Academic/Private Sector

Although aptitude tests, personality scales, and clinical-diagnostic instruments have been administered on computers since the early 1970s, the use of computers to administer organizational scales and surveys is a later development, as are efforts to compare computer and other modes of survey administration.

In an academic setting, Kiesler and Sproull (1986) had users of a computer-mail system at Carnegie Mellon University complete a survey of health and personal characteristics and five items to assess socially desirable responding. Although there were no differences in results for computer and paper versions of the survey on the attitude items assessing health and personal characteristics, computer respondents gave less socially desirable responses. Similarly, Sproull (1986) found that mean responses to an organizational survey administered on computer (electronic mail) and paper did not differ; computer respondents, however, were more likely to choose extreme responses. Also, Feinstein (1986) reported anecdotal evidence from a survey in which sales personnel at the Chevron Corporation were asked their views of the company's marketing strategy on either computer or paper. Whereas the paper respondents engaged in impression management (they had only kind words for their bosses), the computer responses were more forthright (not all the responses were so favorable to management). More recently, Corman (1990) administered a communication network (sociometric) questionnaire in an organization. He found that paper and computer surveys produced comparable data, although the computer-based data had slightly better test-retest reliability and criterion validity.

Several attempts have also been made to compare computer surveys with face-to-face interviews. Liefeld (1988) found that adult shoppers who were questioned via computer, interview, or paper responded similarly on both "yes-no" and rating scale question types. However, for multiresponse knowledge questions, respondents on the computer picked more response options and were more often incorrect. Martin and Nagao (1989) had undergraduate students in an organizational behavior course complete a simulated job interview survey in computer, paper, or face-to-face interview conditions. Respondents in the face-to-face interview condition had higher social desirability scores and inflated their grade point averages and SAT scores significantly more than did those in the computer and paper groups. A comparison of the computer and paper conditions showed that there was more socially desirable responding and overreporting of scholastic aptitude scores on paper than on computer.

Federal Government/Military

The Computerized Executive Networking
Survey System (CENSUS) Project

In 1983, the Navy's Office of Civilian Personnel Management (OCPM) first tasked the Navy Personnel Research and Development Center (NPRDC) with conducting a feasibility study of a computer-based survey system that would automate and speed the process of survey administration. This resulted in the development of several prototypes of the CENSUS system during the mid- and late-1980s. In its original form (CENSUS I), individuals completed surveys on a computer terminal linked to an IBM PC/XT or PC/AT host computer. This configuration allowed up to eight users to complete the survey simultaneously, either on-site or at remote locations using commercial phone connections.

As microcomputers became more sophisticated, CENSUS II was introduced with its multiuser XENIX operating system. CENSUS II allowed up to 16 users to complete a survey simultaneously, either on-site or at remote locations. Although the multiuser capability of the CENSUS prototypes proved an advantage for surveys of large organizations, the system's requirement that respondents be linked to the host computer during administration limited the system's flexibility and usefulness. This requirement resulted in the development of the microcomputer-based assessment surveys and questionnaires (MASQ) system. MASQ mimicked the features of the CENSUS system but did so on single floppy diskettes capable of running on any IBM-compatible microcomputer. Using MASQ, a computer survey could be developed, run, stored, and analyzed without a networked system or a specific operating system. MASQ allowed organizational surveys to be mailed out to respondents on diskettes, which respondents completed on their own personal computers and then mailed back to NPRDC for analysis. Another version, portable-MASQ (P-MASQ) (Rosenfeld, Doherty, Vicino, & Greaves, 1988), allowed surveys to be administered on computers in field settings, enabling organizational surveys to be administered at respondents' work sites.

When the CENSUS project first began, there were no widely available software products that could meet all the requirements necessary to conduct Navy surveys. More recently, however, commercial survey software, such as Ci2 from Sawtooth Software, has become readily available. Thus the most recent versions of CENSUS have adapted commercial survey software to Navy needs. Also, a CENSUS electronic bulletin board allowing for downloading of electronic surveys and uploading of completed surveys has been successfully tested with a sample of 3,600 employees completing the Navy Civilian Personnel Survey (see Tyburski, 1992).[3]

Research Evidence

In the first CENSUS study, Doherty and Thomas (1986) administered a 60-item attitude survey on the civil service system to over 300 civilian

surveys. In this chapter, we have reviewed computer surveys as one mode of administration and suggested factors that should be considered when contemplating their use in organizations. The results of the studies reviewed overwhelmingly suggest that computer and paper modes of administration yield similar results, although individual studies have at times reported differences. This conclusion argues that, where financial and logistical considerations allow, organizations should not hesitate to use computers instead of paper, face-to-face, or telephone modes of administration.

Although researchers who have focused on potential response differences between paper and computer surveys may be disappointed by our conclusion of "no difference," there are advantages associated with the view that there are no consistent differences in the results of computer versus paper organizational surveys. Because respondents who complete computer surveys find them more interesting and report being more aware of their thoughts and feelings than do respondents who use paper surveys, an organizational practitioner may find greater respondent attentiveness and alertness on long computer surveys than on paper equivalents.

As we complete this chapter about computer-administered surveys, we realize that past predictions of a "paperless" society have become increasingly plausible. Certainly in the organizational arena, the paperless survey has clearly moved from science fiction to daily reality.

Notes

1. One feature of computer-administered aptitude testing that may have applicability to computer surveys is *tailored testing* ("Collegians being put to the test," 1992). A future potential advantage of using computer-administered questionnaires is the possibility of tailoring the questionnaire to the individual respondent. In the tailored or adaptive questionnaire, the items selected for administration are based on the respondent's answers to previous items. Research on ability tests has found that tailored tests typically take less than half the time of traditional tests and may provide more precise ability estimates (Moreno, Wetzel, McBride, & Weiss, 1983; Weiss, 1985). The feasibility of developing tailored, computerized, *nonaptitude* psychological tests has only begun to be explored. Given the additional time savings that could be gained from tailored psychological and organizational instruments, this is an approach that should be pursued further.

2. There have been several studies comparing computer and face-to-face interview assessment of nonaptitude psychological measures. Overall, these studies have yielded equivocal results. Lucas, Mullin, Luna, and McInroy (1977) found 30% greater admission of alcohol consumption on a computerized questionnaire than in a face-to-face interview.

Similarly, a study conducted in Scotland found that a computer survey led to a 33% higher admission of alcohol consumption than did a face-to-face interview (Duffy & Waterston, 1984). Skinner and Allen (1983), however, found no differences in responses to alcohol and drug use measures administered in computer and face-to-face interview conditions. Consistent with the results finding greater admission of substance use on the computer, Farrell, Camplair, and McCullough (1987) found that clients reported a significantly greater number of clinical complaints (e.g., mood problems or compulsive behaviors) on a computer than in a face-to-face interview. Matheson and Zanna (1988) found that respondents participating in computer-mediated discussions with other participants reported higher private self-awareness than did those who engaged in discussions in a face-to-face condition. Lindell (1988) found no differences between computer and face-to-face interview conditions on scores on the Tennessee Self-Concept Scale or on a measure of socially desirable responding (the Balanced Inventory of Desirable Responding). Thus there is some suggestion of a tendency for respondents to be more candid on the computer than in face-to-face interview conditions.

3. Recently, the U.S. Air Force has been conducting research and development to automate and speed data collection on Air Force occupational surveys. The effort is designed to enable occupational surveys to be self-administered on a personal computer, optimize the reliability and validity of responses through adaptive scaling procedures, allow for automatic item branching and feedback of information, and provide integration of the system within an Air Force-wide electronic data transmission network (Armstrong Laboratory, 1992).

4. Although these CENSUS studies demonstrated that computer surveys produced responses equivalent to paper surveys, they failed to support the claims that by reducing social desirability bias the use of computers surveys leads to higher-quality data. Rosenfeld et al. (1991) reasoned that whereas respondents in general may not be more candid on the computer, there may be a subgroup of individuals particularly sensitive to social cues for impression management who might respond differently on the computer. This individual differences approach was tested with employed business students. Students completed a survey, which contained the JDI and the Self-Monitoring Scale, either on a personal computer using MASQ or on paper. The results were mixed. Although high self-monitors had higher job satisfaction scores on paper than on MASQ, for low self-monitors, the opposite occurred: Their job satisfaction scores were higher on the computer than on paper. If, as the authors assumed, it is socially desirable to indicate higher levels of job satisfaction, then it is unclear what these results indicate. Furthermore, in the Vicino (1989) study mentioned previously, high and low self-monitors *did not* respond differently on computer and paper instruments that included the Crowne- Marlowe Scale. Thus the idea that high and low self-monitors would respond differently on computer versus paper instruments has not received clear support.

References

Armstrong Laboratory. (1992, July). *Human resources directorate newsletter* (AFHRLRL 80-1). Brooks Air Force Base, TX: Department of the Air Force.
Ben-Porath, Y. S., & Butcher, J. N. (1986). Computers in personality assessment: A brief past, an ebullient present, and an expanding future. *Computers in Human Behavior, 2*, 167-182.

Biskin, B. H., & Kolotkin, R. C. (1977). Effects of computerized administration on scores on the Minnesota Multiphasic Personality Inventory. *Applied Psychological Measurement, 1,* 543-549.

Booker, E. (1990). Scanner users see new benefits. *Computerworld, 24*(49), 51, 60.

Booth-Kewley, S., Edwards, J. E., & Rosenfeld, P. (1992). Impression management, social desirability, and computer administration of attitude questionnaires: Does the computer make a difference? *Journal of Applied Psychology, 77,* 562-566.

Bresolin, M. J., Jr. (1984). *A comparative study of computer administration of the Minnesota Multiphasic Personality Inventory in an inpatient psychiatric setting.* Unpublished doctoral dissertation, Loyola University, Chicago.

Collegians being put to the test with new computerized exams. (1992, March 21). *San Diego Union,* p. A-9.

Corman, S. R. (1990). Computerized versus pencil and paper collection of network data. *Social Networks, 12,* 375-384.

Crowne, D. P., & Marlowe, D. (1960). A new scale of social desirability independent of psychopathology. *Journal of Consulting Psychology, 24,* 349-354.

Davis, F. D., Bagozzi, R. P., & Warshaw, P. R. (1992). Extrinsic and intrinsic motivation to use computers in the workplace. *Journal of Applied Social Psychology, 22,* 1111-1132.

Davis, C., & Cowles, M. (1989). Automated psychological testing: Method of administration, need for approval, and measures of anxiety. *Educational and Psychological Testing, 49,* 311-320.

Davis, L. J., & Morse, R. M. (1991). Self-administered alcoholism screening test: A comparison of conventional versus computer-administered formats. *Alcoholism: Clinical and Experimental Research, 15,* 155-157.

Doherty, L., & Thomas, M. D. (1986). Effects of an automated survey system upon responses. In O. Brown, Jr., & H. W. Hendrick (Eds.), *Human factors in organizational design management—II* (pp. 157-161). North Holland, The Netherlands: Elsevier Science.

Duffy, J. C., & Waterston, J. (1984). Under-reporting of alcohol-consumption in sample surveys: The effect of computer interviewing in fieldwork. *British Journal of Addiction, 79,* 303-308.

Dunn, T. G., Lushene, R. E., & O'Neil, H. F. (1972). Complete automation of the MMPI and a study of its response latencies. *Journal of Consulting and Clinical Psychology, 39,* 381-387.

Edwards, J. E., Booth-Kewley, S., & Rosenfeld, P. (1991, October). *Computer administration of questionnaires: Impression management and social desirability.* Paper presented at the annual meeting of the Military Testing Association, San Antonio, TX.

Erdman, H., Klein, M. H., & Greist, J. H. (1983). The reliability of a computer interview for drug use/abuse information. *Behavior Research Methods and Instrumentation, 15,* 66-68.

Farrell, A. D., Camplair, P. S., & McCullough, L. (1987). Identification of target complaints by computer interview: Evaluation of the computerized assessment system for psychotherapy evaluation and research. *Journal of Consulting and Clinical Psychology, 55,* 691-700.

Feinstein, S. (1986, October 9). Computers replacing interviewers for personnel and marketing tasks. *Wall Street Journal,* p. 35.

Fowler, F. J., Jr. (1988). *Survey research methods.* Newbury Park, CA: Sage.

Frey, J. H. (1989). *Survey research by telephone* (2nd ed.). Newbury Park, CA: Sage.

George, C. E., Lankford, J. S., & Wilson, S. E. (1992). The effects of computerized versus paper-and-pencil administration on measures of negative affect. *Computers in Human Behavior, 8*, 203-209.

Groves, R. M., & Kahn, R. L. (1979). *Surveys by telephone: A national comparison with personal interviews.* New York: Academic Press.

Harrell, T. H., & Lombardo, T. A. (1984). Validation of an automated 16PF administration procedure. *Journal of Personality Assessment, 48*, 638-642.

Hinkle, J. S., Sampson, J. P., & Radonsky, V. (1991). Computer-assisted versus traditional and paper assessment of personal problems in a clinical population. *Computers in Human Behavior, 7*, 237-242.

Hogan, J., & Hogan, R. (1989). How to measure employee reliability. *Journal of Applied Psychology, 74*, 273-279.

Honaker, L. M. (1988). The equivalency of computerized and conventional MMPI administration: A critical review. *Clinical Psychology Review, 8*, 561-577.

Jordon, L. A., Marcus, A. C., & Reeder, L. G. (1980), Response styles in telephone and household interviewing: A field experiment. *Public Opinion Quarterly, 44*, 210-222.

Kantor, J. (1991). The effects of computer administration and identification on the Job Descriptive Index (JDI). *Journal of Business and Psychology, 5*, 309-323.

Katz, L., & Dalby, J. T. (1981). Computer and manual administration of the Eysenck Personality Inventory. *Journal of Clinical Psychology, 37*, 586-588.

Kiesler, S., & Sproull, L. S. (1986). Response effects in the electronic survey. *Public Opinion Quarterly, 50*, 402-413.

Lavrakas, P. J. (1987). *Telephone survey methods: Sampling, selection and supervision.* Newbury Park, CA: Sage.

Lautenschlager, G. J., & Flaherty, V. L. (1990). Computer administration of questions: More desirable or more social desirability? *Journal of Applied Psychology, 75*, 310-314.

Liefeld, J. P. (1988). Response effects in computer-administered questioning. *Journal of Marketing Research, 25*, 405-409.

Lindell, B. J. (1988). Interactive effects of interview method, self-deception and impression management on self-reported data (Doctoral dissertation, Hofstra University). *Dissertation Abstracts International, 49/09B*, 4011.

Llabre, M. M., Clements, N. E., Fitzhugh, K., & Lancelotta, G. (1987). The effect of computer-administered testing on text anxiety and performance. *Journal of Educational Computing Research, 3*, 429-433.

Lucas, R. W., Mullin, P. J., Luna, C. B., & McInroy, D. C. (1977). Psychiatrists and a computer as interrogators of patients with alcohol-related illnesses: A comparison. *British Journal of Psychiatry, 131*, 160-167.

Lukin, M. E., Dowd, E. T., Plake, B. S., & Kraft, R. G. (1985). Comparing computerized versus traditional psychological assessment. *Computers in Human Behavior, 1*, 49-58.

Lushene, R. E., O'Neil, H. H., & Dunn, T. (1974). Equivalent validity of a completely computerized MMPI. *Journal of Personality Assessment, 38*, 353-361.

Martin, C. L., & Nagao, D. H. (1989). Some effects of computerized interviewing on job applicant responses. *Journal of Applied Psychology, 74*, 72-80.

Matheson, K., & Zanna, M. P. (1988). The impact of computer-mediated communication on self-awareness. *Computers in Human Behavior, 4*, 221-233.

Meier, S. T. (1988). Predicting individual differences in performance on computer-administered tests and tasks: Development of the computer aversion scale. *Computers in Human Behavior, 4*, 175-187.

Miller, D. C. (1991). *Handbook of research design and social measurement.* Newbury Park, CA: Sage.

Millstein, S. G. (1987). Acceptability and reliability of sensitive information collected via computer interview. *Educational and Psychological Measurement, 47,* 523-533.

Moreno, K., Wetzel, C. D., McBride, J. R., & Weiss, D. J. (1983). *Relationships between corresponding Armed Services Vocational Aptitude Battery (ASVAB) and computerized adaptive testing (CAT) subtests* (NPRDC Tech. Rep. No. 83-27). San Diego, CA: Navy Personnel Research and Development Center.

Paulhus, D. L. (1984). Two-component models of socially desirable responding. *Journal of Personality and Social Psychology, 46,* 598-609.

Paulhus, D. L., & Reid, D. (1991). Enhancement and denial in socially desirable responding. *Journal of Personality and Social Psychology, 60,* 307-317.

Read, W. H. (1991). Gathering opinion on-line. *HR Magazine, 36,* 51, 53.

Rosenfeld, P., Doherty, L., & Carroll, L. (1987). Microcomputer-based organizational survey assessment: Applications to training. *Journal of Business and Psychology, 2,* 182-193.

Rosenfeld, P., Doherty, L., Carroll, L., Kantor, J., & Thomas, M. (1986, November). *Does microcomputer-based testing encourage truthful responses?* Paper presented at the annual meeting of the Military Testing Association, Mystic, CT.

Rosenfeld, P., Doherty, L. M., Vicino, S. M., & Greaves, J. M. (1988, April). Using portable microcomputers to conduct organizational surveys. In *Proceedings of the 11th Psychology in the Department of Defense Symposium,* p. 501.

Rosenfeld, P., Doherty, L., Vicino, S. M., Kantor, J., & Greaves, J. (1989). Attitude assessment in organizations: Testing three microcomputer-based survey systems. *Journal of General Psychology, 116,* 145-154.

Rosenfeld, P., Giacalone, R. A., Knouse, S. B., Doherty, L., Vicino, S. M., Kantor, J., & Greaves, J. (1991). Impression management, candor, and microcomputer-based organizational surveys: An individual differences approach. *Computers in Human Behavior, 7,* 23-32.

Rozensky, R. H., Honor, L. F., Rasinski, K., Tovian, S. M., & Herz, G. I. (1986). Paper-and-pencil versus computer-administered MMPIs: A comparison of patients' attitudes. *Computers in Human Behavior, 2,* 111-116.

Russell, G. K., Peace, K. A., & Mellsop, G. W. (1986). The reliability of a micro-computer administration of the MMPI. *Journal of Clinical Psychology, 42,* 120-122.

Scissons, E. H. (1976). Computer administration of the California Psychological Inventory. *Measurement and Evaluation in Guidance, 9,* 22-25.

Skinner, H. A., & Allen, B. A. (1983). Does the computer make a difference? Computerized versus face-to-face versus self-report assessment of alcohol, drug and tobacco use. *Journal of Consulting and Clinical Psychology, 51,* 267-275.

Space, L. G. (1981). The computer as psychometrician. *Behavior Research Methods & Instrumentation, 13,* 595-606.

Sproull, L. S. (1986). Using electronic mail for data collection in organizational research. *Academy of Management Journal, 29,* 159-169.

Staw, B. M., Bell, N. E., & Clausen, J. A. (1986). The dispositional approach to job attitudes: A lifetime longitudinal test. *Administrative Science Quarterly, 31,* 56-77.

Temple, D. E., & Geisinger, K. F. (1990). Response latency to computer-administered inventory items as an indicator of emotional arousal. *Journal of Personality Assessment, 54,* 289-297.

Tuckel, P. S., & Feinberg, B. M. (1991). The answering machine poses many questions for telephone researchers. *Public Opinion Quarterly, 55,* 200-217.

Tyburski, D. A. (1992). *Computer enhanced Navy survey system: Final report.* Unpublished manuscript, Navy Personnel Research and Development Center, San Diego, CA.

Tyburski, D. A., Petrey, J. L., Wilson, S., & Kewley, B. (1989). *OCPM-CENSUS bulletin board system user's manual* (NPRDC TN 90-6). San Diego, CA: Navy Personnel Research and Development Center.

U.S. Merit Systems Protection Board. (1988). *Sexual harassment in the federal government: An update.* Washington, DC: Government Printing Office.

U.S. Merit Systems Protection Board. (1989). *Who is leaving the federal government? An analysis of employee turnover.* Washington, DC: Government Printing Office.

U.S. Merit Systems Protection Board. (1990). *Working for America: A federal employee survey.* Washington, DC: Government Printing Office.

Veit, D. T., & Scruggs, T. E. (1986). Can learning disabled students effectively use separate answer sheets? *Perceptual and Motor Skills, 63,* 155-160.

Vicino, S. M. (1989). *Effects of computer versus traditional paper-and-pencil survey administration on response bias among self-monitors.* Unpublished master's thesis, San Diego State University.

Watson, C. G., Manifold, V., Klett, W. G., Brown, J., Thomas, D., & Anderson, D. (1990). Comparability of computer- and booklet-administered Minnesota Multiphasic Personality Inventories among primarily chemically dependent patients. *Psychological Assessment, 2,* 276-280.

Weiss, D. J. (1985). Adaptive testing by computer. *Journal of Consulting and Clinical Psychology, 53,* 774-789.

White, D. M., Clements, C. B., & Fowler, R. D. (1985). A comparison of computer administration with standard administration of the MMPI. *Computers in Human Behavior, 1,* 153-162.

Wise, S. L., Plake, B. S., Eastman, L. A., & Novak, C. D. (1987). Introduction and training of students to use separate answer sheets: Effects on standardized test scores. *Psychology in the Schools, 24,* 285-288.

5

New Methods and Technologies in the Organizational Survey Process

RICHARD A. DUNNINGTON

Three decades of dynamic developments in communications and computer technology have transformed, if not revolutionized, organization survey use and potential. These rapid and ongoing changes make a definitive and inclusive statement nearly impossible; this chapter, however, attempts to capture the highlights of the present state of the technology.

The content of the chapter derives from three sources: (a) the author's 25 years coordinating development of the IBM Opinion Survey Program and 10 years establishing survey programs in other organizations; (b) comments from 60 professionals in a Society of Industrial and Organizational Psychologists (SIOP) workshop concerned with "new methods and technologies of organization surveys" in April 1992; and (c) a bibliographic search of the materials in the academic and nonacademic press published during the past 5 years (Dunnington, 1992).[1]

The years since 1960 have been pivotal. The first 20 years were dominated by mainframe and centralized data processing; during the past 12 years, personal computers and computer workstations dramatically emerged and are now ubiquitous.

When the mainframe computer burst on the scene in the 1960s it made data entry, data reduction, data analysis, and report preparation of large-scale organization surveys feasible and economical. This spawned a profusion of applied statistics, data reduction, and report software as well as behavioral research and survey-guided change and development activities.

The second wave of innovation during the 1980s put enormous computing and communication potential at the fingertips of individual professionals. Major components were personal computers (PCs), fax machines, modems and improved telephone capabilities, and computer-driven graphic technology. Mainframe programs were converted to PC applications, and literally hundreds of new programs were developed to facilitate writing, statistical analysis, project planning, data storage and retrieval, electronic data transmission, and "what if?" kinds of mathematical calculations. It was this decentralization of computing power and the development of new programming techniques and application programs that unleashed a new wave of creative organizational survey innovations and entrepreneurial activity.

This chapter identifies recent developments that pertain to contemporary organizational surveys: surveys that are systematically administered to organization members. Organizational surveys vary greatly in content depending on goals and purposes; the results are generally used to facilitate communication, assessment, development, and change initiatives and to provide research data, including prediction of employee choices using conjoint analysis. They differ from academic research efforts, opinion polls, and market research in that the target population for data collection and feedback usually is specific to a particular organization or organization unit.

Organization of the chapter follows the sequence of activities usually observed in developing an organizational survey. Technologies are reviewed where applicable to each activity. In some instances, a technology or software development may apply to more than one activity and thus is referenced again. Addresses and telephone numbers of products and services discussed are provided in the appendix.

The activities involved in an organizational survey addressed in this chapter include planning, identification of objectives and purposes, survey program design, questionnaire development, questionnaire administration, data analysis, and results reporting. This chapter is concerned with the new technologies and methods that are employed at each step.

Survey Planning

Survey planning forces consideration of the crucial "what, when, and who" questions. It is a continuing process. Survey plans change as survey objectives, survey design, and subsequent survey development steps unfold. Project planning software facilitates the development of a survey plan. Activities, sequences, overlaps, interdependencies, duration, and staffing can all be reflected in the plan. However, the real strength of planning software is facilitating plan modification.

Spreadsheet programs and project planning programs support the planning process. There are several currently available. In addition, Kerzner (1984) has prepared a useful reference on how to do project planning; LeBlond and Perkins (1984) have published a procedure using the Lotus 1-2-3 spreadsheet.

Johnson and Vale (1987) discuss a way to maximize the usefulness of these programs. Finding that the very brief task descriptions required by planning software are not sufficient to capture the complexity of the tasks for those involved in project reviews, they offer the following suggestions:

1. Using outlining or thought processing software, first identify and describe each task, indicating who is involved and any task dependencies. The software automatically numbers each task.
2. Use these numbers as well as the abbreviated task statement called for by the planning software to develop the project plan.
3. For project reviews, incorporate both the Gantt chart from the project planning software and the task detail from the outliner in the review process to facilitate communication. Many word processing programs (e.g., WordPerfect®) now incorporate outlining capability.

Identification of Objectives and Purposes

New methods and technologies facilitate development of surveys that truly meet the needs of organizations, including improving communications, supporting the development of individuals or groups, assessing programs and change initiatives, facilitating employee involvement, and reinforcing vision and values or a particular management style. The first step is to determine which among the many possible goals and options will best serve an organization.

Individual and group interviews, focus groups, and review of documents are the commonly used vehicles for identifying goals and objectives. Recently available software called *groupware* facilitates this process.

Groupware

Groupware programs combine state-of-the-art computer network technology with concepts of effective group meetings.[2] They greatly improve the efficiency of identifying and building consensus around the objectives of a single survey or survey program. They can also help identify topics or issues to be addressed in the questionnaire's content. Currently, the following groupware products are available: Group Systems (Ventana Corp., Tucson, AZ), TeamFocus (IBM, Armonk, NY), VisionQuest (Collaborative Technologies Corp., Austin, TX), OptionFinder (Option Technologies, Inc., Mendota Heights, MN), and Notes (Lotus Development). Designed to improve the effectiveness of brainstorming and thus decision making, each of these systems requires participants to respond to a particular question or issue by simultaneously entering ideas into a computer terminal rather than presenting them orally in a meeting. After completing this task, all the ideas of all the participants are displayed on each computer terminal along with a rating and/or priority scale designed to fit the task at hand; each participant then rates each comment. On completion of this exercise, the system summarizes and displays the ideas on the basis of participant ratings. Participants can be provided a printout of the results while they are in the meeting. A discussion may or may not ensue depending on the meeting's purpose. The advantages of groupware have been described by both distributors, users, and product reviewers as follows:

1. Everyone "talks" at once, using the keyboard. In a traditional hour-long meeting of 15 people, each person has an average of 4 minutes. Using groupware, everyone has potential "air time" of 60 minutes.

2. With exceptions (e.g., Lotus Notes), comments are anonymous; therefore, individuals can give their ideas without embarrassment, intimidation, or fear of retribution.

3. Because participants categorize and rank the ideas independently and the program summarizes them, the meeting summary reflects the areas of consensus.

4. There are substantial savings in meeting time and thus cost as revealed by studies done at IBM, the Boeing Aircraft Company, and Marriott International Headquarters.

Groupware use is not bound by geography. Although VisionQuest is installed in a "decision center room" at Marriott International Head-

Tailoring the survey does not mean, however, that all the questions are unique. Rather, where possible, questions are used that can serve the dual purpose of addressing the identified important topics and also providing comparisons of normative data from other organizations.

Pretesting, whether the survey used is "off the shelf" or tailored to the specific organization, is also a necessity. It ensures that the topics and questions are congruent with the organization's culture and are understood as intended by the survey team.

Groupware

Groupware was discussed earlier as potentially valuable in developing the objectives of a survey. It can be equally valuable in identifying questionnaire topics and pretesting the questions. This can be done in a central location, such as the Marriott Decision Center, or through a computer network. The network has the advantage of allowing for geographic representation. The use of groupware can provide significant time and cost savings for both topic identification and question pretesting; therefore, this application of groupware would be particularly useful for organization climate surveys tailored to meet the unique information needs of a specific organization.

Survey Systems

There are several available survey systems designed to assist in developing a questionnaire; most also handle data reduction and report preparation. Many were initially developed for market research applications and later adapted for organization surveys.

The systems reviewed in this chapter were developed specifically for organization surveys: Survey Software Systems (Insync, NY); the Organizational Universe Survey System (Organization Universe Systems, Valley Center, CA); the mainframe On-Line Opinion Survey (IBM, Armonk, NY), developed and used internally by IBM; and the Ci2 and Ci3 systems (Sawtooth Software, Evanston, IL). In contrast to the others, Ci2 and Ci3 systems rely on other vendor software for data reduction and report preparation.

Three of the systems have questionnaires or banks of questions as part of the system. The Ci2 and Ci3 systems have questionnaire development capability but no question banks. The Organizational Universe Survey System has six major sets of questionnaire items: a basic set of

1,048 questions covering 19 categories based on the Jones organizational universe and the Jones/Bearley organizational hierarchy models, 385 items based on a "stair-step" model of training needs, 363 questions designed for internal and external customer surveys, 300 items appropriate for use with both sales professionals and sales managers, 213 organizational values questions, and a collection of 703 items based on the Malcolm Baldridge criteria for the National Quality Award. The system allows editing and development of new questions to fit local conditions. A hard-copy item pool reference guide is part of the package.

Insync markets five programs. *The Survey Manager*, Insync's basic software system, comes with no resident questions but provides questionnaire development, processing, and reporting capabilities within the system. Four other programs are extensions of *The Survey Manager* program and provide resident questionnaires: ASSESS-TQM measures organization quality using a survey based on the Baldridge National Quality Award criteria; *The Customer Manager* evaluates an organization's customer service effectiveness and includes three resident survey questionnaires that gather customer service effectiveness data from employees, current customers, and lost customers; *The Organization Manager* helps organizations evaluate the quality and effectiveness of their operations; and *TASK* has training assessment capabilities, using four resident questionnaires for assessing training needs, customer satisfaction, courses, and instructors. These programs can also be used to design totally new surveys.

Application of the IBM On-Line Opinion Survey is described by Read (1991). The system is the primary method through which organizational surveys are developed, administered, and analyzed in IBM worldwide. It has a question bank that contains the corporate core questions asked in every survey as well as an extensive inventory of optional questions from which operating units can select additional questions as appropriate. The questions are specific to the culture and reflect the history of question development and survey results use in IBM.

Surveys are administered through computer terminals; therefore, questions are formatted for that medium of presentation. The program has the capability of branching; that is, if a respondent selects a question response predetermined to merit exploration through related questions, these questions appear on the terminal display. This is equivalent to the paper-and-pencil questionnaire that instructs respondents to "skip" to a particular question or set of questions if a question is answered in a certain way.

There is a great deal of flexibility in the design of the questionnaire allowing change in content and order relatively easily. Questions can be added, deleted, and/or tailored to meet the specific needs of an operating location.

Ci2 and the more advanced Ci3 systems are designed for writing and administering computer-aided questionnaires to be used in interviews. The questionnaire author has complete control over question writing, sequencing, presentation, and screen design. Like the IBM on-line system, it provides for all the common types of questions: single response, multiple response, numeric, open-ended, branching, and so on. The ability to skip based on previous answers, combinations of answers, or mathematical computations performed on answers is incorporated. Although developed for use by interviewers, it can be used for diskette mail surveys. The Ci3 system uses names rather than numbers for question referencing; it allows for inserting or deleting questions, with little or no modification of branching or skipping instructions. Help screens are provided; a mouse can be used rather than a keyboard. "Back-up" capabilities allow the interviewer to revisit a question by name, change an answer, and resume the interview.

Survey Administration

For the purposes of this chapter, administration includes completing or answering the survey and entering the responses into a data base. Technology is now providing ways of combining these two elements. This is made possible by the rapid proliferation of PCs and computer workstations and the development of computer networks, that is, systems that allow electronic communication among the various organization units regardless of geographic location.

Computer-Assisted Administration

A number of systems allow for computer-assisted administration: The On-Line Opinion Survey, developed and used by IBM, the Ci2 and Ci3 systems marketed by Sawtooth Software, the VisionQuest program, and the use of an electronic mail or PROFS system available in many organizations with centralized computer facilities.

The IBM On-Line Opinion Survey system, first used in 1986, now is used worldwide. Over 90% of employees at IBM choose to take company-related surveys on-line (Read, 1991).

The system is user friendly. The software provides abundant instruction to assist users through the questionnaire completion process. A small number of questions appear on each screen. The questions and instructions are color-coded to enhance communications. There is opportunity for written comments, and IBM reports that there are a third more write-in responses than with paper-and-pencil questionnaires.

The questionnaire development capability of the system has been mentioned earlier. Some advantages for questionnaire administration are the following:

1. The data entry step is accomplished as the respondent completes the questionnaire. The keyboarding or optical scanning step is eliminated.

2. Response rates are available on a real-time basis for the total survey population as well as subunit, permitting timely follow-up of areas with low response rates to determine if there is a problem needing management attention. Interim results reports are possible, should that be necessary.

3. Employees away from their normal work setting may take the survey at any IBM location by accessing the company's worldwide office system.

4. Survey completion time is reported to be shorter than required by paper-and-pencil administration; it need not be accomplished at one sitting. Because of the unique system of identification numbers and passwords that ensures individual anonymity, the respondent can interrupt questionnaire completion and return at a later time. The process can continue until the employee executes the command to enter his or her set of answers into the survey data set (Read, 1991).

The On-Line Opinion Survey system is not available for purchase at the present time, but IBM is reported to have made the system available on a fee-for-use basis.

Questionnaire on a Diskette

Like the IBM On-Line Opinion Survey system, the questionnaire on a diskette uses PC and computer workstation technology. However, it does not combine the questionnaire completion and data entry aspects of survey administration in the same way. A respondent answering a questionnaire using both approaches would say they are very similar. Instead of calling up the questionnaire from the system, the diskette with the questionnaire would be delivered to the respondent for insertion into the PC or workstation disk drive and then accessed following instructions accompanying the diskette. Data entry is accomplished by delivering the diskette back to a designated processing agent where it is read into the data set.

Insync survey systems programs have questionnaire administration by diskette capability; the Ci2 and Ci3 systems from Sawtooth Software provide for computer administration of surveys through interviews by telephone, face-to-face format, or mailed diskettes.

Electronic Mail (e-mail)

Instead of voice, messages are entered into the system through computer terminals. The survey capability is available, and structured questionnaires can be distributed through the system. The system does not tabulate responses; this must be done by the recipient of the responses. As with voice mail, application is limited to those who are members of the particular e-mail system.

Groupware

In addition to its capabilities and characteristics discussed previously, groupware allows for administration of a fixed alternative questionnaire of modest proportions and simple design. For example, although lacking branching capability to special sets of questions, groupware appears ideal for short, special-purpose questionnaires administered to limited numbers of respondents.

Survey Administration by Telephone

The telephone as the vehicle for questionnaire completion is common practice in marketing and public opinion surveys. It is less common for organization surveys because easy access to a telephone is uneven among employees. Office workers are easily accessible, production workers less so. Some telephone surveys are administered to people at home, but many organizations and employees view this as an invasion of privacy.

The Hay Poll

Using touch-tone telephone technology, the Hay Group Research for Management has developed an alternative to traditional telephone interview surveys. Survey issues and targeted employee populations are identified. Appropriate questions are developed and then recorded for access by the respondents. The questionnaire and instructions are distributed to the survey population, who, at their convenience, dial a dedicated 800 number from any phone to participate in the survey. A voice recording leads them through the questionnaire, prompting a response following the statement of each question. Respondent answers are entered by pressing the appropriate buttons on a touch-tone phone. Although participants are encouraged to read the questions prior to dialing the 800 number, this is not required. The following example illustrates the question and response design:

Overall, how would you rate your company as a place to work compared with other companies you know about or have worked for?

Response	Touch
One of the best	1
Above average	2
Average	3
Below average	4
One of the worst	5

If a respondent is referring to the questionnaire during the interview, it is not necessary that he or she listen to the recorded questions to register an answer. If the answer button is pressed immediately follow-ing the recorded announcement of a question number, the recording moves to the next question rather than stating the question and response alternatives. The respondent can offer comments at the end of the questionnaire or in conjunction with selected fixed alternative ques-tions depending on how the system is programmed for a particular questionnaire. Also, for longer questionnaires where each respondent is given a unique access number, the survey need not be completed in one phone call. By entering their access number on a subsequent call, respondents can continue answering the questionnaire.

Survey results from the Hay Poll are available on a real-time basis, thus allowing monitoring of response rates during administration. The Hay Group offers the client national and industry-specific norms based on more than 2,000 U.S. companies where comparable questions are asked. The open-ended comments can be summarized or presented verbatim in the results report. Respondent anonymity is maintained.

The author is aware of two companies that have used the Hay Poll and compared it to a self-administered paper-and-pencil questionnaire. There was no significant difference in the response rates of management and nonmanagement personnel. The survey results from the two methods were not statistically different. Using a system of identification numbers would make it possible to use a follow-up procedure with nonrespondents.

Computer-Assisted Telephone Interview (CATI)

In the days before computers were widespread, the telephone interview was the data collection workhorse for the social sciences, market research studies, and public opinion polls. What worked well before mainframes, PCs, and computer networks has been further enhanced with the development of the CATI system.

Sawtooth Software markets a CATI system that is an extension of the Ci2 and Ci3 programs. It is designed for telephone facilities with up to 60 interviewing stations. PCs are linked together in a local area network (LAN). The supervisor station for setting up studies and generating reports is an IBM AT or 386-class PC.

Using questionnaires with the attributes described earlier as part of the Ci2 and Ci3 systems, interviewers conduct telephone interviews with a preselected sample of respondents. The system can help in the random selection of individuals and management of the respondent contact process. It can assign quotas to interviewers and monitor their progress, invoke an automatic dialing and follow-up process, and generate status reports of up to 24 ongoing studies.

Organizations historically have used outside CATI services; Westat in Rockville, Maryland is one of several vendors offering such services. CATI survey administration depends on the availability of an up-to-date data base of employees and their telephone numbers. CATI provides fast turnaround and is particularly well suited for narrowly focused studies. Interviews last from 8 to 10 minutes.

Voice Mail

Organizations that have voice mail systems find them an easy way to poll small numbers of people on a question or limited number of topics. Voice mail is an automated and enhanced answering service that can include a survey option. A list of individuals who are part of the voice mail system can be entered as addressees along with a message including the return voice mail number and the system will automatically send the message to each of the addressees. This approach is usable only with those listed in the system, thus limiting its applicability.

Data Entry by Fax

In its May 1992 issue, *PC World* reported on a new product, *Teleform*, that reads responses to a fax questionnaire using a combined forms design package and fax program for *Windows*. The forms module allows creation of a unique document that can include check boxes and hand-printed data that Teleform is able to recognize. Each form includes an identification code. The forms can be distributed individually or use the program's polling feature. When the respondent faxes back the filled-in form to a faxboard-equipped PC, Teleform identifies the form image and does the handwriting and checkmark recognition, converting the information into one of nine file formats.

Teleform could be useful for short surveys demanding fast turnaround, such as those concerned with customer satisfaction or questionnaires to members of a management team who are geographically dispersed.

Data Analysis and Results Reporting

The character of data analysis and results reporting is guided by the objectives of the survey. As noted earlier, the range of possible applications of today's survey technology is enormous. Similarly, the analysis scheme and design of results reports is limited only by the imagination and creativity of the survey designer using the rich array of statistics and graphics software available.

There are three primary types of statistical manipulations commonly used with survey data: descriptive summaries including reduction of the data into dimensions (addressing the "what" and "where" questions), explanatory analyses (addressing the "why" questions), and predictive analyses (addressing the "what if" questions). The potential for doing each of these analyses is determined by the design and content of the survey instrument. The data analysis and results reporting plan must, therefore, be formulated during the questionnaire development phase to ensure that the appropriate variables are included.

Descriptive Statistical Analysis and Report Presentation

Three PC-based survey processing products discussed earlier have powerful processing and report generating power as well as questionnaire development capability.

The Organizational Universe Survey System is an integrated system that incorporates item pools and facilitates questionnaire construction, data entry, reporting, and data transformation for other statistical software. Data can be entered through a keyboard or from a file. The latter allows use of an optical-mark reader or scanner. It includes a graphics module for reports generated by printers that are compatible with Hewlett-Packard Laserjet and IBM/Epson dot-matrix printers.

Insync's Survey Software Systems develops data input screens for keying in survey responses and also accepts optically scanned data. The software analyzes survey data by percentage, mean and standard deviation, frequencies, and the mean, mode, or median, formatted in tables or graphs. The software also performs cross-tabulations to analyze selected questions against others to develop tables showing responses for various demographic breakouts.

The IBM On-Line Opinion Survey system, a mainframe system, produces statistical reports that display the mean, a t test of significant differences between data lines, the number of responses in the data base for each data line, invalid responses, the percentage response for each category, and the percentage of favorable, neutral, and unfavorable responses. Historical data comparisons, where permitted by the questions, are built into the reports. Graphics capability and special report design capability are included in the system. Write-in comment reports are also generated.

The Microcomputer Survey System II (MCSSII), developed by Dr. William Macey of Personnel Research Associates, Inc., in the mid-1980s, is designed for IBM-compatible PCs; it has a track record of successful use by many organizations. Like others described earlier, the program was designed specifically for organization surveys. Direct key entry of data is supported, as is optical scanning. The program, if run on a PC (640K RAM needed, minimum), can handle up to 250 items. The number of respondents is limited only by the memory limits of the hard disk. MCSSII is able to track surveys over time, matching current with previous survey content, and automatically compares current with previous results where the items are the same.

Results are reported using Hewlett-Packard Laserjet printers and HP softfonts. Twenty standard report formats are available, and the option of custom-designed reports is provided as part of the system. A purchaser can select as many standard reports as desired; three are included in the base price of the system. Additional reports are sold separately.

Reporting Results on Diskette

The previously described systems provide hard copy reports formatted and organized to meet the needs of the average user. For example, management at various levels in the organization would be provided a data report or reports showing results by question and/or topic for the entire organization, subunits, demographics, geographic cuts, written comments, and so on. Depending on the size of the questionnaire, a manager might need to refer to several sources to better understand a particular issue or survey result.

The Skidaway Group (Savannah, GA) reports survey data on a diskette as well as providing hard copy reports. The diskette permits a client to see the data displayed through a series of screens done in color, highlighting favorable, neutral, and unfavorable results by topic and question. The user can quickly explore specific topics or questions by various demographic and organization unit information that is elicited in the questionnaire. The graphic presentation and ease of operation make it an attractive and user-friendly survey report format.

Explanatory and Predictive Analyses

Explanatory and predictive analyses are more commonly conducted by the academic community, market researchers, and public opinion pollsters. These analyses often incorporate behavioral data in addition to organization survey data. The dependent and independent variables are carefully identified, building on prior research, theories, and models, specifying through hypotheses the relationships expected among the variables.

Conjoint analysis is a methodology designed to help identify the importance or value of various attributes influencing the selection of a particular option from among a set of available choice alternatives. It addresses the "what if" questions about new or revised services or product features. The product could be a personnel program, such as executive compensation or benefits.

The results of conjoint analysis are believed to be more predictive of behavior than questions that ask the respondent to rank or rate the importance of various attributes (i.e., descriptive data reflecting important differences among attributes). It is particularly useful where most of the attributes might be rated important but the subtle underlying differences in importance influencing behavior could be missed.

Temple (1990) describes a study using conjoint analysis designed to determine which on-line information service attributes were most important to users, both librarians and end users. A diskette questionnaire was administered to 281 subjects. Nineteen attributes were assessed, including frequency of information update, response time for searches, and availability of customer support, among others.

To uncover the most important attributes, the respondent was presented with several hypothetical combinations of service attributes, a modified paired-comparison methodology. These configurations were different combinations of the attribute levels (e.g., cost of service at $1 to $5 a minute, frequency of information update—daily, weekly, monthly, quarterly, semiannually); the respondent assigned preference ratings to these configurations. As the questioning unfolded, new sets of combinations were presented based on the respondent's previous choices. This is possible using computer-administered survey technology but difficult, if not impossible, using paper-and-pencil questionnaires.

One application of conjoint analysis in organizational studies would be to cafeteria benefit programs, where it is important to understand user trade-offs among benefit alternatives so that employee satisfaction and cost savings could be maximized.

Summary and Conclusions

New methods and technologies developed over the past 30 years have revolutionized organizational surveys, providing more options in all phases of the survey process. Clients, respondents, and survey professionals are all benefiting.

Clients' Benefits

The rapid changes occurring within society and reflected in organizations make survey-generated information increasingly important and relevant to organization leaders. Global competition, technology, the economy, legislation, and changes in values all place great demands on business leaders to seek up-to-date information on the human resource as well as the financial, production, and marketing aspects of their organizations.

Currently available organizational survey technology can provide relevant information rapidly and cost-effectively and with minimal disruption. Organizational surveys can be an important management tool for leaders who are striving to improve competitiveness through increased employee involvement and empowerment, downsizing, culture change, and change initiatives. The information provided by surveys permits periodic readings of management and nonmanagement perspectives of the organization. This information can enhance the decision-making process. Survey feedback using a diskette suggests that "hands on" involvement of management in the analysis of survey results can further enhance the use of the data.

Respondents' Benefits

There are many benefits for the respondent from use of the new technologies. Computer-administered surveys provide greater flexibility in questionnaire completion. The respondent need not complete the questionnaire at one sitting. This permits accommodation to the ongoing flow of work and thoughtful reflection on the questions asked, which may generate more interest and satisfaction with the process.

Branching techniques in computer-administered surveys are often invisible to the respondents but result in questions that appear more focused on their interests and concerns. This is done without "skip" instructions and thick documents of questions that many find confusing and overwhelming.

Skillful use of sampling reduces the number of questionnaire contacts per employee—targeting the appropriate individuals for special topics. The new technologies of voice mail, fax, CATI, and the Hay Poll all permit greater responsiveness to the needs of the respondent as well as the client.

Survey Professionals' Benefits

The survey professional now has more control over the organizational survey activities. The new technologies permit the survey professional to more skillfully select from among the many options those that will do the job most effectively. It offers opportunity for innovation on a real-time basis. The wide range of options for questionnaire development, survey design, administration, data analysis, and results reporting increase the potential for the survey to more completely meet the needs of the clients and thus enhance the perceived contribution of the survey professional.

The period covered by this chapter has been an exciting time for those of us in the survey business. Today's emerging technologies will surely make the future just as exciting.

Appendix: Contact Information for Products and Services Discussed in Text

BMDP [Computer program]. BMDP Statistical Software, 1440 Sepulveda Boulevard, Los Angeles, CA 90025, (213) 479-7799

Carl DiPietro Associates, 9114 Willow Gate lane, #A2, Bethesda, MD 20817, phone/fax (301) 365-5313

Group Systems, Ventana Corporation, 1430 East Fort Lowell Road, Suite 100, Tucson, AZ 85719, (602) 325-8228

Hay Poll—Touch-Tone Telephone Survey Technology, Hay Group, 229 South 18th Street, Rittenhouse Square, Philadelphia, PA 19103, (215) 875-2423

Insync, Survey Software Systems [Computer program]. 1675 Third Avenue, New York, NY 10128, (800) 828-8714, (212) 996-5600

MCSSII [Computer program]. Personnel Research Associates, Inc., 657 E. Golf Road, Suite 301, Arlington Heights, IL 60005, (708) 640-8820

OptionFinder [Computer program]. Option Technologies, Inc., 1275 Knoll-wood Lane, Mendota Heights, MN 55118, (612) 450-1700

Organizational Universe Survey System [Computer program]. Organizational Universe Systems, 12665 Cumbres Road, Valley Center, CA, (619) 749-0811

Sawtooth Software [Computer program]. 1007 Church Street, Suite 302, Evanston, IL 60201, (708) 866-0870

SAS/STAT [Computer program]. SAS Institute, Inc., Box 8000, SAS Circle, Cary, NC 27511, (919) 677-8000

Skidaway Group, 6 Pelham Road, Savannah, GA 31411, (912) 598-0355

SPSS/PC+ [Computer program]. SPSS, Inc., 444 N. Michigan Avenue, Chicago, IL 60611, (312) 329-2400

SPSS-X [Computer program]. SPSS, Inc., 444 N. Michigan Avenue, Chicago, IL 60611, (312) 329-3500

TeamFocus [Computer program]. IBM Corporation, Old Orchard Road, Armonk, NY 10504, (914) 765-2178

Teleform [Computer program]. Cardiff Software, Inc., 531 Stevens Avenue, Bldg. B, Solana Beach, CA 92075, (800) 659-8755

VisionQuest [Computer program]. Collaborative Technologies Corporation, 8920 Business Park Drive, Austin, TX 78759, (512) 794-8858

Westat, 1650 Research Boulevard, Rockville, MD 20850, (301) 251-1500

Notes

1. The resulting bibliography was used in and distributed at the SIOP workshop and is available for a nominal fee on request.

2. Corporate experience with groupware was reported by William Bulkeley (1992) and by David Kirkpatrick (1992).

3. VisionQuest was recently demonstrated to me by Carl DiPietro, the Decision Center's creator, at Marriott's international headquarters in Washington, DC. DiPietro has recently established his own consulting firm.

References

Bulkeley, W. M. (1992, January 28). "Computerizing" dull meetings is touted as an antidote to the mouth that bored. *Wall Street Journal*, pp. B1-B2.

Dunnington, M. J. (1992). *Annotated bibliography—Organizational surveys.* (Available from Richard Dunnington & Associates, 30 Boulder Hill Road, Ridgefield, CT 06877, 203-438-0591)

Henry, G. T. (1990). *Practical sampling.* Newbury Park, CA: Sage.

Johnson, R. H., & Vale, C. D. (1987). *Microcomputer applications for I/O psychologists.* Unpublished notebook.

Kerzner, H. (1984). *Project management: A systems approach to planning, scheduling, and controlling.* New York: Van Nostrand Reinhold.

Kirkpatrick. D. (1992, March 23). Here comes the payoff from PCs. *Fortune*, pp. 93-100.

LeBlond, G. T., & Perkins, T. D. (1984). *Lotus 1-2-3 for business.* Indianapolis: Que Corporation.

Read, W. H. (1991). Gathering opinion on-line. *HR Magazine, 36*, 51, 53.

Temple, M. (1990, December). *Marketing research methods for online information.* Paper presented at Online Information 90, London. (Available from Michael Temple, Vice President, Ketron, Inc., Great Valley Corporate Center, 350 Technology Drive, Malvern, PA 19355, 215-648-9000)

6

Consortium Surveys

GARY W. MORRIS
MARK A. LoVERDE

During the latter half of the 1980s and continuing into the 1990s, two major trends in American business have been *benchmarking* and the *industry consortium*. In benchmarking, organizations seek to identify ways to improve their business processes (see Camp, 1989). They do this through a systematic examination of the comparable business processes and practices of either highly successful organizations or organizations renowned for a particular business process (i.e., "best practices"). Generally, a benchmarked organization is similar to a benchmarking organization on certain relevant characteristics. For example, both organizations may be large high-tech American manufacturers.

A consortium, on the other hand, is a cooperative effort among a number of organizations. Consortium members almost always include companies or industries but may also include universities and state or federal governments. Although consortiums are generally nonprofit, a major goal of a consortium is usually to help its member companies improve their competitiveness in the global marketplace (Barron, 1990). The efforts of a consortium are most often geared toward research, product development, or standard setting (Mandell, 1990).[1] Consortium goals may range from manufacturing research (Thomas, 1990) to the development of an artificial intelligence environment for mathematical modeling and analysis (Greenberg, 1990) to basic and applied business marketing research (Lilian, 1990).

Although the above examples are in line with the traditional conception of a consortium as a marketing or manufacturing tool, there are also a number of human resource-oriented consortia. The Life Insurance Marketing Research Association (LIMRA) is a trade association, which, in addition to marketing, consumer, and financial divisions, has a division that provides human resources research and support to its member organizations. Like LIMRA, many human resources consortia are organized along industry lines. The Banking Administration Institute (BAI), for example, provides human resources consulting services to banks and other financial institutions (Burns, 1988). Similar consortia also exist among utilities, railroads, and telecommunications companies. Unlike LIMRA and BAI, however, most such consortia do not maintain professional full-time staff.

The purpose of this chapter is to describe the application of the consortium concept to employee attitude surveys. We discuss how consortium employee attitude surveys can be viewed as a limited form of external benchmarking. We also consider the activities involved in a survey consortium, the responsibilities of consortium members, the characteristics of good consortium partners, the advantages and disadvantages of being a survey consortium member, and some alternatives to a survey consortium.

As a point of clarification, our use of the term *consortium survey* refers to an employee attitude survey effort that a group of companies (the consortium) share in common according to some formally agreed-on rules. This "survey" could be a complete instrument or, more commonly, a set of core questions that member companies incorporate into their own unique research questionnaires. Member companies share information that they obtain using this common set of research questions. As with most employee attitude surveys, the survey items are generally designed to measure attitudes and perceptions about various attributes of the working environment—organizational culture, management practices, physical working conditions, awareness of competition, comfort with change, and so on.

This chapter largely reflects our experiences and opinions because very little research or professional literature exists on this topic. There are two reasons for this state of affairs. First, relatively few formal survey consortia have been established. Second, existing consortia typically prefer to keep a low profile and maintain a high degree of confidentiality.

The Survey Consortium

The model of survey consortium discussed in this chapter is that used by the Telecommunications Employee Survey Consortium (TESC). TESC was formed in 1985 and is composed of companies in the telecommunications industry. Currently, there are nine member companies, including our company, Ameritech. All are primarily North American companies, though most have some international interests.

TESC is also a member of a much larger consortium of companies. As a member of this consortium, many of TESC's practices and characteristics are, of necessity, similar to those of the larger consortium. This larger consortium, however, maintains higher confidentiality requirements than TESC and is not directly discussed in this chapter.

The purpose of this consortium, as reflected in its mission, is to "share important and current information, gathered from member companies, for use in strategic and operational planning and decision making." This mission is amplified through a set of objectives, of which two are pertinent to the discussion here: (a) to share and disseminate information on survey programs, attitude assessment, survey data use, and the relationship of attitudes to organizational performance and (b) to disseminate the consortium norms on a 2-year interval. It is this latter objective that forms the primary reason for the formal existence of the survey consortium.

Requirements for Membership

Companies must meet or agree to uphold several standards to be a part of TESC. The most obvious standard is to be a member of the telecommunications industry. Further, member companies must support the consortium through payment of dues, participation in biannual meetings, and, as the need may arise, participation in special research projects or lobbying efforts. Last, member companies must maintain an active survey research program that meets the specifications described below. Any company wishing to become a member of TESC must convince the current members that it has an established survey research program, will add value to the existing membership, and will abide by the consortium's requirements and bylaws.

Member companies must agree to conduct a representative survey of their organization at least biennially. Their survey must include at least 22 questions from a core set of 26 that the consortium tracks.[2] Companies must also submit their data in a prescribed format so that norms can be published on these core questions on a biennial basis.

TESC Core Questions

The response format for all 26 core questions is a 5-point Likert-type scale with anchors appropriate to the item stem. Examples of questions and response formats are "I like the kind of work that I do" (*strongly agree* to *strongly disagree*); "The people I work with cooperate to get the job done" (*strongly agree* to *strongly disagree*); and "Considering everything, how satisfied are you with your job?" (*very satisfied* to *very dissatisfied*).

These questions measure intrinsic job satisfaction, employee perception of teamwork, and overall job satisfaction, respectively. The remaining 23 core questions measure employee opinions regarding pay, benefits, job security, opportunity for advancement, downward communications, participatory climate and upward communications, career development opportunities, training, reward and recognition, productivity, physical working conditions, and autonomy.

The questions have been used for a number of years and were researched in depth. Companies using them understand how employees interpret and respond to them. The items form a stable base for understanding how employees react and respond to questions on new or topical areas.

As stated above, all TESC members must use 22 or more of the core questions every time they survey. The questions must be incorporated intact and cannot be altered. Compliance to this requirement is monitored. A designee of the consortium reviews the surveys that each company uses and issues a compliance report. Companies that alter questions could be placed on probation and ultimately asked to leave the consortium.[3]

TESC Norms

Member Company Norms

Member companies submit information (i.e., raw response data) on core questions during the year that they survey. If a sufficient number of companies have surveyed during a given year, norms will be constructed and issued to all members. However, due to the limited number of companies in TESC, norms are usually published biennially. An outside firm constructs the norms using specifications supplied by the consortium.

Table 6.1 TESC Normative Information (fictitious) on All Exempt Personnel for the Question "Considering Everything, How Satisfied Are You With Your Job?" (in percentages)[a]

	Favor-able	Neutral	Unfavor-able	Very Satisfied	Satis-fied	Neither	Dissat-isfied	Very Dissat-isfied
Median of (7) companies	73	15	12	20	53	15	10	2
Arithmetic average of (7) companies	72	15	13	21	51	15	10	3
Range								
High	91	23	17	42	59	23	13	4
Low	60	7	2	14	46	7	2	0

a. Based on 26,557 responses.

Normative information is provided for each core question that was administered by at least three companies. Separate reports would routinely be built for various demographic subgroups: exempt workers, nonexempt workers, different management levels, and different non-management job clusters appropriate to the industry (e.g., clerical, customer contact, telephone installation, and maintenance). Separate reports might also be built for racial/ethnic, gender, and age subgroups if a sufficient number of companies have collected information on these demographic variables. Norms are not typically constructed for survey dimensions. Table 6.1 represents the type of information provided for a given item in one of the reports.

National and Special Norms

As noted above, TESC is also affiliated with a larger consortium composed of several industry groups in addition to telecommunications. It publishes norms yearly in a manner similar to TESC, though with more demographic breakdowns and with industry group breakdowns. It also allows a member company to select any group of three or more companies that they want to be normed against and to purchase a norm report incorporating this select group. Thus TESC members are able to compare themselves not only against companies within their own industry but against excellent companies in other American industries.

Benefits of the Survey Consortium

The primary benefits of the consortium survey approach accrue from sharing information and resources—norms, costs on special projects, and so on. Benefits also accrue, however, simply from the congregation of companies into a consortium. The adoption and enforcement of rigorous surveys standards by a consortium, for example, has the tendency to solidify and uniformly upgrade survey methodology both within the member companies and across that consortium. This positive influence on survey practices may also extend to companies outside that consortium. In this section, we explore the benefits of membership in a survey consortium, who gets them, and how.

Sharing of Information

As we have stated above, survey consortia exist primarily for the purpose of sharing information—via meetings, networking, and published documents such as norms, manuals on survey practices, and so forth. The information that is shared falls into two main categories: current practices and results. The first category primarily benefits survey practitioners by enabling them to do their jobs better and add value to their function. The latter category primarily affects management decision makers.

Information on Current Practices

The exchange of information about current survey practices of consortium members provides a valuable opportunity to learn from the experiences of others. New or less experienced representatives get the opportunity to learn from survey veterans who have knowledge and skills that are not present in the newer member company. Just as important, however, veterans learn from each other. Every organization faces different challenges and opportunities; even common challenges elicit different responses from different organizations. Hence survey practitioners in different companies grow in different ways. When they get together, they can share and learn from each other.

Information on current survey practices comes from three places. Informal exchange of information comes from *networking*. The consortium provides a ready network of contacts to bounce ideas off of, ask questions of, check the reputation of vendors, and so on. Formally, *consortium meetings* provide an open forum for the exchange of ideas as well as the opportunity to hear presentations about survey-related matters by consortium members or invited speakers. A survey consortium also provides an opportunity to exchange survey instruments, manuals and other documents, and information not generally made available. This latter practice becomes especially valuable when the consortium distills the information and publishes it in a *survey practices manual* for members.

The consortium meeting. TESC meetings are controlled by the needs of the members and, apart from the typical business sections of the meeting, are like miniconventions or seminars that deal with a specific range of topics. Meetings consist of four basic agenda items: business issues, committee and special reports, an invited address, and a roundtable session. The latter three items provide opportunities for information exchange and education.

In the section dedicated to committee and special reports, members share their personal research results with the general membership. In each session, there are usually two to three 30- to 60-minute presentations. For example, members recently presented "Models for Communicating Survey Results" (Ramos, 1991) and "Facilitating Cultural Change Through Survey Procedures" (Morris, 1991).

In addition to presentations by members, a guest speaker also presents research at every meeting. The guest speaker is either a nationally recognized expert or on the cutting edge of survey research technology. Three recent guest speaker addresses were "The Motivation Climate Analysis (MCA): A System for Improving Motivational Climate" (Katzell, 1990), "Trends in Attitude Results Over the Last 20 Years" (Fralicx & Schroeder, 1991), and "Redefining Employee Surveys: Give Your Organization the 'Competitive Advantage' " (Stum, 1991).

Such sessions provide TESC members with opportunities to learn and informally exchange ideas about the newest survey research and organizational intervention processes. Indeed, many of the invited speakers join the session both before and after their presentations and contribute to the general discussions of the consortium. Although such interactions may not occur in all consortia, they have been extremely worthwhile parts of the TESC meetings.

The last session of the meeting, the roundtable, is in many ways the most valuable part. In the roundtable, representatives from each company get an opportunity to share their recent experiences with their peers. The emphasis in this session is on the ramifications of various employee opinion survey research programs. Representatives discuss all facets of this common link, frequently sharing copies of their most recent surveys, general feedback results, and, sometimes, survey communication packets. At this time, representatives may also share and discuss survey-related articles that have appeared in the professional and academic literature.

Consortium members also tend to share general information about the survey process, such as how they obtained top management buy-in and how they kept costs down. They even share nonconfidential information about the action plans and/or process changes that have resulted from the survey process. In that vein, TESC recently published an internal document that listed a compendium of actions initiated as a result of survey findings.

In addition to discussing issues related to survey research, consortium members also share information about general human resource practices within their company. The larger consortium that TESC belongs to has a formal roundtable process where members are solicited in advance to share information with their colleagues. Any member who wants to share something submits a memorandum, or Roundtable Summary, to the consortium chair. The memorandum briefly describes each item that is to be discussed. In addition, the member indicates the company's willingness to share any written reports that describe the topic to be discussed. The following entries, edited from a recent consortium meeting, are typical:

> We are developing a Customer Service Survey to measure and track the service quality of our payroll vendor. The survey is designed to measure customers' expectations for service as well as the actual service they receive.

> Completing development of indices for our corporate survey for Diversity, Quality, and Partnership (self-managed work teams). Also working on streamlining our survey and developing a process to report data "up" the organization.

> A new employee satisfaction scale has been implemented in our corporation. Questions are grouped into factors that measure key drivers of employee satisfaction and motivation.

> Last year we made a trial of an employee opinion survey via telephone using voice messaging technology. This year we conducted our full survey this way. Major benefit: We were able to generate reports the day after the cut-off date. Major drawback: 10% drop in response rate.

This larger consortium maintains one-line descriptions of all items discussed in roundtables, by year of discussion. A member wishing to do research on "Pay for Performance," for example, would begin the process by searching the data base for related roundtable entries and calling peers in other companies.

The roundtable can also be used to request information or collaboration from others. Two recent requests edited from the Roundtable Summary were as follows:

> We are planning to conduct an in-depth study of career development within our company. We would like to talk with anyone who currently employs central staffing and/or succession planning systems.
>
> We are working on plans to prepare for the implementation of the new Americans with Disabilities Act. We are interested in what other companies are doing.

To summarize, the consortium meeting yields substantial information to members. Members get state-of-the-art information, learn what innovative companies are doing, and, to a degree, see the future in human resource thinking unfold before them. They are privy to a wealth of unpublished research information that is, from the practitioners' point of view, at the cutting edge of the discipline.

Manual of current survey practices. Recently, the larger consortium conducted a benchmarking study of its members. The resulting confidential document provided detailed information that allowed members to compare their survey practices to those of the other member companies. A member who, for example, wished to determine if the company's survey cost per respondent was unusually high could compare the company's costs for different stages of the survey process to the mean costs for the other members. Likewise, members wishing to increase their response rate might identify ways of doing so by examining the survey practices of member companies with high response rates. In addition, if a representative was given an assignment to determine how management pay was linked to survey results, the representative could identify member companies that had linked pay to survey results and contact them directly.

As one might imagine, much of the information in this document is sensitive and meant for consortium members alone. Yet, surprisingly enough, members have been very good about maintaining the confidentiality of the information. To the knowledge of these authors, there have never been any unauthorized leaks.

Information on Survey Results: Norms

While it is true that results other than norms may be shared by companies, the information that consortium members agree to share formally and continuously are the *norms*. Norms are "descriptive statistics that are compiled to permit the comparison of a particular score (or mean) with the scores (or means) earned by the members (or groups of members) of some defined population" (Angoff, 1991, p. 533). Applying Angoff's definition to our discussion, norms are essentially benchmarks against which decision makers can compare the performance of their companies.

Even though normative information has several interrelated uses, dealing with the uses as distinct concepts is helpful in understanding them. The most obvious use of normative information is to help *understand one's own results*, perhaps even uncover causal relationships (Burns, 1988). As Marks (1982) pointed out, "We are more sure of where we stand when we have some standard of comparison" (p. 688). As an example, one of the companies in TESC conducted a survey in 1990 for the first time in about 3 years. Overall, employee attitudes were dramatically more negative than in the prior survey. Coincidentally, the outside speaker at the following TESC meeting reviewed the results of a study (Moore, 1989) that documented a rather steep decline in the favorableness of employee attitudes in American industry over the past 10 years. The Hay Group (1991) has reported similar findings regarding the decline in positive work attitudes.

Although the above company could have taken comfort in learning that their results were consistent with a general trend, this finding did not provide the full picture. What the company needed to determine was how much of the decline was due to internal company issues and/or management practices beyond the general decline in attitudes across the country. With good longitudinal internal and external norms, it is possible to make such determinations. Thus two norm issues—company versus norm group and time periods (e.g., 1988 vs. 1990)—are of concern. If the company were in the same position relative to the norm both times, then the drop would likely be a function of external factors. If the company's position changed faster over time than the norm (which it did for this particular company), then some company-specific issues would probably also be influencing the results.

Another use of normative information is to determine the kind of actions that should be taken as a result of the survey findings. This determination can be as simple as identifying the differences between company results and norms and *prioritizing* actions based on the degree of difference.

Normative comparisons can also help to identify the critical issues that a company needs to address if it wants to increase its competitive edge. This use of normative comparisons is, essentially, a form of benchmarking. As mentioned, benchmarking is a means of identifying best practices and importing those best practices (or pieces of them) into one's own company to radically improve performance (Camp, 1987; Gerber, 1990). With regard to the impact of human resource practices on employees and employee satisfaction, the only real means of benchmarking is through attitude assessment and normative comparison. This comparison stage is then followed by an investigation of the practices of those companies that have outstanding results. It is in this arena that the survey consortium approach can be of great value, especially in those consortia where members are able to request special norms reports.

By isolating companies into a special norm report, as TESC can do, a company is able to compare itself to other "excellent" companies. A comparison of profiles can tell a company what it needs to work on to be an excellent company. For example, if a company's mean for "satisfaction with career opportunities" is lower than the norm, the company can begin to investigate the reasons for this result.

As a case in point, one TESC company recently compared itself to a special norms report and found that there was a particularly large gap on items relating to career opportunities. This large difference from the "excellence" norm emerged during a recessionary time where there was little movement and virtually no opportunity for promotion within the company. The affected company found that "excellent" companies had better methods of communicating job openings and allowed more employee-initiated job-bidding procedures. In addition, excellent companies invested in more career development and career planning programs for their employees. Although the excellent and affected companies had similarly limited career opportunities, the employees in the excellent companies responded more positively because of the career programs.

In addition to comparing attitude profiles, overall level differences can also provide important information. If, for example, a company averages 10 points below the norm, it may determine that it has much room for improvement. Such a finding might prompt the company to adopt the reengineering of major business processes as a means of moving forward as opposed to relying solely on a quality effort. Quality efforts tend to engender incremental as opposed to dramatic levels of improvement in a short period of time.

As a point in passing, the figure of 10 percentage points used above is for illustration purposes only. TESC and the larger consortium provide no *formal* decision rules for determining "practically significant" differences. As a rule of thumb, however, because of the large sample sizes that they routinely deal with, most consortium members do not consider a difference of less than 5 percentage points to be practically significant.

As a last issue, normative comparisons can help companies by providing evidence of excellence and progressiveness. For instance, benchmarking is a necessary element in winning the Malcolm Baldridge Award for quality (Gerber, 1990). Several hundred points in the award equation are apportioned to human resource practices and employee satisfaction (Riemann, 1990). Favorable attitude survey results, relative to excellent companies, may aid in winning the award. Even if a company is not involved in award competition, such information can be used to create a positive image marketing tool for an organization and its products. In light of the shortages of skilled workers projected by the *Workforce 2000* report (Johnston & Packer, 1987), a company may also be able to use favorable survey results to help recruit from a shrinking applicant pool.

The Importance of Consortium Norms

Actions determined through norm-based data comparisons may lead to changes in the way that management interacts with employees. As such they have the potential to affect a company's bottom line and competitive stance (see Hinrichs, 1991; Ulrich, Halbrook, Meder, Stuchlik, & Thorpe, 1991). The validity of these important norm-based conclusions depends in large part on the relevance and accuracy of the norms used. The need for relevant and accurate norms underscores the importance of stringent data collection standards, consortium norms, and good consortium partners.

Although norms have historically been advocated as interpretive aids (e.g., Burns, 1988; Ernest & Baenen, 1985; Marks, 1982; Verheyen,

1988), other authors (Bracken, 1992; Lees-Haley & Lees-Haley, 1982) have written convincingly about the danger of the incautious use of norms. The latter group have argued that "bad" norms are worse than no norms at all. After they detailed several problems that may result from using external norms to interpret data, Lees-Haley and Lees-Haley (1982) concluded that "the most useful norm for your employee opinion data is your own data" (p. 89) trended over time. Though less negative about external norms, Marks (1982) cautioned users:

> To compare the results from your organization with those of other organizations . . . may be very difficult, indeed statistically inaccurate, [unless] . . . results come from a *comparable source* . . . collected in a *comparable manner*. A comparable source means a work organization involved in a same or similar industry. . . . Comparable manner refers to the way the question is asked at your site and if it was asked in the same or similar way elsewhere. Items worded differently or having different response scales tend to generate different patterns of response. (pp. 688-689, emphasis in original)

Bracken (1992) also cautioned about the use of external norms but specifically exempted good consortia:

> If you have an ongoing survey program, you can look into joining the Mayflower Group, a consortium of major U.S. companies that have been sharing norms for decades. The membership requirements for Mayflower are stringent, but the group takes great care to address many of the typical concerns about creating a high-quality data base. (p. 53)

In summary, a good consortium with rigorous standards and high criteria for membership is extremely important if one is to be able to trust the norms provided and use them to aid in survey-related decisions. In a consortium, one knows who the companies are, how the data was collected, and what questions were used.

Good Consortium Partners

Because the worth of norms is dependent on consortium members, we briefly consider the characteristics of good consortium partners.

The major requirement is *comparability* (Marks, 1982). Marks defined comparability largely in terms of industry similarity. Acknowledging Marks's definition as the ideal, we suggest a different definition that is less stringent regarding what constitutes a comparable source but which also addresses some of the practical concerns that could make or break a consortium.

The first characteristic of a good consortium partner is similarity of environment rather than industry. That is, consortium partners should be subject to similar cultural, social, economic, market, and legal factors. For example, a Taiwanese manufacturer of low-priced consumer electronics would not be a good consortium partner for a highly regulated American utility. Instead, a regulated American telecommunications or transportation company might be a better partner.

A second characteristic is comparability of size. In general, smaller companies should seek smaller partners, and larger companies should seek larger partners. There are three reasons for this recommendation. The first reason pertains to how employees in different sized companies perceive the work experience (e.g., more or less specialized, more or less able to affect overall company performance). The second reason pertains to the development of norms and reporting of results. If results are weighted according to company size or are simply combined, the results from a much larger company may overwhelm results from a smaller one. Conversely, if the results from a smaller company are given equal weight to those of a larger company, the resulting norms may be unduly affected by the smaller sample and may be more unstable and unreliable. Perceived equity is the third reason for seeking organizations of comparable size. If the efforts, resources, and sample sizes required of all consortium members are similar, a small organization will be subjected to a relatively greater burden than its larger partner company. Conversely, if requirements are allocated based on company size, the benefits (e.g., cost savings) of including smaller members in the consortium may be negligible for much larger members.

A third characteristic of a good consortium partner is comparability of survey goals. Companies seeking to aggressively change their corporate culture or identify specific actionable issues will need very different information (and hence benefit from different core items) than companies who survey to "take the corporate temperature."

Finally, good consortium partners should share a comparable level of commitment. If commitment to surveying generally is lacking within a member company, that company may be unable to fulfill its responsibility to survey its employees and provide data to the consortium on a regular basis. In addition to sharing a commitment to surveying, good consortium partners should be committed to the consortium (Bracken,

1992). This commitment includes a willingness to share in the costs and other resource requirements of consortium membership (e.g., volunteering to be on a committee). More important, partners must share a comparable commitment to remaining in the consortium. A consortium without a stable core of members is a consortium with meaningless norms.

Sharing of Resources

Consortium members share many resources: item pools, communications, plans, and so on. In a limited fashion, members also share labor and monetary resources. For example, a recent TESC collaborative effort was the construction of a quality questionnaire that is based on the Baldridge Award criteria. Consortium members contributed their "quality" questionnaires to a subcommittee of the consortium, and the subcommittee used information from these surveys to build a consortium questionnaire. Member companies were encouraged to use items from the questionnaire in order to test them out. Several thousand responses were gathered for some items, several hundred for others, with little data available for some infrequently used items. Those items for which sufficient samples were available were factor analyzed. A report of this research effort was produced and disseminated to the membership. The report provided normative, demographic, and factor information that could be used by members interested in administering this questionnaire.

Companies may also share the costs of consultants. TESC, for instance, uses consultants to solve mutual problems. By undertaking a joint effort, each member gets the full benefit of the goods and services contracted for, with the costs spread out among all of the members. The consortium pays once for services rendered instead of having each company pay separately. This results in lower "unit" cost. Similarly, consortium members have been able to negotiate more favorable consulting and data processing rates due to volume when a number of companies have agreed to use the same vendor.

Consortium Influence on Survey Practices

Consortium membership appears to have a positive influence on several survey issues: the credibility of the survey program, allegiance to the survey process and to organization development, and the quality of the survey program. The fact that a consortium surveys with the same instrument on a regular schedule lends legitimacy to the process. To the extent that consortium membership is valued by an organization's decision makers, it helps get upper management to buy in to good survey practices and stabilizes survey commitment. It also helps to make continuing organizational development a reality. If a partner continues a survey for very long, the company will need to do something with the results. If the company does not use the results, employees will lose interest and stop responding.

Last, if a company stays in a consortium it will need to maintain a quality survey process, at least one that meets minimum consortium standards. Consortium membership, however, tends to increase the quality of survey practices and procedures beyond these minimum standards. For example, the previously discussed exchange of information about what works well and what does not is conducive to a cycle of continuous improvement. Thus consortium membership tends to drive excellence into members' survey practices. In addition, because of information sharing outside the consortium, a partner company also fosters improvement in the practices and procedures of reputable consultants, other industrial members, and other industries as well.

Responsibilities of Consortium Members

Overall, there are several areas of responsibility that companies must accept to be consortium members. Most of them are outlined in the section that describes TESC and include payment of dues, agreements to uphold and abide by the bylaws of the consortium, and so forth. The most critical of the responsibilities, however, is to adhere to specified survey standards so the survey data shared within the consortium will be meaningful.

These survey standards often include rigid guidelines for sampling, sample sizes, and frequency of survey efforts. Consortium standards also require that members use, at a minimum, a common core of survey items and demographics. These items and their response formats must comply with some established form and must be administered in a prescribed manner. Survey administration requirements may be outlined that require all companies to survey at the worksite on company time and to use the method yielding the highest survey completion rate.

Data analysis and processing requirements also often dictate that members adhere to specific requirements regarding the format of the data file and the medium on which it is provided.

Although these requirements are necessary for a consortium to be successful, they also constitute the downside of consortium membership. A consortium member may, for example, find that very few "core items" are relevant to the goals of their survey effort; yet as a consortium member the company is required to use these items. Similarly, the requirement to conduct surveys on a regular basis, while critical to the currency of the consortium norms, may not always be greeted with enthusiasm by management or employees within a member's company.

Technical Survey Standards

Survey standards may be thought of as falling into three groups: item standards, sampling standards, and reporting standards. The following paragraphs outline the major "technical" standards in each group that are usually incorporated in a consortium.

Item Standards

The first item standard is so obvious that it is often overlooked—the consortium's core items must be relevant to its members' goals. Core items should be only those items that are relevant to the survey purposes of the majority of consortium members. Including each member's "pet" items will result in an unnecessarily large number of core items and will damage the credibility and value of both the consortium and the survey effort back in the company.

A second desirable item standard is that all core items be pretested. Pretesting helps to ensure that the items are not ambiguous or otherwise confusing to survey respondents. At a minimum, this pretesting should include a review of potential items by someone external to the consortium. For an established consortium, potential core items may be pretested by including them as optional items that members may use in a survey. Depending on the results of these "trials," items may or may not be included as core items in future surveys. For a new consortium, pretested core items may be selected from previous surveys of member companies or purchased from reputable survey vendors.

Third, a consortium should maintain strict guidelines for item use. Often, individual consortium members are under pressure to modify items to please some officer or special interest group in the company. As we have stated, even slight modifications may substantially alter the meaning of an item and negate the comparability of results. At least one consortium with which we are familiar will not accept data from a member's survey if one comma is out of place. These strict standards ensure that resulting information for its members is relevant and directly comparable. Such standards also provide a powerful ally in countering upper management requests for item modification.

Sampling Standards

Sampling standards also help ensure the relevance and comparability of results. Sample size requirements ensure that each member's data are within certain sampling error parameters. These requirements also ensure that the burden of providing data is equitably distributed among members. Furthermore, sampling method/representativeness requirements help to minimize the likelihood of systematic sampling errors. Finally, survey frequency requirements help to ensure the currency of the norms provided to members.

Reporting Standards

Reporting standards generally do not directly benefit the survey practitioner. They do, however, speed and simplify the development of the consortium data base from which norms and other information can be extracted. These standards include such things as data coding standards, data file format, and data transmission media.

Alternatives to Consortiums

What alternatives are available to a company that does not belong to a consortium, cannot comply with the many requirements of a consortium, or does not have the time to wait until a consortium can be formed? Such a company has at least two options. One, a company can follow Lees-Haley and Lees-Haley's (1992) recommendation and dispense with external norms altogether. Two, a company can follow Marks's (1982) recommendation and employ a consulting firm that makes norms available as part of its services. Most large consulting firms, particularly those that specialize in organizational surveys, will have normative information of some kind. Before choosing a consultant, however, one should read Bracken's (1992) article. It provides a reasonable, detailed review of the information to consider before choosing a consulting firm and norm base.

Summary and Conclusions

In this article, we have defined and discussed the consortium employee attitude survey approach and have portrayed it as a limited form of benchmarking. We have discussed the many benefits of this approach, including the exchange of survey practices information and the dissemination of consortium norms and have pointed out how the standards that lead to these benefits may, at times, be the greatest disadvantage of consortium membership. In addition, some viable alternatives to the survey consortium approach have been described.

We have provided insights into the workings of one survey consortium, TESC, and based our discussion on that model. In this way, some practical ideas and information have been provided to readers who may be interested in adopting this approach. On the downside, we recognize that other equally valid approaches were likely omitted.

As at the beginning of this article, we wish to stress that what we have written is based more on our experiences, opinions, and observations than on any pool of research or professional literature. Others, even members of the same consortium, may disagree with the views expressed in this article. We welcome their input and hope they will add their views to the dearth of publicly available literature on this topic.

Notes

1. The November-December 1990 issue of *Interfaces* magazine provided numerous examples of research consortia.
2. These two requirements are also placed on TESC by the larger consortium to which TESC belongs.
3. To date, very few alterations have been detected, and those changes were due to printing errors.

References

Angoff, W. H. (1991). Scales, norms, and equivalent scores. In R. L. Thorndike (Ed.), *Educational measurement* (2nd ed., pp. 508-600). Washington, DC: American Council on Education.

Barron, J. (1990). Consortia: High-tech co-ops. *Byte, 15,* 269-270.

Bracken, D. (1992). Benchmarking employee attitudes. *Training & Development, 46*(6), 49-53.

Burns, T. J. (1988). Learning what workers think. *Nation's Business, 76,* 32.

Camp, R. C. (1989). *Benchmarking: The search for industry best practices that lead to superior performance.* Milwaukee, WI: Quality Press/American Society for Quality Control.

Ernest, R. C., & Baenen, L. B. (1985, May). Analysis of attitude survey results: Getting the most from the data. *Personnel Administrator,* pp. 71-80.

Fralicx, R., & Schroeder, M. (1991, April). *Trends in attitude survey results over the last decade.* Paper presented at the meeting of the Telecommunication Employee Survey Consortium, San Diego.

Gerber, B. (1990, November). Benchmarking: Measuring yourself against the best. *Training,* pp. 36-44.

Greenberg, H. J. (1990). An industrial consortium to sponsor the development of an intelligent mathematical programming system. *Interfaces, 20*(6), 83-93.

Hay Group, Inc. (1991). *The 1991-92 Hay Employee Attitude Study.* Philadelphia, PA: Author.

Hinrichs, J. (1991). Commitment ties to the bottom line. *HR Magazine, 36*(4), 77-80.

Johnston, W., & Packer, A. (1987). *Workforce 2000: Work and workers for the 21st century.* Indianapolis, IN: Hudson Institute.

Katzell, R. A. (1990, October). *The motivation climate analysis (MCA): A system for improving motivational climate.* Paper presented at the meeting of the Telecommunication Employee Survey Consortium, Phoenix, AZ.

Lees-Haley, P. R., & Lees-Haley, C. E. (1982, October). Attitude survey norms: A dangerous ally. *Personnel Administrator,* pp. 51-53.

Lilian, G. L. (1990). Industry-university cooperation at Penn State's Institute for the Study of Business Markets. *Interfaces, 20*(6), 94-98.

Mandell, M. (1990). The consortium: An idea whose time has come (or gone)? *Across the Board, 27,* 30-35.

Marks, M. L. (1982). Conducting an employee attitude survey. *Personnel Journal, 61,* 684-691.

Moore, D. G. (1989). *Recent trends in employee attitudes in the United States.* Chicago: Standard & Associates, Inc.

Morris, G. W. (1991, April). *Facilitating cultural change through survey procedures.* Paper presented at the meeting of the Telecommunication Employee Survey Consortium, San Diego.

Ramos, R. (1991, April). *Models for communicating survey results.* Paper presented at the meeting of the Telecommunication Employee Survey Consortium, San Diego.

Reimann, C. (1990, April 23). How to win the Baldridge Award. *Fortune,* pp. 106-116.

Stum, D. L. (1991, October). *Redefining employee surveys: Give your organization the "competitive advantage."* Paper presented at the Telecommunications Employee Survey Consortium, New Orleans.

Thomas, M. E. (1990). The manufacturing research center at the Georgia Institute of Technology. *Interfaces, 20*(6), 69-74.

Ulrich, D., Halbrook, R., Meder, D., Stuchlik, M., & Thorpe, S. (1991). Employee and customer attachment: Synergies for competitive advantage. *Human Resource Planning, 14*(2), 89-103.

Verheyen, L. G. (1988). How to develop an employee attitude survey. *Training and Development Journal, 42*, 72-76.

PART III

Applications

7

Surveying Pregnancy
and Single Parenthood

The Navy Experience

MARIE D. THOMAS
PATRICIA J. THOMAS

Women have entered the labor force in large numbers in the last two decades, including mothers of small children. For example, in 1990, more than 50% of women who had given birth to a child in the past year were in the labor force, whereas only about 30% of these mothers had worked in 1970 (Eckholm, 1992).

As women in general and mothers in particular continue to seek employment outside the home, questions have been raised about whether women can adequately manage both work and family roles (Crosby, 1991). Pregnancy (Wallace, 1982), single parenthood (Lewin, 1992; Wright, 1989), and day care (Eckholm, 1992) are issues many organizations must now consider when managing their work forces. Such issues took on a political tone, as debates about family values dominated the media during the months leading up to the 1992 presidential election. Even Murphy Brown, a sitcom character, became the focus of arguments about single motherhood.

AUTHORS' NOTE: This chapter was written by government employees as part of official duties; therefore the material cannot be copyrighted and is in the public domain. The opinions expressed in this chapter are those of the authors. They are not official and do not represent the views of the Department of the Navy.

145

The issues raised by these debates are not new to the military, although events occurring in the early 1990s have brought them to the forefront. The unprecedented mobilization of women in the reserves during Operation Desert Shield/Storm raised questions about sending mothers into battle. Reports of women returning from the Persian Gulf pregnant and rumors about a "Love Boat" filled the media. As a result of congressional concern over the impact on children of deploying mothers and the excellent performance of women in the Persian Gulf War, a Presidential Commission on the Assignment of Women in the Armed Forces was established. Its purpose was to assess the laws and policies affecting the assignment of women and to report to the president its findings and recommendations for further legislative and administrative actions. Women's capacity to bear children and the possible effect of pregnant women on morale and mission accomplishment were topics of particular concern to the commissioners.

The perception that an unreasonable number of Navy women are pregnant and that many of these pregnant women are single is widespread among Navy personnel. Yet, until 1988, there was no systematic way of estimating how many pregnant women or single parents are in the Navy (P. J. Thomas & Edwards, 1989). Moreover, no empirical data existed regarding descriptive characteristics of the people involved—their age, tenure, rank, and so on. Such data are required to evaluate and possibly modify policies, develop interventions, and estimate the need for support services. In addition, by periodically measuring the rates, trends can be monitored, enabling the Navy to be proactive if pregnancy and single parenthood are shown to have a negative impact on the military mission.

A commonly used method to gather data on such topics has been the survey. To illustrate the application of survey methodology to organizations, this chapter will discuss a series of surveys conducted by the Navy Personnel Research and Development Center (NPRDC) on pregnancy and parenthood among Navy personnel. These Surveys of Pregnancy and Parenthood have been administered every 2 years since 1988. The first part of the chapter reviews some of the important changes that have occurred with regard to women in the military so as to place the surveys within a context. A discussion of the steps involved in designing, administering, and analyzing the surveys follows. Results related to the perceptions about pregnancy mentioned above are then reviewed. We describe how the survey results have been used by the Navy as well as important issues we encountered in the survey process. Finally, the "Conclusions" section presents applications to civilian organizations.

Women and the Military

Women in the military are a twentieth-century phenomenon, whose fluctuating population and functions have been closely tied to U.S. wars. When their country called, women answered. When wars ended, their numbers fell precipitously, and the few that remained in uniform served in support jobs that were consistent with current female roles (P. J. Thomas, 1978). The All Volunteer Force and the decline in the pool of eligible young men interrupted this pattern in the early 1970s, and the recruitment of women for the armed forces began for the first time under peacetime conditions. From less than 2% of the military in 1972, their representation expanded to 11% in 1991, when more than 200,000 women were serving in the Army, Air Force, Navy, and Marine Corps (Becraft, 1991).

Expansion of the roles of women has accompanied the increases in numbers. The first female pilots graduated from flight training in 1973. At the direction of the Congress, women entered the service academies for the first time in 1976. The first women reported aboard a ship that was not designated as a transport or hospital ship[1] in 1979. Although women are still prevented from serving in military jobs classified as combat positions, they are found in combat support functions and deployed throughout the world.

Implications of Increased Participation

The Women's Armed Services Integration Act of 1948, which established the permanent status of women in uniform, included a number of restrictive clauses. Regulations pertaining only to women were also enacted in each of the services. The military had stricter entry standards for women than men, requiring that they be older and better educated and score higher on tests to be eligible for enlistment. Women's husbands were not given the medical and commissary benefits available to the wives of military men. By not being allowed to serve in ships, women were denied the assignments they needed to reach the higher ranks in the Navy. These gender-specific policies have been overturned by the courts, after being challenged by military women. Most of the changes that followed were accomplished with little disruption, because they essentially required that women's treatment be brought into consonance with men's. Revisions in pregnancy policies were an exception.

Concerns About Pregnancy

Until 1972, women who became pregnant were involuntarily discharged from the military. In reality, it may have been motherhood, not pregnancy per se, that was being controlled because women who became mothers through marriage to a man with children or through adoption also were discharged (P. J. Thomas & M. D. Thomas, 1993). When the dismissal policy was first modified, it allowed for headquarters to retain pregnant women on a case-by-case basis. In 1975, however, the Department of Defense made pregnancy separations voluntary. Since that time, policies have been enacted to discourage the discharge of pregnant women and require the retention of those in whom the military has invested a great deal of training or bonus money.

Complaints about pregnant women's effect on the military mission followed soon after the mandatory discharge policy was abandoned (P. J. Thomas & Edwards, 1989). Pregnant women were said to be absent from work a great deal of time due to prenatal medical care and illness. Military manpower studies were undertaken to investigate the nonavailable time of women (e.g., P. J. Thomas, M. D. Thomas, & Robertson, 1993). In the first of the Navy studies, Olson and Stumpf (1978) analyzed absences that were recorded in Navy personnel and medical data tapes to assess the impact of the voluntary separation policy on absences and attrition. In addition, coworkers were surveyed about pregnant women in the work group and the new pregnancy policy. The authors found that women lost less time than men. More than two thirds of the survey respondents who had worked with a pregnant woman felt that the pregnancy had no impact on productivity. Conversely, male personnel who had never worked with a pregnant woman felt that there would be an impact on the work group (Olson & Stumpf, 1978).

The Army also gathered data regarding pregnancy and absences using a diary methodology and supervisors' memories of the recent past (Savell, Rigby, & Zbikowski, 1982). Had it relied on only one of these sources, very different conclusions would have been reached. While the real-time diary data indicated that there was not a significant gender difference in absences, enlisted supervisors thought that women had lost more time than men for medical reasons (20 hours versus 8 hours) over the past 4 weeks.

Despite the lack of evidence that military women are absent more than men, pregnancy and childbirth do exact a toll. Pregnant and convalescing women lose time from work for medical reasons that are not applicable to men or to women who are not pregnant. They must be excused from hazardous work environments and tasks that might endanger their health or that of the unborn child. They have an impact upon the military medical, child care, and housing systems by creating a greater need for services and straining the budgets of the providers. A woman transferred from her job because of pregnancy may create a personnel vacancy that usually cannot be filled quickly.

Debates over increasing the role of women in the military often focus on pregnancy and its potential effect on combat or combat support units. With regard to pregnancy, some feel that military women have made *too much* progress over the past two decades. Mitchell (1989), for example, stated that pregnancy is the "only 'temporary disability' that service members can inflict upon themselves without fear of punishment. It is also the only temporary disability that earns a service member the right to decide for herself whether to stay in the service or get out, notwithstanding the desires of her commander or the needs of the service" (p. 168).

Concerns About Single Parents

Single parents are another group that are often viewed as a problem— a problem that is related, in the minds of some, to pregnant women. Although male single parenthood is a growing phenomenon, women are 5 times more likely to be single parents than men are (U.S. Department of Commerce, 1988). Because women who are single parents may be never-married mothers, pregnancy and single parenthood become entwined. For the military, this relationship appears self-evident, because there was no single parent "problem" when the number of women in the armed forces was low.

Children have an impact on the military for several reasons. First, they create a need for child care, recreational, and educational services. Second, children increase the demand for housing and medical services. Third, direct costs are also involved because each child results in a higher subsistence allowance for a military parent. Fourth, parenthood in the military has a potential impact on job performance to an extent much greater than in most civilian work settings. Military personnel are often required to work extended hours or are called back to work to perform unexpected tasks. Also, members of the armed forces can be assigned to geographic locations where their families cannot accompany them or to ships at sea for months at a time. Although married parents find child-rearing and military duties difficult to reconcile when such situations arise, the stress brought on by the demands of conflicting roles is much greater for single parents. When they fail to satisfy both parental and job responsibilities, their children and the mission of their military unit may suffer.

Policies have been enacted to reduce the possible negative impact of single parents upon the resources and performance of military units. In most of the services, single parents cannot enlist unless they relinquish custody of their children to a legal guardian. In the Navy, they cannot regain custody during their first enlistment except under extraordinary circumstances. If they do regain custody, the Navy may discharge them.

Contingency child care plans are of vital importance to the military because of the unpredictability of personnel requirements. As witnessed in the Persian Gulf War, both active-duty and reserve components may be mobilized on short notice. Children of these personnel must be cared for during the parents' absence. Even during peacetime, military evolutions require that parents be absent for several weeks or months at a time. Furthermore, day-to-day work may extend beyond the hours of child care centers. Making arrangements for child care when such circumstances arise is especially difficult for single parents, who have no spouses to take over during their absence. To ensure that appropriate arrangements are made in advance, the armed forces have enacted policies that affect only single personnel with children[2] or parents who both are in the military.

Why Gather Information About
Pregnancy and Single Parenthood?

The notion that pregnancy and single parenthood are "problems" for the military seems to be widespread, despite the lack of empirical evidence of such problems. The Navy, more than other military branches, has attempted to assess the validity of these perceptions through surveys, analysis of personnel data, and field research. Therefore the rest of this chapter will focus on Navy surveys of pregnancy and parenthood.

Prior to the 1988 Navy-wide Survey of Pregnancy and Parenthood (P. J. Thomas & Edwards, 1989), pregnancy rates were typically based on the number of service women who were hospitalized at Navy facilities for reasons associated with bearing and delivering children (Hoiberg,

1982). As a pregnancy rate, such a figure is an underestimate, because it does not include pregnancies terminated by elective abortion. In addition, service women who obtained obstetric services from civilian or other military health care providers would not be counted.

Accurate pregnancy rates are important for the Navy, in part, because of the work restrictions experienced by pregnant women. For example, pregnant women must be transferred off ships by the end of the 20th week of gestation, and replacements may not arrive for several months. Even before 20 weeks, pregnant women cannot deploy with their ships unless medical evacuation can be managed in less than 6 hours. Restrictions on the types of work and hazards to which pregnant women can be exposed limit the jobs in which these women can be placed. For efficient personnel management, the Navy needs to know what percentage of women will be pregnant at any given time.

A similar situation exists for single parents. The Navy Women's Study Group (Secretary of the Navy, 1987) reported that many commands view single parents as an administrative burden. Problems seemed to center on child care and parents' lack of flexibility in dealing with changing work hours (P. J. Thomas & Edwards, 1989). It is difficult to estimate needs for military child care if there is no systematic way of determining the number of parents and children who require such services.

Although pay records contain the number of dependents supported financially by a service member, they fail to indicate whether such children live in the Navy member's household. Orthner and Nelson (1980) attempted to estimate the number of single parents by analyzing the emergency forms that are completed whenever Navy personnel are transferred from one command to another. They estimated that approximately 4,500 enlisted personnel were single parents with dependent children living in their households. This figure was an underestimate because the authors did not count as single parents any personnel who had specified custodians for their children. Several years later, Kerce (1988) replicated Orthner and Nelson's methodology. Although she arrived at a figure of 18,800 single Navy personnel who were also parents, she concluded that only 3,540 were, by the Orthner and Nelson definition, single parents. The Navy Study Group's Report on Progress of Women in the Navy (Secretary of the Navy, 1987) made note of the lack of information on single parents and indicated that there was no way of knowing if their numbers were changing. The group recommended that a system to monitor such figures be developed.

Navy Surveys of Pregnancy and Single
Parenthood: Issues, Logistics, and Impact

In 1988, NPRDC began a 3-year study of pregnancy and single parenthood among enlisted personnel and their impact on the Navy. The first step was to develop reliable estimates of pregnancy and single parenthood. Data for these estimates were collected as part of the 1988 Navy-wide Survey of Pregnancy and Parenthood (P. J. Thomas & Edwards, 1989). The findings proved to be so useful that NPRDC personnel were asked to administer a survey every 2 years to monitor pregnancy, single parenthood trends, and other related concerns (M. D. Thomas & P. J. Thomas, 1990).

The remainder of the chapter will focus on some of the steps involved in designing, administering, and analyzing these surveys. Issues and decisions that arose at each step will be illustrated by examples taken from the surveys. In addition, results will be presented to demonstrate the types of data collected.

Survey Content

While it might seem that determining pregnancy and single parenthood rates would be a straightforward task, the creation of each of the Surveys of Pregnancy and Parenthood was time consuming and often frustrating. Many decisions about survey content had to be made. For example, an early decision was that both women and men needed to be surveyed, even though many perceived the survey to be dealing with "women's" problems. Including men in the survey sample required the creation of two surveys, because most questions about pregnancy are relevant only to women. Therefore two forms of the survey were developed for each administration, with the men's form essentially a subset of the women's form.

In addition, each survey administration required decisions about the types of demographic data to be collected. How demographic questions are asked should be determined by the types of analyses that will be conducted. In our Navy surveys, we are frequently required to compare the findings with civilian data. Thus it is critical to include appropriate demographic questions that will permit direct comparisons to Census or other population data. Researchers need to control the tendency to collect more demographic data than will used. Not controlling this tendency results in an unnecessarily long survey and may lower the response rate. For example, items on race/ethnicity are often included in Navy surveys. Several respondents in the 1992 sample refused to indicate their race/ethnicity, however, stating that these descriptors are not relevant to the survey topics. In a period of heightened awareness of racial and gender issues, we might have been more sensitive to such a concern when developing the 1992 version of the survey. Pretesting, however, did not indicate that an item about race/ethnicity would be a problem.

The Surveys of Pregnancy and Parenthood were large-scale endeavors with approximately 10,000 surveys mailed out for each administration. Using these surveys simply to develop pregnancy and single parenthood rates would have represented a missed opportunity to collect additional information on these topics that military leaders needed. For example, single parents and parents in dual military couples must officially designate custodians for their children (i.e., complete a Dependent Care Certificate), but headquarters does not oversee this requirement. Thus the survey has been used to monitor compliance with this regulation. In addition, in 1988 and 1990, both men and women were "quizzed" on their knowledge of and experience with Navy policies regarding pregnant women and single parents. Their responses provided the Navy with information regarding the extent to which supervisors of pregnant women were knowledgeable about pregnancy regulations.

In the surveys, women are asked if they are currently pregnant. Responses to this question are used to establish a "point-in-time" pregnancy rate that is monitored for trends. In addition, women who had been pregnant while in the Navy are asked about the outcomes of all such pregnancies. With this information, abortion, miscarriage/still-birth, and live birth rates are developed. Navy respondents are asked if their most recent (or current) pregnancy had been planned. If it was unplanned, they are asked whether they had been using contraceptives and, if so, what type. While such questions may appear to be very intrusive, contraceptive failure is of concern to an organization that also serves as the primary medical provider.

A final comment on survey content: Creating a survey in an organization like the Navy is a cooperative effort. While some of the additional questions were included in the three surveys at the researchers' request, the final instruments had to meet the needs of the Navy. The military is a hierarchical organization, with many levels to its "chain of command." Each survey went through a lengthy approval process, with many different people exercising their rights to insert, modify, and delete questions. It is not unusual for our surveys to be changed at each level of approval. This can be frustrating for two reasons. First, a long lead time is required. We allow at least a month simply for the approval process. Second, military personnel who may have little or no training in psychology or survey methodology have the final say over the inclusion and phrasing of survey questions. We recognize, however, that these same leaders must take responsibility for any political fallout from the survey results. If the data become front-page news, the leaders will have to defend them inside and outside the organization. Mutual cooperation in these efforts is therefore absolutely necessary.

Sampling

The process of selecting a sample generally occurs while the survey is undergoing review. Early on, we decided a simple random sample would not be appropriate for a survey on pregnancy and parenthood. Women make up approximately 10% of the enlisted Navy and therefore they would make up approximately 10% of a random sample. Because pregnancy was a major focus of the surveys, and relatively few Navy women are pregnant at any given time, however, it became necessary to select large samples of women.

Each administration of the survey has used a sample of Navy personnel that was stratified within gender.[3] Enlisted women and men are treated as separate populations and the resulting samples for men and women are approximately equal in size. In 1988 and 1990, samples were stratified by paygrade (E2, Seaman Apprentice, to E9, Master Chief Petty Officer) and job classification (whether the job was primarily sea or shore based). Job classification was included because pregnancy among women in ships requires reassignment, whereas pregnancy at a shore command does not cause as much personnel turbulence. In addition, some believe that the pregnancy rate is higher among women whose jobs often take them out to sea. In 1992, only paygrade was used for stratification, because (despite perceptions) job classification was not related to pregnancy or single parenthood rates in the two prior survey administrations.

Once the stratification variables were determined, a random sample was chosen from within most strata. All women in the highest paygrades (i.e., the population of E8 and E9 women) were selected because the numbers were so small.

Officers were surveyed for the first time in 1992. The stratification method used to select the officer sample was similar to that for the enlisted personnel. Women and men officers were treated as separate populations and stratification was based on rank (O1, Ensign, to O5, Commander). Response rates vary greatly by sex and paygrade. Women are more likely to respond to Navy surveys than are men. Enlisted service members in higher paygrades and officers are much more likely to return surveys (their response rates generally exceed 70%) than are personnel in lower paygrades. During sample selection, response rates from previous surveys are taken into account when determining the size of each stratum. For example, lower paygrade male sailors and female E2s tend to have very low response rates, and, therefore, they were oversampled in the 1990 and 1992 surveys. While oversampling helped in 1990, the response rates in 1992 for female and male personnel in the lowest paygrade surveyed (E2) were poor (17% and 9%, respectively). The cell size for E2 males was considered inadequate.

These low rates bring up the question of nonresponse bias. Whether nonresponse has an effect on survey results depends on the percentage of the sample who do not respond and the extent to which the nonrespondents are systematically different than the entire population (Fowler, 1988). Such bias is never completely independent of a survey's issues (Alreck & Settle, 1985). While unlikely to affect single parenthood rates because of the low incidence among E2s, the low response rate of women in this paygrade is of concern because they are at high risk for pregnancy. In fact, the pregnancy rate for E2s, as estimated from three sets of survey data, has been the least stable of any paygrade.

Administration

Surveys are mailed directly to personnel at their commands. Each survey has a cover page that explains its purpose and informs the respondent that his or her responses are anonymous, confidential, and voluntary. Because surveys are anonymous, no targeted follow-up is possible. For the 1990 administration, reminder postcards were sent to everyone in the sample 4 weeks after the surveys were mailed; this procedure is believed to have helped increase the response rates. We were unable to follow this procedure with the 1992 survey.

Data Analysis Issue: Poststratification Weighting

For Navy purposes, percentages of all respondents answering questions in a specific manner are often the preferred units of analysis. For other analyses, breakouts by organizational level are frequently needed. The Navy might want to know what percentage of the single parents in the sample have filled out a Dependent Care Certificate or what percentage of the sample's pregnant women were assigned to a ship at the time they became pregnant. Sometimes the data are used to estimate population values—for example, the percentage of Navy personnel who are single parents or the percentage of women who are pregnant at a given time.

When estimates of population values are derived from a sample, *poststratification weighting* is often performed. This operation makes adjustments for deviations between the way a characteristic is distributed in the sample and its distribution in the population (Henry, 1990). As an example, consider the factors relevant to computing a Navy-wide estimate of the single parenthood rate. Relative to men, a much higher percentage of women are single parents with custody of their children. In the 1990 survey sample, 10.9% of the women and 2.6% of the men were single parents. In terms of the actual number of single parents, however, there are many more male than female single parents in the Navy because about 90% of the Navy's enlisted force are men. Women made up 44% of the 1990 sample, while they would constitute only about 10% of the enlisted population. The overall Navy single parenthood rate based on the uncorrected sample would have been 6.6%; the weighted single parenthood rate was 3.1%. Weighting appropriately reduced the contribution of the women's percentage to the overall estimate.

The weighting procedure is relatively simple. Each stratum's proportion in the population and its proportion in the sample is determined. The population proportion is divided by the sample proportion to provide weights for the strata. These weights are then applied to the number of events in a response option. The new weighted frequencies are totaled and a weighted percentage can be determined.

Another example will further clarify the procedure. In the 1992 survey, approximately 6.5% of the enlisted women in the sample were pregnant at the time of the survey (135 of 2,080 respondents). Because of response rates, however, women in the lower paygrades were underrepresented among the respondents. For example, E4s constitute 24.1% of the female enlisted force. They made up only 12.5% of the survey sample, however (even with a 55% response rate). The weight for E4 women therefore is $(.241)/(.125) = 1.93$. This weight is then multiplied by the number of current pregnancies (23) found in the sample for this group. The weighted number of E4 pregnancies is (23)(1.93) = 44.4. This weighting procedure was followed for all paygrades. It had the effect of increasing the "influence" of the lower paygrades, whose representation in the population is larger than the sample representation and who are more likely to be pregnant, and decreasing the "influence" of the higher paygrades, who have high response rates but low pregnancy rates. In total, the weighted number of pregnancies became 174.44; the overall weighted pregnancy rate was therefore (174.44)/(2080) = 8.39%.

Weighting has no effect on the *percentage* of women in a paygrade stratum who are pregnant. If the Navy had not needed an overall rate, no weighting would have been undertaken.

Survey Results

In this section, we will focus on the concerns that generated the original research: Are an excessive number of Navy women pregnant at any given time? Are most of them young and single?

The point-in-time pregnancy rate for enlisted women has been very consistent, ranging from 8.4% to 8.9% in the three administrations of the Survey of Pregnancy and Parenthood. Figure 7.1 shows the percentage of pregnant women in the three surveys by paygrade, which is highly correlated with age ($r = .85$). The rate of pregnancy is highest for women who are E4 and below. In terms of age, in 1992, almost 65% of the women who were pregnant at the time of the survey were under the age of 25.

Most of the higher paygrade women (E6 and above) who were pregnant at the time of the 1992 survey were married. There is some validity to the perception that many of the younger pregnant women are single; 64% of the pregnant E2s and 49% of the E3s were single. Many of the pregnant E3s were cohabiting with, presumably, the father-to-be. More than half of the pregnant E2s, however, were single, never married, and not living with a man.

More than half (59%) of the pregnancies reported in the 1992 survey were unplanned. This has been a consistent finding over the three surveys. Of the women who became pregnant unintentionally, 56% reported that they had been using birth control. The two most common methods used by women who became pregnant were condoms and the contraceptive pill.

Abortion rates tend to be low (between 15% and 17%), except among E2s. This low abortion rate is probably at least partly the result of the

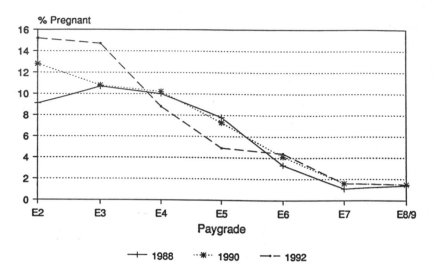

Figure 7.1. Percentage of Pregnant Women by Paygrade

passage of the FY79 Defense Appropriations Act, with its attached antiabortion amendment. This act prohibits the military from performing or paying for the abortions of active-duty women or dependents except in very limited circumstances. While it is difficult to ascertain the effect of this bill on the number of abortions obtained by Navy women, hospitalization data for Navy women for several years preceding the FY79 Defense Appropriations Act showed that induced abortions consistently outnumbered births in Navy hospitals (Hoiberg & Ernst, 1980).

**Impact of Navy Pregnancy and
Parenthood Surveys**

Based on the three survey administrations, we reached some conclusions about Navy enlisted women and pregnancy. First, pregnancy rates are stable. Second, pregnancy rates seem to be comparable to the available civilian data. These and other data have led us to conclude that pregnancy is not an out-of-control problem. Our findings have allowed some of the concern over the negative effect pregnant women were presumed to be having on the Navy to dissipate. Most pregnant enlisted women are, however, under the age of 25, and many of the pregnant women in the lowest paygrades are unmarried. It seems clear that additional efforts are needed to reduce the rates of pregnancy and single parenthood among the most junior personnel. The Navy has made major strides toward this goal by improving and increasing the amount of sex education presented to enlisted personnel during training, making a wide variety of contraceptives available, and reducing the wait for gynecological appointments.

Single parenthood rates estimated from the survey data are higher than corresponding civilian rates. The data indicate, however, that career personnel, not first-termers, have the highest rates of single parenthood. Most single parents are not young, unmarried women but older personnel who have achieved this status through divorce. This finding quieted those advocating the discharge of all single parents.

The survey data have been put to other uses. For example, the finding that less than half of single and dual military parents had a contingency child care plan led the Chief of Naval Personnel to issue a message to all commands directing that this deficiency be corrected. A second example also involves child care requirements. Military planners responsible for child development centers asked that survey data be reanalyzed to develop estimates of the number of parents in the Navy, by marital and spouse employment status, and the number of children by age categories (M. D. Thomas & P. J. Thomas, 1992). Prior to gathering the survey data, no systematic way of estimating such numbers existed.

Ethical and Practical Concerns

Privacy. Personnel in the military are more accustomed to invasions of privacy than are civilians and therefore may be more willing to answer questions that civilians would refuse to consider. They also are used to "following orders," a trait especially pleasing to survey researchers, who can expect good response rates, even to mail-out surveys. The questions included on the surveys we have been discussing, especially for women, were very personal and, sometimes, potentially embarrassing. Women were asked about abortions and contraceptive use and about some demographic characteristics of the biological father of their child. With items like these, a guarantee of anonymity and confidentiality was crucial.

Even though the cover sheet of the survey states that no one will see the returned surveys except the researchers, respondents sometimes have expressed fears of being identified. Several women officers refused to report their job specialty code because there were so few women with their code that they were sure they could easily be identified. Not surprising, at times, respondents chose not to answer certain questions. Perhaps more surprising is the fact that most respondents *did* answer all of the questions. While most organizational surveys do not request the types of personal information that we routinely ask, it is important to keep privacy in mind when designing and administering surveys, especially those containing sensitive items (see Hosseini & Armacost, this volume).

Surveying emotional issues: The effect of current events. When surveying an emotional issue, response rates and results can be affected by contemporary events. For example, the Navy experienced several highly publicized incidents of sexual harassment and assault in 1991. Throughout 1992, women's roles in the military were being scrutinized and debated by the Presidential Commission on the Assignment of Women in the Armed Forces. In the midst of this turmoil, our 1992 survey was sent out, asking very personal questions about pregnancy. We were also attempting to assess attitudes toward women in the military and in combat. Some personnel in the sample saw the survey as another attempt to discredit women in the military and complained to senior officers. Fortunately, only a small minority felt this way.

The primary evidence that current events were important to the respondents was the quantity of written comments on the surveys. The 1990 survey had contained a comments section, and some respondents took advantage of it to express their views. On the 1992 survey, however, more than one third of the respondents wrote at least two sentences. We received four-page essays, reports of personal experiences, and comments on the individual items. Many women wrote about the positive and negative aspects of Navy life. Some men expressed frustration with the current Navy climate, believing that women were already playing too great a role in the Navy. Other men believed that women should be given equal opportunities in all areas of the military. The survey touched a nerve and provided the respondents with a chance to express their feelings.

It is likely, though, that, had the survey gone out 6 months later, it would have provoked less of a reaction. One might question whether current events biased the 1992 sample, with personnel who held stronger views on the survey topics being more likely to respond. Surveys performed in the Navy are built around deadlines that must be met, regardless of possible intervening events. Therefore repeating surveys with controversial themes every few years enables researchers to have more confidence in their results.

Conclusions

This chapter has discussed an application of organizational surveys to the study of pregnancy and parenthood. While the Navy has been concerned about pregnancy and single parenthood for several years, the 1992 presidential election campaign has elevated these issues to public debate.

Although the specific examples in this chapter may not be relevant to most organizations, the issues discussed do apply to different settings. An organization has a "problem"; a survey is performed. Based on the results, an organizational change is effected. At some point, the survey is repeated. The Navy example also demonstrates how emotionally charged issues can be studied and how researchers can help to separate myth from reality.

While the debate surrounding Murphy Brown's new status as single mother raised the discussion of pregnancy and single parenthood to the forefront, it must be remembered that Murphy Brown, her life, her career, her pregnancy, and her single parenthood are fiction. For many Navy women and men, the challenges of balancing career and parenthood are all too real. Organizational surveys have helped the Navy accurately estimate the scope of these issues and to take initiatives to address them in the 1990s workplace.

Notes

1. Title 6015 of U.S. Code 10 prohibited the assignment of Navy women to any ships, other than hospital ships and transports, until it was amended in 1978 to permit their assignment to noncombatant ships.
2. A single person who claims a parent or other relative as a dependent is also covered by the policy.
3. Stratification reduces the confidence limits of the responses (i.e., reduces error).

References

Alreck, P. M., & Settle, R. B. (1985). *The survey research handbook.* Homewood, IL: Irwin.

Becraft, C. (1991). *Women in the U.S. armed services: The war in the Persian Gulf.* Washington, DC: Women's Research and Education Institute.

Crosby, F. (1991). *Juggling: The unexpected advantages of balancing career and home for women and their families.* New York: Free Press.

Eckholm, E. (1992, October 6). Finding out what happens when mothers go to work. *The New York Times,* pp. 1, 12.

Fowler, F. J., Jr. (1988). *Survey research methods.* Newbury Park, CA: Sage.

Henry, G. T. (1990). *Practical sampling.* Newbury Park, CA: Sage.

Hoiberg, A. (1982). *Health status of women in the U.S. military* (NHRC Rep. No. 82-32). San Diego, CA: Naval Health Research Center.

Hoiberg, A., & Ernst, J. (1980). Motherhood in the military: Conflicting roles for Navy women? *International Journal of Sociology of the Family, 10,* 265-280.

Kerce, E. W. (1988). *A profile of Navy family configurations* (NPRDC Tech. Note 88-40). San Diego, CA: Navy Personnel Research and Development Center.

Lewin, T. (1992, October 5). Rise in single parenthood is reshaping U.S. *The New York Times,* pp. 1, 16.

Mitchell, B. (1989). *Weak link: The feminization of the American military.* Washington, DC: Regnery Gateway.

Olson, M. S., & Stumpf, S. S. (1978). *Pregnancy in the Navy: Impact on absenteeism, attriting, and work group morale* (NPRDC Tech. Rep. 78-35). San Diego, CA: Navy Personnel Research and Development Center.

Orthner, D. K., & Nelson, R. S. (1980). *A demographic profile of U.S. Navy personnel and families.* Greensboro, NC: Family Research and Analysis, Inc.

Savell, J. M., Rigby, C. K., & Zbikowski, A. A. (1982). *An investigation of lost time and utilization of a sample of first-term male and female soldiers* (Tech. Rep. 607). Alexandria, VA: U.S. Army Research Institute for the Behavioral and Social Sciences.

Secretary of the Navy. (1987). *Navy study group's report on progress of women in the Navy.* Washington, DC: Author.

Thomas, M. D., & Thomas, P. J. (1990, 25 October). *Survey of pregnancy and single parenthood.* Briefing given to RADM J. M. Boorda (Chief of Naval Personnel), Washington, DC.

Thomas, M. D., & Thomas, P. J. (1992). *Population statistics: Navy parents and children* (NPRDC TN 92-4). San Diego, CA: Navy Personnel Research and Development Center.

Thomas, P. J. (1978). Women in the military: America and the British Commonwealth. *Armed Forces and Society, 4,* 623-636.

Thomas, P. J., & Edwards, J. E. (1989). *Incidence of pregnancy and single parenthood among enlisted personnel in the Navy* (NPRDC Tech. Report 90-1). San Diego, CA: Navy Personnel Research and Development Center.

Thomas, P. J., & Thomas, M. D. (1993). Mothers in uniform. In F. Kaslow (Ed.), *The miliary family in peace and war.* New York: Springer.

Thomas, P. J., Thomas, M. D., & Robertson, P. (1993). *Absences of Navy enlisted personnel: A search for gender differences* (NPRDC Tech. Report 93-3). San Diego, CA: Navy Personnel Research and Development Center.

U.S. Department of Commerce. (1988, September). *Households, families, marital status, and living arrangements: March 1988* (Current Population Reports Series P-20, No. 432). Washington, DC: Government Printing Office.

Wallace, P. A. (1982). Increased labor force participation of women and affirmative action. In P. A. Wallace (Ed.), *Women in the workplace* (pp. 1-24). Boston: Auburn House.

Wright, D. W. (1989). Single parents in the workplace: Conserving and increasing human capital. In G. L. Bowen & D. K. Orthner (Eds.), *The organization family: Work and family linkages in the U.S. military* (pp. 80-96). New York: Praeger.

8

Understanding Sexual Harassment Through Organizational Surveys

AMY L. CULBERTSON
PAUL ROSENFELD

One of the things that became quite evident . . . during the hearings was that the Senate did not grasp the seriousness of sexual harassment and the pervasiveness of it.

Anita Hill (quoted in "Anita Hill
Urges Women Judges," 1992, p. B3)

As the number of working women has grown—women now represent 40% of the U.S. work force (Nasar, 1992)—the awareness of sexual harassment as an organizational issue has also increased. While the occurrence of sexual harassment in the workplace is not a new phenomenon, for decades it was an organizational problem that was "widely practiced but systematically ignored" (MacKinnon, 1979, p. vii). In the aftermath of claims of sexual harassment raised by Anita Hill[1] at the Senate confirmation hearings of Clarence Thomas, and news coverage

AUTHORS' NOTE: This chapter was written by government employees as part of official duties; therefore the material cannot be copyrighted and is in the public domain. The opinions expressed in this chapter are those of the authors. They are not official and do not represent the views of the Department of the Navy.

of the allegations of sexual assault involving Navy personnel at the 1991 Tailhook convention, sexual harassment has gone from being an organizational issue of some concern to a high priority area requiring quick and effective action. The fallout from these highly publicized incidents has led to an increased focus on the prevalence, causes, and consequences of sexual harassment in organizational settings.

The heightened attention has resulted in organizations becoming increasingly aware that sexual harassment often has both individual and organizational costs and consequences. Victims of sexual harassment commonly report negative physical and psychological effects (Culbertson & Rosenfeld, in press; Jensen & Gutek, 1982; Terpstra & Baker, 1991). Sexual harassment also results in organizational costs, from the payment of damage awards due to litigation to "hidden" costs resulting from stress, decreased work effectiveness, absenteeism, and turnover (Terpstra & Baker, 1991). In the federal government, sexual harassment cost an estimated $267 million during the period from May 1985 through May 1987 (U.S. Merit Systems Protection Board [USMSPB], 1988). In the military, sexual harassment could be costing as much as $40 million annually due to losses in productivity and increased absenteeism (Maze, 1992). Similarly, studies in the private sector have reported that sexual harassment costs a typical *Fortune* 500 company approximately $6.7 million every year due to lowered morale and productivity, along with increased absenteeism and turnover (Sandroff, 1988). Costs due to sexual harassment may increase in the future. With the passage of the Civil Rights Act of 1991, employees who have been sexually harassed may now sue for up to $300,000 (depending on the size of the organization) in compensatory and punitive damage awards (Eskenazi & Gallen, 1992). Previously, under federal statutes, victims were only able to sue for back pay and reinstatement (Smolowe, 1992).

Because sexual harassment can have such serious consequences for organizations, attention is being given to preventing its occurrence as well as protecting organizations from liability. Thus organizations are issuing policy statements, providing training, and establishing and publicizing grievance procedures to address sexual harassment (Benton-Powers, 1992; Krohne, 1992; Segal, 1992; Terpstra & Baker, 1991). One component—the sexual harassment survey—is, however, an often overlooked aspect of integrated programs aimed at reducing sexual harassment in the workplace.

A survey can serve many purposes in an organization's efforts to combat sexual harassment. A sexual harassment survey allows an organization to identify the extent to which sexual harassment is occurring. Victims of sexual harassment rarely report the incidents, particularly to supervisors or other authorities (Culbertson & Rosenfeld, in press; Culbertson, Rosenfeld, Booth-Kewley, & Magnusson, 1992; USMSPB, 1981, 1988). As Hotelling (1991) noted, "Sexual harassment remains an invisible and elusive problem because its victims are extremely hesitant to report its occurrence" (p. 499). Thus a survey may be the best way to determine how widespread sexual harassment is in an organization.

A sexual harassment survey can be used to gather information that will assist managers or the human resource management (HRM) department in the design of training programs and grievance procedures. In addition to determining an overall rate of sexual harassment, surveys can provide specific data concerning what types of harassment are occurring, who the harassers are (e.g., coworkers, supervisors), what actions victims take, and the consequences victims—and the organization—may suffer due to sexual harassment.

A survey of sexual harassment is also important as an evaluation tool to gauge the effectiveness of organizational policies and practices over time. By administering the survey on a periodic basis, it is possible to determine whether (a) training has resulted in employees having a better understanding of what constitutes sexual harassment, (b) the organization's efforts at preventing sexual harassment are viewed as sincere, (c) the amount of harassment occurring in the workplace has been reduced, and (d) the types of actions employees have taken after being harassed have changed. This evaluation function is essential to providing feedback on how effective efforts have been in combatting harassment.[2]

There are reasons that organizations may be hesitant to conduct surveys of sexual harassment. First, management may not be convinced that sexual harassment is a problem. They may fear that surveying (or discussing) the potential presence of sexual harassment is equivalent to acknowledging its occurrence (Strom, 1991). Second, focus on this issue may strain relationships between men and women in the workplace. This may be due in part to findings that indicate men and women perceive the existence and seriousness of sexual harassment differently (see Terpstra & Baker, 1991). Third, conducting an organizational survey can be a costly, time-consuming, and labor-intensive effort (Booth-Kewley, Rosenfeld, & Edwards, this volume; Edwards & Thomas, this volume).

The reasons for conducting organizational surveys of sexual harassment must be weighed against these potentially negative factors. In deciding whether to survey or not, managers should be aware that sexual harassment is common in many organizational settings. As Sandroff (1988) has noted, "Every employee-attitude survey that we've conducted for the private sector shows at least 15 percent of female employees have been sexually harassed in the last 12 months" (p. 71).[3] Furthermore, in purely financial terms, the overall costs of not assessing the extent of sexual harassment and dealing with it can be high. For example, Johns-Manville Corporation paid $100,000 in 1979, Ford paid $187,023 in 1981, and Montana Power Company paid $73,390 in 1983 in damages due to litigation on sexual harassment (Terpstra, 1986).

Although Edwards and Thomas (this volume) thoroughly describe the main steps involved in conducting an organizational survey, certain additional issues need to be considered when doing a survey of sexual harassment. For the past 4 years, we have been the primary investigators on a Navy-wide survey project that has assessed sexual harassment among active-duty Navy personnel (see Culbertson & Rosenfeld, in press; Culbertson et al., 1992). This experience has resulted in our learning a number of lessons that can help improve the sexual harassment survey. In this chapter, we describe these "10 rules of thumb" that we recommend be considered by others conducting sexual harassment surveys.

Conducting Sexual Harassment Surveys: Ten Rules of Thumb

Rule 1: Don't Survey in a Vacuum; Know What Others Have Done

Before a sexual harassment survey is conducted, it is important to become familiar with what other surveys have found. Surveys of sexual harassment developed by other organizations can be reviewed to determine if the questions, the procedures, and the types of analyses are applicable to your organization. A working knowledge of the results from other surveys is also necessary to allow your subsequent findings to be interpreted in context. Knowing what others have found may prevent needless panic reactions or a hesitancy to deal with seemingly negative findings. If organizations similar to your own (i.e., same industry) have conducted sexual harassment surveys, it is particularly important to review their work before beginning your own.

Although sexual harassment surveys have been administered since the mid-1970s (see Saal, 1990), the first large-scale, scientifically sampled sexual harassment survey was conducted with U.S. federal government employees (USMSPB, 1981). In that study, 42% of the female and 15% of the male respondents indicated that they had been sexually harassed (i.e., had experienced one or more forms of sexually harassing behaviors, such as uninvited sexual teasing, jokes, remarks or questions, or uninvited pressure for dates) during the 2-year survey period of 1978 to 1979. A follow-up survey found virtually the same percentages (42% females, 14% males) for the 2-year period between 1985 and 1987 (USMSPB, 1988).

In the largest and most comprehensive sexual harassment survey ever conducted, approximately 38,000 active-duty personnel in the Army, Navy, Air Force, Marine Corps, and Coast Guard were mailed a survey assessing the occurrence of sexual harassment. The 1988 Department of Defense (DoD) Survey of Sex Roles in the Active-Duty Military (Martindale, 1991) found that 64% of female and 17% of male military personnel had experienced some form of sexual harassing behaviors during the 12 months prior to the survey.

Our own large-scale effort, known as the Navy Equal Opportunity/Sexual Harassment (NEOSH) survey, was initially administered to 10,070 active-duty personnel in October 1989. We found that 42% of female enlisted and 26% of female officers indicated that they had been sexually harassed during the prior 12 months while on duty or while on base or ship while off duty. A small percentage of male enlisted (4%) and male officers (1%) indicated they were sexually harassed during the 1-year survey period. Similar to the other two surveys described above, the NEOSH found the most common forms of harassment for women were unwanted sexual teasing, jokes, remarks, or questions. Generally, as the harassment became more severe in nature, its reported occurrence decreased (Culbertson et al., 1992).

In addition to these large-scale government and military surveys, other sexual harassment surveys have been administered in college and university settings (e.g., Barak, Fisher, & Houston, 1992; Fitzgerald et al., 1988). Although there are differences in rates of sexual harassment that have been obtained, several consistent findings are reported on nearly all major surveys: (a) Victims of harassment are usually those lowest in the organization (i.e., having the least power and status); (b) coworkers and supervisors are the most common perpetrators of sexual harassment; (c) the less serious harassment behaviors occur more frequently; and (d) few victims of sexual harassment file grievances.

Rule 2: Know Thy Organization:
Design the Survey With Your Organization in Mind

Sexual harassment surveys come in many forms. It is important when designing a survey of sexual harassment that it is adapted to fit the particular needs of the organization. Several factors should be considered during the survey design process.

Focused versus omnibus survey. A decision that needs to be made is whether the entire survey should be devoted to sexual harassment or whether it will be part of an omnibus survey that covers other topics. One criterion should be: How serious an issue is sexual harassment for your organization, and thus how much information do you need to collect? A way to determine the seriousness is to consult with the human resource management (HRM) department to determine the number of informal and formal complaints or grievances that have been filed. You also may want to talk with union representatives or others in the organization (e.g., Equal Employment Opportunity Counselors, legal staff) who have their fingers on the pulse of the work force. Interviews or focus groups with employees (Kolbert, 1992) also can be conducted, but it is better to keep the discussion general rather than asking about personal experiences. Using an outside consultant can be an effective way to gather information regarding the seriousness of the problem without it being threatening to members of the organization. Based on such preliminary data, decide whether the survey should be devoted to sexual harassment or should include other topics. Survey costs can be reduced by having several related topics surveyed at the same time.

Type of work force. The survey you design or adapt and the manner in which it is administered need to be tailored to the type of work force in the organization (e.g., white collar, military). Decisions concerning the readability level of the items (see Edwards & Thomas, this volume), the examples of sexual harassment provided, and the method of administration used (see Booth-Kewley et al., this volume) should be selected to best fit your work force.

Female-to-male ratio. Studies have consistently found that the overwhelming majority of sexual harassment victims (90%-95%) are women (Koen, 1989). Also, women in nontraditional jobs—those that have historically been occupied by men—are subject to harassment more than other women (Gruber & Bjorn, 1982; Lafontaine & Tredeau, 1986). Typically, women in nontraditional jobs are far outnumbered by men in the work force. If your organization has departments that were recently gender integrated, or if the ratio of female employees to male employees is small, conducting a survey of sexual harassment is highly recommended. Where the number of women is very small, however, an alternative form of data collection may be considered, such as anonymous interviews, a comments/suggestion box, or a telephone "hot line." For example, the Du Pont corporation has instituted a 24-hour hot line staffed by specially trained employees who answer questions related to sexual harassment and attempt to resolve problems before they escalate into public complaints (Solomon, 1991).

Although women victims are the focus of most sexual harassment surveys, from a legal standpoint, sexual harassment is gender neutral. Males as well as females can be victims of sexual harassment; individuals can be harassed by members of their own gender. Though the majority of victims are women harassed by men (Koen, 1989), it is important to realize that sexual harassment of men does occur and also needs to be addressed.

Guaranteeing anonymity. When designing an original sexual harassment survey or adapting an existing model to an organization, careful attention should be given to protecting the identities of those responding. Factors such as the size of the organization and unique organizational characteristics (e.g., a tendency for "leaks" and "rumors") will influence how many safeguards are needed to ensure that respondents are anonymous and their responses are kept confidential. If respondents have doubts about whether they will remain anonymous, the result may be a large number of missing responses on particularly sensitive items, a lower response rate, or responses that are less than truthful.

In all cases, the respondents' data need to be grouped with the responses of others, and no individual data should be analyzed or reported. It is also recommended that you avoid asking for identifying information such as name, social security number, or department in which the respondent works. In addition, ask respondents to place the completed surveys in a sealed envelope, and set up a survey drop box or similar arrangement where respondents can return their surveys without being identified (Scarpello & Vandenberg, 1991). Finally, where appropriate, indicate that completed surveys will be destroyed after the information is entered into a computer data base.[4]

While these safeguards may appear excessive, it is our experience that many respondents are apprehensive about being identified on sexual harassment surveys. We are aware of a large-scale sexual harassment survey where a code had been placed on each survey to assist the survey team in properly administering and subsequently processing the data. A number of respondents returned the surveys with the coding information cut out, however, apparently out of concern that they could be identified.

Asking demographic questions. With concerns for protecting anonymity in mind, it is important to include a few demographic items to allow for meaningful analyses (e.g., male versus female) to be done. In addition to asking respondents their gender, also ask about their level in the organization (e.g., manager, supervisor) and the type of position they hold (e.g., technical, administrative, clerical). As the examples imply, it is best to use general categories to prevent respondents from feeling they could be identified. In addition, you may want to ask respondents how long they have worked with your organization and any other demographic information important to your organization (e.g., race/ethnic status).

Rule 3: Include a Definition of Sexual Harassment on Your Survey

Defining exactly what sexual harassment is has been a difficult and evolving process. During the 1980s, both the social science and the legal definitions of what constituted sexual harassment changed (Gruber, 1990). Definitions of sexual harassment range from the rather narrow scope of sexually explicit advances to very broad definitions that include all negative gender-related comments and behaviors. The difficulty in clarifying the definition of sexual harassment reflects the fact that perceptions of what sexual harassment is differ from one individual to the next as well as between men and women (Gutek, 1985). A number of researchers have noted this ambiguity:

> Sexual comments or physical contact that one woman finds offensive or objectionable may not cause another women any discomfort on her job at all. (Saal, 1990, p. 218)

> An incident of harassment that is considered mildly offensive by one individual might be seen as serious enough to warrant a formal complaint by another individual. (Terpstra & Baker, 1991, p. 184)

A number of definitions of sexual harassment have been proposed, with the most widely accepted and well-known having been promulgated by the Equal Employment Opportunity Commission (EEOC) in 1980. They define sexual harassment as follows:

Unwelcome sexual advances, requests for sexual favors and other verbal or physical conduct of a sexual nature constitute sexual harassment when

1) submission to such conduct is made either explicitly or implicitly a term or condition of employment;
2) submission to or rejection of such conduct by an individual is used as the basis for employment decisions affecting the individual; or
3) such conduct has the purpose or effect of substantially interfering with an individual's work performance, or creating an intimidating or hostile working environment. (EEOC, 1980, p. 25024)

The EEOC definition of sexual harassment encompasses two general components: quid pro quo (literally, "this for that") and hostile environment. Quid pro quo occurs when an individual suffers a loss of specific job benefits because of submission to or rejection of unwanted sexual overtures. In the hostile work environment form of sexual harassment, unwanted sexually oriented materials or behaviors (e.g., jokes) create a work environment that is hostile or abusive and interferes with an individual's work performance (Johnson & Lewis, 1991).

Although other definitions have been proposed,[5] the fact that the federal government, and the military services, have used the EEOC definition argues for its adoption. Not only is it currently the definition of choice by these and other organizations, the EEOC definition has been used by the courts in deciding legal cases involving sexual harassment as a violation of Title VII of the Civil Rights Act of 1964. While the language of the EEOC definition is somewhat complex, an understanding of it should be one of the goals addressed in an organization's prevention of sexual harassment training program.

On sexual harassment surveys, we and others have found it useful to clarify the EEOC definition by noting: "Both men and women can be victims of sexual harassment; both women and men can be sexual harassers; people can sexually harass persons of their own sex" (Culbertson et al., 1992, p. 8).

Rule 4: Assess the "Sexual Harassment Climate" of Your Organization

When designing a survey of sexual harassment, it is important to include questions that let you assess the "sexual harassment climate" in your organization. The sexual harassment climate may be thought of as the atmosphere of the organization that may condone or support sexual harassment. As Hotelling (1991) has noted, "Exploration of the problem

Table 8.1 Sample Sexual Harassment Climate Questions

Sexual harassment is a problem in this organization.
Actions are being taken in this organization to prevent sexual harassment.
The leadership of this organization enforces our policy on sexual harassment.
People in this organization who sexually harass others usually get away with it.
I feel free to report sexual harassment without fear of bad things happening to me.
This organization's sexual harassment training is taken seriously.
I understand this organization's definition of sexual harassment.

---

of sexual harassment is not complete without examination of the cultural context within which it occurs" (p. 498).

Social psychologists have noted that behavior is a function of both the person and the situation (see Tedeschi, Lindskold, & Rosenfeld, 1985). Sexual harassment climate data allow the survey team to determine the degree to which situational or organizational factors are contributing to the occurrence of harassment. This information can assist in identifying problems or causes of sexual harassment in the organization. Also, climate items can be completed by all respondents, even those who have never directly experienced sexual harassment. Climate items allow all respondents to provide feedback on the effectiveness of the organization's policies, training, and procedures to combat this behavior. Table 8.1 includes some sample sexual harassment climate items. These can be used with typical Likert scales anchored from 1 (strongly disagree) to 5 (strongly agree).

Rule 5: Decide How to Measure the Overall Rate of Sexual Harassment

One reason surveys have found widely different estimates is that there is no generally agreed upon method of collecting and calculating the rates of sexual harassment. One summary of the results of sexual harassment surveys found rates of 33% to 69% in the general population, 42% to 59% in the public sector, 36% to 75% in the private sector, and 28% to 37% in the academic sector (Gruber, 1990). While differences in sample size, survey time period, and response rate can account for some of these differences, it may be that something more fundamental has led to this divergence.

We believe a key factor is that sexual harassment has been measured quite differently in previous surveys (Culbertson & Rosenfeld, in press).

Some surveys have asked respondents directly if they have been sexually harassed (*direct query* method), while others have asked respondents whether they have experienced certain unwanted sexual harassment behaviors (*behavioral experiences* method). Being aware of these differing approaches is important, for each will influence the kind of data collected and the way the overall rate of sexual harassment is determined.

Direct query method. The direct query method asks respondents directly if they have been sexually harassed while engaged in work or work-related activities. On the NEOSH survey, respondents were asked if they have been sexually harassed during the past year while they were either on duty or off duty but on the base or ship[6] (Culbertson et al., 1992). The percentage answering in the affirmative to these questions provides an estimate of sexual harassment.

The direct query approach has the advantage of leaving the decision of whether a sexually oriented behavior is considered sexual harassment to the respondent, rather than leaving the determination to the survey team. This approach has been criticized, however (in research using college samples), for underestimating the occurrence of behaviors that should be in the sexual harassment category but are not labeled as such by the respondent (Barak et al., 1992; Fitzgerald et al., 1988).

As the national consciousness regarding sexual harassment continues to be raised in the aftermath of the Anita Hill-Clarence Thomas hearings and the Tailhook convention, we believe that employees will have a greater understanding of what sexual harassment is and less hesitancy to indicate that they have been harassed. For example, Sandroff (1992) found in a survey of *Fortune* 500 HRM executives and readers of *Working Woman* magazine that just 15% of the female respondents were unclear about what sexual harassment is.

Although past research has suggested that individuals may not label all unwanted sexually harassing behaviors as sexual harassment, our research takes the approach that sexual harassment is more than just experiencing sexual harassment behaviors (Culbertson & Rosenfeld, in press). This view supports the idea that "sexual harassment is, after all, a matter of individual perception" (Terpstra & Baker, 1991, p. 185).

Behavioral experiences method. Rather than asking respondents directly if they have been sexually harassed, other surveys ask whether respondents have experienced any of a series of unwanted sexual harassment behaviors (Martindale, 1990; Tyburski, 1992; USMSPB, 1981, 1988). This circumvents the issue of people not labeling certain behaviors as sexual harassment. This approach to calculating an overall rate of sexual harassment may be problematic, however. One reason is that there are no standard, agreed-upon means of categorizing unwanted sexual behaviors[7] (Gruber, 1992).

Furthermore, it is doubtful whether a *single* instance of a relatively mild form of unwanted sexual behavior, such as one whistle, would qualify as sexual harassment under the hostile environment clause of the EEOC definition. This appears to be the criterion applied by the Supreme Court in the 1986 *Meritor Savings Bank v. Vinson* case. The court held that "environmental sexual harassment can violate Title VII if it is severe or pervasive enough to actually affect the alleged victim's work conditions and create a hostile environment. However, remarks that simply offend someone's feelings but are not pervasive harassment creating a hostile environment would not violate Title VII" (USMSPB, 1988, p. 44).

Although an overall rate does provide a global indicator of the extent of harassment in an organization, it is important to understand the imprecise nature of measurement in the sexual harassment area. As Martindale (1990) states, "Although the term incidence has been used to refer to these kinds of percentages, it is incorrect to refer to self-report data from any survey of sexual harassment as incidence data, since the term incidence implies a level of measurement precision not currently attainable" (p. 10).

We recommend that, when calculating overall rates of harassment, you use the same methodology over time and compare the results of your most recent survey administration with those of prior administrations, instead of comparing with other surveys that may use a different methodology. Whether you end up using the direct query (our choice) or behavioral experiences approaches, it is important that employees understand what sexual harassment is and isn't through periodic training.

Rule 6: Go Beyond an Overall Rate: Gather Information on the Types and Frequencies of Harassment Behaviors

Regardless of how you decide to measure and calculate the overall rate of harassment, you will want to collect information on the forms and frequency of unwanted sexual harassment behaviors. The overall rate of sexual harassment is important, but it rarely tells the whole story. It is recommended that the survey gather information about the kinds of unwanted sexual harassment behaviors experienced and their frequency. A finding that certain severe behaviors are occurring, such as

Table 8.2 Forms of Sexual Harassment Behaviors in the U.S. Merit Systems Protection Board Survey

Actual or attempted rape or assault
Unwanted pressure for sexual favors
Unwanted deliberate touching, leaning over, cornering, or pinching
Unwanted sexual looks or gestures
Unwanted letters, telephone calls, or materials of a sexual nature
Unwanted pressure for dates
Unwanted sexual teasing, jokes, remarks, or questions

actual or attempted rape or assault, would require immediate action on the part of the organization.

Types of sexual harassment behaviors. A variety of different categories or forms of sexually harassing behaviors have been used in previous surveys. Probably the best known are the seven categories, shown in Table 8.2, that were used in the USMSPB surveys. Other surveys have expanded this list (Culbertson et al., 1992; Martindale, 1990) or have used completely different category systems (see Gruber, 1992, for a review).

Frequency of sexual harassment behaviors. In addition to the type of sexual harassment experiences, sexual harassment surveys should assess the frequency of sexual harassment behaviors. This is important because the perceived severity of the harassment is often a combination of factors, including both the form and the frequency of unwanted sexual behaviors (Terpstra & Baker, 1991). For example, the "milder" forms of sexual harassing behaviors (e.g., jokes, whistles) may be perceived as worse by victims if they occur frequently compared with a more severe form (e.g., pressure for dates) if it occurs only once. Thus we and others typically include the following frequency scale: never, once, once a month, 2-4 times a month, once a week or more (Culbertson et al., 1992; USMSPB, 1981, 1988).

Rule 7: Gather Additional Information About the Sexual Harassment Experience

In addition to asking survey respondents if they were sexually harassed, and the types and frequency of harassment behaviors, most surveys gather additional information about the total sexual harassment

Table 8.3 Additional Areas to Assess in Organizational Sexual Harassment Surveys

---

Characteristics of Victims:
  Gender
  Level in the organization
Characteristics of Perpetrators:
  Gender
  Level in the organization
  Work relationship to victim
Actions Taken After the Harassment:
  Informal actions
  Formal actions
Consequences of Sexual Harassment:
  Organizational
  Individual

---

experience. These additional areas are listed in Table 8.3. We review key findings about the sexual harassment experience below.

Characteristics of victims. Demographic items on sexual harassment surveys allow you to determine characteristics of victims of harassment. Additional information to gather on victims relates to marital status, racial/ethnic group, and age. Remember that, depending on the size of your organization, the more information you collect may increase the perception among respondents that they can be identified.

If you assess characteristics of victims, you are likely to find that women, particularly those low in organizational status and power, are far more likely than men or more powerful women to be victims of sexual harassment (Culbertson et al., 1992; Martindale, 1990; Riger, 1991; USMSPB, 1981, 1988). In the federal government, women in nontraditional jobs, those working in a predominantly male environment or having an immediate supervisor who is a male, who are single or divorced, or between the ages of 20-44 were more likely to be sexually harassed (USMSPB, 1988). Data gathered among federal government employees suggest that men may be more at risk for sexual harassment if they work in office/clerical, or trainee positions; work in a predominantly female work group or have a female supervisor; and are divorced, separated, and between the ages of 20 and 44 (USMSPB, 1988).

Characteristics of perpetrators. Many sexual harassment surveys ask about the characteristics of the perpetrators of the harassment. The findings are very consistent: Women victims are almost always harassed by male perpetrators but very rarely by other females. Although the majority of male victims report harassment by female perpetrators, several surveys have found that a sizable proportion of male harassment (22%-40%) is perpetrated by other males (Culbertson & Rosenfeld, in press; Culbertson et al., 1992; Martindale, 1991; Quenette, 1992; USMSPB, 1981). Ask victims whether the perpetrators of the harassment were male, female, or both male and female (because individuals can be harassed by a group of people).

Sexual harassment surveys have also gathered information on the organizational level of the perpetrator and his or her work relationship with the victim. Several large-scale surveys have found coworkers to be the most frequent perpetrators of harassment, although a sizable percentage of supervisors are also involved in sexual harassment (Culbertson & Rosenfeld, in press; Culbertson et al., 1992; Martindale, 1990; USMSPB, 1988). Similarly, in the private sector, the 1988 Working Woman Survey found that most harassment complaints were brought against either a female victim's immediate supervisor (36%) or another individual who had greater power than the victim (26%; Sandroff, 1988). The U.S. Merit Systems Protection Board (USMSPB, 1988) used the following categorization scheme to classify perpetrators: (a) immediate supervisor, (b) higher-level supervisor, (c) coworker, (d) subordinate, (e) other employees, (f) others or unknown. We recommend you use this or a similar system to categorize perpetrators of harassment.

Actions taken after the harassment. It is important on surveys of sexual harassment to ask victims what actions they took after the harassment experience.[8] Surveys have found that the most common actions are to ignore the behavior, to tell the person(s) to stop, and to avoid the person (Culbertson et al., 1992; Martindale, 1990; USMSPB, 1988). Victims rarely report experiences of sexual harassment—either to their supervisor or to other authorities within the organization (Riger, 1991). Only 5% of those harassed in the federal government took any formal action (USMSPB, 1988). Sandroff (1988) reports only 1.4 complaints per 1,000 women harassed.

Surveys have attempted to determine why victims don't use formal grievance or complaint procedures. Explanations of this hesitancy of victims to file a grievance include the power differentials between the harasser and victim (Hotelling, 1991), fear of retaliation, loss of privacy, and negative consequences in the workplace (Sandroff, 1988). When victims are asked directly on surveys why they didn't file a grievance, common reasons include the belief that reporting the harassment would make the work situation unpleasant, that nothing would be done, that they feared reprisal, and the belief that they would be blamed or labeled a troublemaker (Culbertson & Rosenfeld, in press; Culbertson et al., 1992; Martindale, 1990; USMSPB, 1988). In general, most victims do not believe that the benefits of making a formal complaint are greater than the negative consequences of doing so.[9]

Rule 8: Look Down the Road:
Assess Consequences to the Organization and to Individuals

Surveys have found that sexual harassment has both organizational and individual consequences. For instance, on the USMSPB (1988) survey, victims were asked if they used any sick leave, annual leave, or leave without pay after being sexually harassed. The survey found that an average of 13% of both female and male victims used sick leave after the harassment, costing an estimated $26 million during the 2-year study period. In addition, 12% of both female and male victims used annual leave after being harassed, with the approximate value of leave taken equaling $25.6 million. Finally, 2% of female and 4% of male victims used leave without pay, with the approximate amount lost in salaries of $9.9 million. In addition, there are the costs due to turnover ($36.7 million) and decreases in individual and work group productivity ($204.5 million). It is important to include questions such as these to help quantify the impact of harassment in your organization.

It is also important to assess individual consequences of harassment, often quantified in terms of psychological, physical, and interpersonal effects. Jensen and Gutek (1982) reported that 80% of female victims felt disgust after the experience and 68% experienced anger. Gutek (1985) also found that 38% of victims reported the harassment affected their feelings about the job. Culbertson and Rosenfeld (in press) found anger and disgust were the most common psychological reactions among active-duty female Navy victims.

Surveys have also considered the physical effects of sexual harassment. Crull (1982) found that 63% of the victims who sought assistance from the Working Woman's Institute reported they had physical symptoms, such as nausea, headaches, and tiredness, that they believed were brought on by the sexual harassment. Culbertson and Rosenfeld (in press) assessed physical effects, including headaches, difficulty sleeping, nausea, loss or gain of appetite, and other reactions that often occur as a response to stress. A sizable percentage of victims did report physical effects due to the harassment (57% enlisted women, 32% officer women), with headaches and difficulty sleeping being the most common.

Interpersonal relations, both on and off the job, also can be negatively affected due to sexual harassment. Gutek (1985) found that 28% of victims reported that the harassment had affected their relations with others at work. Data from federal government employees showed 15% of employees reported that the harassment worsened their ability to work with others (Tangri, Burt, & Johnson, 1982). Responses from military personnel found that a number of victims report the harassment did negatively affect their feelings about their command and working with their coworkers (Culbertson et al., 1992). Thus the survey team should attempt to quantify consequences, to both the organization and the individuals in the organization, in terms of psychological, physical, and social/interpersonal effects. These data not only help underscore the seriousness of the problem, they also allow a dollar-value estimate to be made of the costs of harassment.

Rule 9: Presenting the Findings: Don't Shoot the Messenger

The hardest part of the sexual harassment survey process may come at the end—when the results are presented to management. As is often the case, sexual harassment surveys are done because there is some evidence of an existing problem. Furthermore, managers may believe that the survey itself is the solution to the problem. Others commission sexual harassment surveys for *impression management* purposes (see Giacalone & Rosenfeld, 1989, 1991). That is, the survey is an attempt to publicly demonstrate their concern and make it appear to others that they are aggressively trying to solve the problem. Unfortunately, surveys by themselves rarely solve problems, but they can provide information that raises additional questions about the problem being studied. Also, the results of a sexual harassment survey may give a harsh reality to a problem that previously only existed in rumor or innuendo.

Because the results of sexual harassment surveys are often neither pleasant nor conclusive, the presenter of the findings may face the "shoot the messenger" phenomenon. When negative findings are obtained, managers unwilling to accept the seriousness of the problem may, in turn, blame the bearer of bad *t* tests.

The presenter of the results of a sexual harassment survey also faces his or her own biasing tendencies. Psychologists have found that people have a cognitive bias to present information more positively than it actually is. As Taylor and Brown (1988) have noted, "Evaluators who must communicate negative feedback may mute it or put it in euphemistic terms thus rendering it ambiguous" (p. 201). When presenting the results of a sexual harassment survey, this tendency may lead to "sugarcoating" the findings and making them overly positive. In the long run, an overly positive portrayal helps no one and will serve to maintain the organization's sexual harassment problems, if they exist. To address these issues, the following points should be considered when providing feedback.

Present the survey results orally. Managers love glossy management reports, but the results of sexual harassment surveys should be first presented orally. One likely impact of the results of the survey will be a discussion of the problem and what steps are required to continue to address sexual harassment. It is important that top management and those individuals who need to make the necessary decisions for further actions be present for the oral report and discussion. Also, as this chapter has indicated, there is much ambiguity and confusion in the area of sexual harassment. An oral presentation is better than a written report so that the presenter can answer questions and clarify misconceptions.

Emphasize successes thus far. While we advocate a clear, honest, and unbiased presentation of the survey results, it is wise to try to identify some successes. When presenting our surveys, we have been able to point out that most individuals in the Navy have had prevention of sexual harassment training, know how to use the grievance system, and feel that their leaders are trying their best to deal with the problem (Culbertson et al., 1992). Presenting successes lets management avoid the feeling that the survey is simply a "hatchet job." Credit can be taken for things that are going well and the negative survey findings may then be taken more seriously.

Put your data in perspective. Managers will want to know how your survey data compare with those of other organizational surveys. After reading this chapter, you are now well aware of many of the methodological issues involved in conducting surveys of sexual harassment and the pitfalls of comparing results using different methodologies. The best advice is to use your first administration of the survey as a baseline and compare future years' results to this initial baseline. Do not change your survey format from one administration to another. By maintaining the same definition and core set of questions, you are able to look at trends over time and get a good view of how effective your efforts to combat sexual harassment have been.

Look at the big picture. Throughout this chapter, we have noted the problem of focusing on the overall rate of sexual harassment as a bottom line figure. Managers, however, often want to get to the bottom line. Unfortunately, it is more complicated than that, a point that needs to be made both orally and in the written report. Looking at the big picture also means framing the presentation of the results in terms of sexual harassment as a larger societal problem, not only one that occurs in a particular organization. Using these guidelines, we've found that the results of our sexual harassment surveys—the good and the bad—can be presented honestly and professionally.

Rule 10: No Survey Stands Alone: Develop an Integrated SH Program

The sexual harassment survey should never be a substitute for a multicomponent program aimed at addressing sexual harassment in your organization. In fact, organizations may be able to protect themselves from litigation regarding sexual harassment if they have previously implemented an integrated program to deal with this problem. In addition to a survey, organizations should develop and implement an organizationwide policy regarding sexual harassment that contains the following components: (a) the organization's definition of sexual harassment; (b) the organization's complaint or grievance procedure, including how to file complaints and carry out investigations and the appropriate punishments for engaging in various forms of sexual harassment; and (c) a training program that is periodically delivered to educate employees on all components of the organization's program (Benton-Powers, 1992; Krohne, 1992; Segal, 1992; Terpstra & Baker, 1991).

The results of the sexual harassment survey play a central role in this integrated program by assessing what is occurring in the workplace, providing management with specific information regarding harassment and its consequences, and giving evaluation information on the effectiveness of policies and training programs. While some organizations have the resources to develop and implement an integrated program in house, others may wish to hire consultants to help with its establishment. Consultants can assist in conducting the sexual harassment survey, can review the results with management, and, based on these results, may develop or revise the organization's policy and complaint procedures. Consultants can also help design a training program tailored to the needs of your organization. They can deliver the training or train in-house staff to deliver it (Sandroff, 1988). Finally, outside consultants may be perceived as more impartial or "fairer" than in-house staff and may raise expectations that change is at hand. As Dov Eden (1991, p. 36) has noted, "[The consultants'] very arrival boosts expectations and triggers a positive self-fulfilling prophecy as members throughout the client organization believe 'Now we're doing something about our problems!' "

Conclusions

Previous surveys have confirmed that sexual harassment is a problem that exists in all sectors of the workplace, whether in the federal government, the military services, or private organizations.[10] In the wake of the national consciousness-raising on sexual harassment, organizations have accelerated their efforts to reduce its future occurrence. Surveys play a key role in this transformation process. As organizations accelerate their initiatives to reduce the future occurrence of sexual harassment, surveys will play a major role in determining how effective these efforts will be.

Notes

1. Articles that appeared on the 1-year anniversary of Anita Hill's Senate testimony attest to the hearing's lasting impact on perceptions of organizational sexual harassment. As the *Los Angeles Times* noted in an editorial, "Hill's testimony sparked an extraordinary national debate over the definition of harassment and the extent of the problem. For months after her appearance—and Senate confirmation of Thomas—sexual harassment was Topic A on talk shows and around office water coolers" ("The legacy of Anita Hill," 1992, p. B9). One measure of Anita Hill's impact is that surveys conducted a year after her testimony found that more people believed her charges of sexual harassment (43%) than believed Clarence Thomas was telling the truth (39%). This reversed the findings of surveys taken at the time of the October 1991 testimony, which indicated that a greater percentage believed Thomas (54%) than Hill (27%). The reversal has been attributed to "a greater understanding of the nature and pervasiveness of sexual harassment" (Puente, 1992, p. 10A).

2. As Rosenfeld, Edwards, and Thomas note in the introductory chapter of this volume, organizational surveys can also facilitate organizational communication. A sexual harass-

ment survey can communicate a powerful message to employees that management is committed to dealing proactively with sexual harassment, takes the issue seriously, and is concerned enough about how employees are treated to solicit their input.

3. A *New York Times*/CBS News national telephone survey conducted during the October 1991 Anita Hill-Clarence Thomas Senate hearings found that 38% of women reported that they had been the target of unwanted sexual remarks or advances from men for whom they worked (Kolbert, 1991). A 1992 *Business Week*/Harris Poll survey of 400 women corporate executives found that 27% had been sexually harassed (Depke, 1992). Tyburski (1992) recently reported sexual harassment rates of 49% of females and 18% of males among a Navy-civilian-employee sample who completed a modified USMSPB survey.

4. If the sexual harassment survey is part of an ongoing research project or if the survey team plans to publish the results, it may be prudent to avoid destroying the original survey data. At a subsequent time, further analyses may be needed that could require checking the data file against the original survey questionnaires.

5. Saal (1990, p. 217) describes the Alliance Against Sexual Coercion (AASC) definition as "any sexually oriented practice that endangers a woman's job, that undermines her job performance and threatens her economic livelihood." He describes the Working Women United Institute (WWUI) definition as "any repeated and unwanted sexual comments, looks, suggestions or physical contact that one finds objectionable or offensive and that causes one discomfort on the job" (p. 217). Although there are many proposed definitions of sexual harassment, some believe that the construct has yet to be satisfactorily defined. In March 1993, the Supreme Court agreed to determine whether sexual harassment in the workplace should be considered behaviors of a sexual nature that are simply offensive or must inflict psychological harm to the victim (Fitzgerald, 1987; Savage, 1993).

6. This wider interpretation of the work environment recognizes and accommodates the Navy's unique situation (e.g., on the base, aboard ship), where members often work, live, and relax in the same environment.

7. Gruber (1990, 1992) has described some of the problems that have emerged with the use of various category schemes. There is great variation in the number of behavioral categories used: Some surveys have as few as two categories (e.g., verbal and physical), while others have seven or more (e.g., Culbertson et al., 1992; Martindale, 1991; USMSPB, 1981, 1988). If the categories are too general, then specific information is lost, which may result in the underreporting of harassment; if the categories are too narrow, then a much higher rate of harassment is likely to be found, and the big picture may get lost. Often the categories used in sexual harassment surveys are not mutually exclusive or exhaustive.

8. Some common categories of actions asked in surveys are (a) I ignored the behavior or did nothing, (b) I avoided the person(s), (c) I asked/told the person to stop, (d) I made a joke of the behavior, (e) I threatened to tell or told others, (f) I reported the behavior to the supervisor, (g) I went along with the behavior (USMSPB, 1988).

9. The publicity associated with the Anita Hill-Clarence Thomas hearings has increased the number of sexual harassment complaints filed. In the entire fiscal year 1991 (October 1-September 30), the EEOC received 6,883 sexual harassment complaints. This was surpassed during the first 9 months of fiscal year 1992 when 7,407 sexual harassment complaints reached the EEOC (Edmonds, 1992).

10. Although this chapter has focused on sexual harassment in the United States, there are indications that sexual harassment is an organizational and societal problem in other

countries including France (Riding, 1992), India (Sengupta, 1992), Japan (Holden, 1992; Taga, 1992; Weisman, 1992), Kenya (Mbugguss, 1992), and New Zealand (Gavey, 1991).

References

Anita Hill urges women judges to push for change. (1992, October 10). *Los Angeles Times*, p. B3.

Barak, A., Fisher, W. A., & Houston, S. (1992). Individual difference correlates of the experience of sexual harassment among female university students. *Journal of Applied Social Psychology, 22*, 17-37.

Benton-Powers, S. M. (1992). Sexual harassment: Civil Rights Act increases liability. *HR Focus, 69*, 10.

Crull, P. (1982). Stress effects of sexual harassment on the job: Implications for counseling. *American Journal of Orthopsychiatry, 52*, 539-544.

Culbertson, A. L., & Rosenfeld, P. (in press). Assessment of sexual harassment in the active-duty Navy. *Military Psychology*.

Culbertson, A. L., Rosenfeld, P., Booth-Kewley, S., & Magnusson, P. (1992). *Assessment of sexual harassment in the Navy: Results of the 1989 Navy-wide survey* (NPRDC TR-92-11). San Diego, CA: Navy Personnel Research and Development Center.

Depke, D. A. (1992, June 15). It happens often. *Business Week*, p. 47.

Eden, D. (1991). Applying impression management to create productive self-fulfilling prophecy at work. In R. A. Giacalone & Paul Rosenfeld (Eds.), *Applied impression management* (pp. 13-40). Newbury Park, CA: Sage.

Edmonds, P. (1992, October 2). Year later, harassment's "real to more people." *USA Today*, p. 6A.

Equal Employment Opportunity Commission (EEOC). (1980). Interpretive guidelines on sexual harassment. *Federal Register, 45*, 25024-25025.

Eskenazi, M., & Gallen, D. (1992). *Sexual harassment: Know your rights*. New York: Carroll & Graf.

Fitzgerald, L. F. (1987). Sexual harassment: The definition and measurement of a construct. In M. A. Paludi (Ed.), *Ivory power: Sexual harassment on campus* (pp. 22-44). Albany: State University of New York Press.

Fitzgerald, L. F., Shullman, S. L., Bailey, N., Richards, M., Swecker, J., Gold, Y., Ormerod, M., & Weitzman, L. (1988). The incidence and dimensions of sexual harassment in academia and the workplace. *Journal of Vocational Behavior, 32*, 152-175.

Gavey, N. (1991). Sexual victimization prevalence among New Zealand university students. *Journal of Consulting and Clinical Psychology, 59*, 464-466.

Giacalone, R. A., & Rosenfeld, P. (1989). *Impression management in the organization*. Hillsdale, NJ: Erlbaum.

Giacalone, R. A., & Rosenfeld, P. (1991). *Applied impression management*. Newbury Park, CA: Sage.

Gruber, J. E. (1990). Methodological problems and policy implications in sexual harassment research. *Population Research and Policy Review, 9*, 235-254.

Gruber, J. E. (1992). A typology of personal and environmental sexual harassment: Research and policy implications for the 1990s. *Sex Roles, 26*, 447-464.

Gruber, J. E., & Bjorn, L. (1982). Blue-collar blues: The sexual harassment of women autoworkers. *Work and Occupations, 9,* 271-298.

Gutek, B. A. (1985). *Sex and the workplace.* San Francisco: Jossey-Bass.

Holden, T. (1992, July 13). Revenge of the "office ladies." *Business Week,* p. 42.

Hotelling, K. (1991). Sexual harassment: A problem shielded by silence. *Journal of Counseling & Development, 69,* 497-501.

Jensen, I., & Gutek, B. A. (1982). Attributions and assignment of responsibility in sexual harassment. *Journal of Social Issues, 38,* 121-136.

Johnson, P. R., & Lewis, K. E. (1991). Hostile work environments: Extending the base of sexual harassment. *Equal Opportunities International, 10,* 5-9.

Koen, C. M., Jr. (1989). Sexual harassment: Criteria for defining hostile environment. *Employee Responsibilities and Rights Journal, 2,* 289-301.

Kolbert, E. (1991, October 11). Sexual harassment at work is pervasive, survey suggests. *The New York Times,* pp. A1, A18.

Kolbert, E. (1992, August 30). Test-marketing a president. *New York Times Magazine,* pp. 18-21, 60, 68, 72.

Krohne, K. A. (1992, August). Conduct unbecoming. *Naval Institute Proceedings, 118,* 53-56.

Lafontaine, E., & Tredeau, L. (1986). The frequency, sources, and correlates of sexual harassment among women in traditional male occupations. *Sex Roles, 15,* 433-442.

The legacy of Anita Hill. (1992, October 10). *Los Angeles Times,* p. B9.

MacKinnon, C. A. (1979). *Sexual harassment of working women.* New Haven, CT: Yale University Press.

Martindale, M. (1990). *Sexual harassment in the military: 1988.* Washington, DC: Defense Management Data Center.

Martindale, M. (1991). Sexual harassment in the military: 1988. *Sociological Practice Review, 2,* 200-216.

Maze, R. (1992, April 27). Sexual harassment squanders millions. *Navy Times,* p. 23.

Mbugguss, M. (1992, February). A debate in Kenya. *World Press Review, 39,* 26.

Meritor Savings Bank FSB v. Vinson, 106 S.Ct. 2399 (1986).

Nasar, S. (1992, October 18). Women's progress stalled? Just not so. *The New York Times* (National ed., Sec. 3), pp. 1, 10.

Puente, M. (1992, October 5). Year later, Hill has edge in "he said, she said" saga. *USA Today,* p. 10A.

Quenette, M. A. (1992). *Navy-wide personnel survey (NPS) 1991: Management report of findings* (NPRDC TR 92-20). San Diego, CA: Navy Personnel Research and Development Center.

Riding, A. (1992, May 3). The French stop to rethink official wink at harassment. *The New York Times,* p. 9.

Riger, S. (1991). Gender dilemmas in sexual harassment policies and procedures. *American Psychologist, 46,* 497-505.

Saal, F. E. (1990). Sexual harassment in organizations. In K. R. Murphy & F. E. Saal (Eds.), *Psychology in organizations: Integrating science and practice* (pp. 217-239). Hillsdale, NJ: Lawrence Erlbaum.

Sandroff, R. (1988, December). Sexual harassment in the Fortune 500. *Working Woman,* pp. 69-73.

Sandroff, R. (1992). Sexual harassment: The inside story. *Working Woman, 17,* 47-51.

Savage, D. G. (1993, March 2). Court to clarify definition of sexual harassment. *Los Angeles Times,* pp. A1, A9.

Scarpello, V., & Vandenberg, R. J. (1991). Some issues to consider when surveying employee opinions. In J. W. Jones, B. D. Steffy, & D. W. Bray (Eds.), *Applying psychology in business: The handbook for managers and human resource professionals* (pp. 611-622). Lexington, MA: Lexington.

Segal, J. A. (1992). Seven ways to reduce harassment claims. *HR Magazine, 37,* 84-86.

Sengupta, R. (1992, February). A symbol of urban anomie. *World Press Review, 39,* 25.

Smolowe, J. (1992, October 19). Anita Hill's legacy. *Time Magazine, 140,* 56-57.

Solomon, C. M. (1991, December). Sexual harassment after the Thomas hearings. *Personnel Journal, 70,* 32-37.

Strom, S. (1991, October 20). Harassment cases can go unnoticed. *The New York Times,* pp. 1, 22.

Taga, M. (1992, February). Scoffing at "sekuhara." *World Press Review, 39,* 26.

Tangri, S., Burt, M. R., & Johnson, L. B. (1982). Sexual harassment at work: Three explanatory models. *Journal of Social Issues, 38,* 55-74.

Taylor, S. E., & Brown, J. D. (1988). Illusion and well-being: A social psychological perspective on mental health. *Psychological Bulletin, 103,* 193-210.

Tedeschi, J. T., Lindskold, S., & Rosenfeld, P. (1985). *Introduction to social psychology.* St. Paul, MN: West.

Terpstra, D. E. (1986). Organizational costs of sexual harassment. *Journal of Employment Counseling, 23,* 112-119.

Terpstra, D. E., & Baker, D. D. (1991). Sexual harassment at work: The psychosocial issues. In M. J. Davidson & J. Earnshaw (Eds.), *Vulnerable workers: Psychosocial and legal issues* (pp. 179-201). New York: John Wiley.

Tyburski, D. A. (1992). *Department of the Navy Sexual Harassment Survey—1991* (NPRDC TR-92-15). San Diego, CA: Navy Personnel Research and Development Center.

U.S. Merit Systems Protection Board (USMSPB). (1981). *Sexual harassment in the federal workplace.* Washington, DC: Government Printing Office.

U.S. Merit Systems Protection Board (USMSPB). (1988). *Sexual harassment in the federal government: An update.* Washington, DC: Government Printing Office.

Weisman, S. R. (1992, April 17). Landmark harassment case in Japan. *The New York Times,* p. A3.

9

Quality of Work Life Surveys in Organizations

Methods and Benefits

ELYSE W. KERCE
STEPHANIE BOOTH-KEWLEY

A great deal has been written about the importance of work in people's lives. The way that people respond to their jobs is thought to have important consequences for their personal happiness, the productivity of their organizations, and even the stability of society (Sheppard, 1975). Middle-class work has been described as a key source of identity, self-respect, and social status and the most central life activity (Fineman, 1987). The principles of the quality of work life (QWL) movement of the 1970s held that it is possible to structure work in such a way that it is meaningful and brings out the talent and ingenuity of people. These ideas have been given less attention in the past decade, as many organizations have concentrated on meeting the challenge of foreign competition and a stagnant economy. Nevertheless, the technological and social forces that motivated the concern with QWL issues are still present.

AUTHORS' NOTE: This chapter was written by government employees as part of official duties; therefore the material cannot be copyrighted and is in the public domain. The opinions expressed in this chapter are those of the authors. They are not official and do not represent the views of the Department of the Navy.

One such force is the change that has occurred in the composition and values of the work force. First, workers are now better educated and approach work differently than workers in the past. Workers want fulfillment and growth on the job, and they want more than a salary and benefits. Second, as Efraty and Sirgy (1990) note, the psychological contract between the employee and the organization seems to have changed in accordance with changes in employee values. Both workers and managers express a strong interest in higher level need satisfaction, with self-improvement and quality of life assuming increasing importance. It is also no longer enough for an employee simply to perform in a dependable manner; today's organizations increasingly require highly motivated employees who can display creative and innovative behaviors based on technical competence. Management's challenge is to motivate such employees in new ways so that they will perform their jobs effectively and without extensive supervision. While pay continues to be a basic motivator, other values such as self-worth, leisure time, and better communication with management are becoming more important to employees.

In this chapter, we will define *quality of work life* and look at how its meaning has evolved as the labor force has changed, discuss how organizations use surveys to monitor QWL, offer suggestions for the content of QWL surveys, and summarize some of the benefits for organizations and individuals that can be realized through the measurement and improvement of QWL.

Defining QWL

QWL is a way of thinking about people, work, and organizations. The term has been used at various times to refer to a movement, a group of methods or approaches to management in organizations, or a variable reflecting the affective evaluations of individuals (Nadler & Lawler, 1983). The QWL movement developed in the late 1960s and early 1970s. During this period, employment surveys conducted at the University of Michigan in 1969 and 1973 assessed the effects of job experiences on the individual, and a number of projects were initiated that had the goal of having labor and management work collaboratively to improve QWL. At about the same time, there was also interest on the part of the U.S. government, which led to such activities as the creation of a federal productivity commission and sponsorship of a number of joint management-labor QWL experiments (Mills, 1981).

QWL also refers to a group of methods or technologies for making the work environment more productive and more satisfying to workers. These methods are distinguished from other productivity or organizational development efforts in that their focus is on outcomes for the employees rather than for management. These QWL methods include participative problem solving, work restructuring, job enrichment, innovative rewards systems, and improvements in the work environment. Participative problem-solving activities are intended to involve members at all levels of the organization rather than targeting only first-level employees. Work restructuring is undertaken to make jobs more consistent with individual needs and the social structures within the work setting. Restructuring activities may take the form of job enrichment or the facilitation of autonomous work groups, to name but two possibilities. Job enrichment is a strategy for increasing the complexity, variety, and challenge in a job. Its advocates believe that most work tasks fail to challenge individuals adequately or meet their needs for growth and stimulation.

As a variable, QWL is measured by assessing an individual's reaction to work or the personal consequences of the work experience (Nadler & Lawler, 1983). The work attitudes that have been studied most frequently are job satisfaction, job involvement, work commitment, and organizational commitment (Loscocco & Roschelle, 1991). As with other topic areas reviewed in this volume, organizational surveys typically have been used to measure work attitudes and QWL.

At one time, a positive QWL environment was defined as one in which employers and workers could fulfill their economic responsibilities to one another and to society. Such an environment would provide workers with stable employment, adequate income, benefits, fair treatment, due process, and a safe and secure place to work (Mirvis & Lawler, 1984). Each of those attributes remains an important aspect of QWL; however, the definition has expanded to meet the expectations of today's labor force.[1]

Today's workers have been found to have a lower respect for authority and a greater desire for self-expression, personal growth, and self-fulfillment. In short, they expect work that provides opportunities to fulfill higher-order needs. With these changing values in mind, most theorists (e.g., Mirvis & Lawler, 1984) have expanded the definition of a positive QWL environment to include characteristics such as job challenge commensurate with individuals' levels of education, autonomy, responsibility, good coworker relations, good supervision, and the opportunity to develop individual interests and abilities. Organizations, however, typically have been slow to recognize that this new generation of workers holds work-related attitudes that are different than those of prior generations, and organizations have failed to restructure work and its incentives to meet workers' needs.

The factors that lead workers to evaluate their work in a positive manner also may change as the work force becomes more culturally diverse or as more U.S. organizations open international operations. The definition of QWL is a matter of values and standards that are dependent to a large extent upon one's cultural context. North American and Western European workers differ from those in Japan or Mexico, for example, in that they value individual achievement and tolerate personal risk-taking to a greater extent (Hofstede, 1984). The need for dependence on leaders also varies in strength among various cultures. In many Third World countries, subordinates expect superiors to behave autocratically and may be uncomfortable if their superiors consult them. At the opposite end of the power-distance continuum are countries such as Denmark and Sweden, where a democratic workplace is valued. Thus, in some societies, improving the quality of work life may involve offering greater security while, in others, it may involve greater challenge and autonomy or more democratic management styles. For organizations operating internationally, it is important to recognize that different cultures have different need hierarchies and that the saliency of various work goals may also differ as a result.

Factors That Determine QWL

A long-standing debate has centered on the question of whether personal factors or structural factors (e.g., characteristics of the job) are principal determinants of perceived QWL. The basic assumption of the *dispositional approach* is that personal attributes such as dispositional tendencies are the primary influence on QWL (e.g., Staw, Bell, & Clausen, 1986; Staw & Ross, 1985). The *structural approach* assumes that situational variables such as characteristics of the job have the greatest effect on QWL (Herman & Hulin, 1972; Loscocco, 1990). It suggests, for example, that QWL will always be poor on jobs that are routine, lacking in autonomy, and low in personal meaning because such jobs do not satisfy human needs. A third approach, based on *expectancy theories,* suggests the possibility that individuals come to the workplace with different goals and needs that they seek to fulfill through work as well as different perceptions of job characteristics (Hackman & Lawler, 1971; Mitchell & Biglan, 1971). Although individuals' particular needs, values, and dispositions shape their work attitudes, this approach recognizes that a single, pervasive need structure cannot be assumed. Differences in needs are therefore assumed to account for variation in work attitudes among employees in the same jobs.

Advocates of the dispositional position argue that individuals tend to be consistent in their job attitudes over time (e.g., Staw & Ross, 1985). Based on their longitudinal assessment of the job attitudes of people who changed jobs, Staw et al. (1986) concluded that enduring dispositional attributes exert as strong an influence on job attitudes as do objective job characteristics.

Most studies investigating the effects of personality on work attitudes (e.g., Levin & Stokes, 1989; O'Reilly, 1977; Witt, Beorkrem, & Andrews, 1991) have, however, found that aspects of the job have a more powerful impact on job attitudes than do dispositional characteristics. Nevertheless, affective variables may moderate the association between the structural variables and job satisfaction (Levin & Stokes, 1989; Newton & Keenan, 1991). Taken together, these studies suggest that dispositional variables should be considered when studying job satisfaction even though structural variables probably have a greater impact and are more relevant for managers seeking to improve the quality of work life of their workers.

In the structural approach, high QWL is defined by the existence of a certain set of organizational conditions and practices. High QWL is assumed to occur when jobs are enriched, supervision is democratic, employees are involved in their jobs, and the work environment is safe. Extensive evidence (e.g., Herman & Hulin, 1972; Loscocco, 1990) has been accumulated to indicate that such structural factors do have a significant effect on job attitudes.

Rather than specifying the job characteristics that promote QWL, those who favor an integrative approach to QWL equate high QWL with a workplace in which individuals feel safe, are satisfied, and are able to grow and develop as human beings. This definition acknowledges that things such as democratic decision making and enriched jobs are not desirable or important to everyone (Lawler, 1973; Schneider, 1976). This approach focuses on the *interaction* of structural and personal influences, with QWL determined by the degree to which the full range of human needs are met.

Individuals bring different needs to the workplace and will likely experience high QWL to the extent that these needs are satisfied.

Generally, QWL increases in a linear fashion as outcomes approach or exceed an individual's personal standard.[2] The greater the person-environment congruence, the more positive an individual's affective experiences are likely to be. Further, the more positive the affective experiences, the more the person will be motivated to act in ways that lead to a good fit with the environment (Efraty & Sirgy, 1990). Given the values of today's workers, it will probably become increasingly difficult to find people whose needs will be satisfied by jobs lacking in variety, autonomy, or feedback (Salancik & Pfeffer, 1977).

QWL Surveys: Research and Measurement Issues

QWL assessments are typically undertaken for research, diagnostic, or evaluation purposes. Although many QWL researchers advocate the use of a combination of data-gathering techniques, organizational surveys are included in most assessments. For a more comprehensive QWL assessment, survey data may be combined with that obtained from organizational records and observational methods (e.g., Harrison, 1987). The use of standardized instruments, rather than locally developed survey items, saves time and allows for comparison with results from other organizations.

QWL surveys typically measure the job-related perceptions and attitudes of individuals. The work attitude studied most often is job satisfaction. Although job satisfaction is a simple way of conceptualizing QWL, it does not, however, by itself adequately reflect the impact of the work environment on employees (Mirvis & Lawler, 1984). While survey-based research on job satisfaction has found that workers are generally satisfied with their jobs (Strauss, 1974), researchers using the case study method have frequently found that workers are angry, unhappy, and bored.

To understand this discrepancy, each of the problems that have driven QWL research must be considered. Over the years, efforts to improve QWL have been directed at one of four basic problems: equity (with regard to pay), security (of employment), alienation, and anomie (Westley, 1979).[3] Dissatisfaction is a response to a sense of relative deprivation in security and equity only (Herzberg, Mausner, & Snyderman, 1959). To reflect the extent of alienation and anomie, QWL surveys need to include measures of job involvement and job characteristics in addition to measures of satisfaction. It is also useful to include measures for

Table 9.1 Measures Used in QWL Surveys

Overall job satisfaction
Facet satisfactions:
    pay
    benefits
    working conditions
    chances for advancement
    job security
    coworkers
    physical surroundings
    resources and equipment
    chances to develop skills
    supervision
    opportunity for personal growth and development
Job Characteristics:
    skill variety
    task identity
    task significance
    autonomy
    feedback
Job involvement

assessing discrepancies between what the respondent values and what the job provides.

The typical survey used to assess QWL in organizations includes some or most of the measures shown in Table 9.1.

Survey Instruments

Job satisfaction. Job satisfaction is an individual's affective response to his or her job overall or to facets of the job. Quinn and Staines (1979) used the terms "facet-free" to refer to measures of global job satisfaction and "facet-specific" to refer to measures of specific job components. Organizations should focus on a global measure of job satisfaction when they are interested in the overall level of satisfaction in certain segments of the work force at a particular point in time. When an organization is interested in improving the satisfaction of its employees by making specific changes, or is seeking to explain employees' negative behaviors, facet-specific measures should be included.

Measures of global job satisfaction may consist of a single item (e.g., "All things considered, how satisfied are you with your job?") or multiple-item scales. Single-item satisfaction measures have sometimes been criticized on grounds of reliability, but the evidence does not generally support this contention (Scarpello & Campbell, 1983). Rather, these measures have been shown to be relatively stable and reproducible. Because of their high reliability, however, single-item satisfaction measures are insensitive to change and are of limited value for evaluating effects of QWL programs.

We generally recommend the use of multiple-item indices of global job satisfaction, of which there are several examples available. The 1977 Quality of Employment Survey operationalized global job satisfaction as the mean of 5 items. In addition to a direct "How satisfied are you with your job?" question, other items sought to determine if respondents would take the same job over again and how their current jobs compared with their ideal job (Quinn & Staines, 1979).

Another multiple-item scale of global job satisfaction is Brayfield and Rothe's (1951) Index of Job Satisfaction (IJS). This scale consists of 18 items with 5 response options expressing degrees of agreement with the statements. The corrected internal consistency reliability coefficient for this scale is .87. Evidence for the high validity of the index rests upon the nature of the items, the method of construction, and its differentiating power when applied to two groups that could be assumed to differ in job satisfaction (Miller, 1991). Its use is recommended when a precise measure of global job satisfaction is desired. Some sample items from the IJS are: "My work is like a hobby to me," "I am fairly well satisfied with my job," and "I definitely dislike my work."

Organizations are often concerned with improving specific aspects of the work situation with which employees are dissatisfied. To determine where their efforts should be concentrated or to evaluate the success of their efforts, organizations may want to use facet satisfaction measures.[4] Empirical data have shown that the sum of facet satisfactions is not necessarily equivalent to a global job satisfaction measure. In their investigation of the reasons for the relatively low correlations between the two types of measures, Scarpello and Campbell (1983) hypothesized that an individual's global judgment of overall job satisfaction may include variables not typically measured by facet satisfaction instruments. Global measures of job satisfaction appear to include consideration of satisfaction with occupational choice, career progress, and life off the job in addition to facet satisfactions. Through interviews, these researchers also identified five facets that are not usually included in facet scales but that were significantly related to global measures of job satisfaction. These five additional facets were flexibility of work hours, adequacy of tools and equipment, adequacy of work space, degree to which coworkers facilitate work, and pleasantness of interactions with people at work.

Facets of job satisfaction are emphasized in a dimensional conceptualization of job satisfaction. One of the earliest and most widely used facet measures is the Job Descriptive Index (JDI) (Smith, Kendall, & Hulin, 1969). The JDI measures satisfaction with five facets of the job: work, pay, promotion, coworkers, and supervision. The response format is a 3-point scale calling for "yes, no, or ?" responses.

The Minnesota Satisfaction Questionnaire (MSQ) developed by Weiss, Dawis, England, and Lofquist (1967) also measures facet satisfactions. The content of the MSQ is broader than that of the JDI, and respondents indicate their satisfaction on a 5-point response scale. The short form of the MSQ contains 20 items, which ask how satisfied the respondent is with such aspects of the job as "the chances for advancement on this job" and "the freedom to use my own judgment." It has been used in numerous studies, has adequate psychometric properties, and has intrinsic and extrinsic satisfaction scales.

The Job Diagnostic Survey (JDS) was developed to implement the theory that work satisfaction, internal motivation, high quality performance, and low absenteeism and turnover result when employees experience meaningful work, autonomy, and feedback on their jobs (Hackman & Oldham, 1975). An underlying assumption was that work is experienced as meaningful to the extent that it provides skill variety, task identity (the task is performed from beginning to end with a visible outcome), and task significance. In addition to measuring the job's meaningfulness, autonomy, and feedback, the instrument also provides measures of overall satisfaction and satisfaction with job facets such as security, pay, coworkers, supervision, and opportunity for personal growth and development. Also included in the JDS is a measure of growth need strength. Items in the scale are presented in a "would like" format, giving respondents an opportunity to indicate how much of certain specified conditions they would like to have in their jobs.

The JDS has sound psychometric characteristics, making it suitable for assessing the level of motivation and satisfaction of employees as well as the motivating potential of their jobs. Internal consistency reliabilities are generally satisfactory, and most of the scales have adequate discriminant validity (Hackman & Oldham, 1975).

Although the instruments discussed above are among those that have been most rigorously developed, similar measures have been tested in other studies and could be adapted for use by organizations. Whether single-item or multiple-item satisfaction measures are used, there is a general consensus that multiple-point rating scales (e.g., 7-point scales) are superior to a dichotomous "yes-no" format. Also, job satisfaction items that solicit evaluative responses are preferable to those soliciting descriptive responses.

Job characteristics. The job characteristic measures typically included in QWL surveys differ from job satisfaction measures in that the former scales are primarily descriptive rather than evaluative. Thus, instead of assessing respondents' reactions to their jobs, items assess the extent to which various characteristics are descriptive of their jobs. Job characteristic instruments use a variety of item formats and response scales. Respondents may, for example, be asked directly to indicate the amount of each characteristic they perceive to be present in their jobs. When items of this type are used, additional information can be obtained by also asking respondents how much of each characteristic they would like their job to have. This strategy allows individual differences in what is valued in a job to be measured. Another type of job characteristic item asks respondents to indicate the degree to which they agree or disagree with a number of statements about the characteristics of their job.

Some instruments, such as Hackman and Oldham's (1975) JDS, include both types of items. Job characteristics measured by the JDS are skill variety, task identity, task significance, autonomy, and feedback from the job itself.

Another instrument for measuring job characteristics is the Job Characteristics Inventory (JCI), which was developed by Sims, Szilagyi, and Keller (1976). They were concerned that a perceptual measure of job characteristics should have a reasonable degree of correspondence to objective attributes of the job and have the power to discriminate between jobs. The JCI has six scales covering the dimensions described by Hackman and Lawler (1971). These scales are variety, dealing with others, autonomy, feedback, task identity, and friendship opportunities. The authors were able to demonstrate adequate scale reliabilities as well as convergent and discriminant validity.

Job involvement. Job involvement has been defined as (a) the extent to which self-esteem is affected by level of performance or (b) the degree to which individuals are identified psychologically with their jobs—that is, the importance of work to the self-image of the person (Rabinowitz & Hall, 1977). Researchers have variously conceptualized job involvement as an individual difference variable, a situationally determined variable, or a function of the individual-job interaction.

The majority of studies of job involvement have used items adapted from a scale developed by Lodahl and Kejner (1965). Their original scale consisted of 20 items in a Likert format with 4 response options (strongly agree, agree, disagree, strongly disagree). For inclusion in large surveys, however, the authors have also suggested the use of a shortened, 6-item scale. Items making up the abbreviated scale were those loading highest on the first general factor (nonacceptance of items expressing very high job involvement) as identified in the 20-item set. "The major satisfaction in my life comes from my job" is an example of the content of the items suggested for the shortened scale. The abbreviated scale has an estimated reliability of .73, and 76% of the variance in the 20-item scale can be accounted for by these 6 items.

Other measures. A battery of instruments developed as part of the Michigan Quality of Work Program (Seashore, Lawler, Mirvis, & Cammann, 1983) can also be used to assess various work-related concerns. Module 1 of the Michigan Organizational Assessment Questionnaire (MOAQ) is well suited to the assessment of individual-level attitudes and beliefs; the other modules assess group processes, supervisor behaviors, and so on.

Although situational variables have been shown to be the best predictors of perceived QWL, it has become increasingly accepted that dispositional factors also play an important role. If this is true, it is useful for QWL surveys also to include measures that tap individual differences in affective or dispositional tendencies. It is generally accepted that affect consists of two dominant and relatively independent dimensions: positive affect and negative affect. Watson, Clark, and Tellegen (1988) have developed two 10-item scales that constitute the Positive and Negative Affect Schedule (PANAS). Both scales consist of a list of words that describe feelings and emotions; respondents are asked to indicate the degree to which they have experienced each feeling on the average or during a specific time frame. The authors report that both the positive and the negative scales are internally consistent, demonstrate appropriate stability, and have adequate convergent and discriminant validity (Watson et al., 1988).

The Job Affect Scale (JAS) is a modification of the PANAS (Brief, Burke, George, Robinson, & Webster, 1988). It is designed to measure positive and negative affect at work. The JAS is similar to the PANAS, except that work is the referent: The respondent is asked to indicate the extent to which he or she experienced each of 20 feelings (10 positive and 10 negative) at work during the past week. The JAS has acceptable internal consistency reliability and convergent and discriminant validity (see George, 1989).

The opportunity to satisfy higher-order needs at work is assumed to be a primary source of the motivation to work. With this in mind, it is useful to include measures of *need strength* in comprehensive assessments of QWL. The concept of higher-order need was implemented as "gruwth need strength" by Hackman and Oldham (1975) in their development of the JDS. Here, the strength of growth needs was indicated by items such as "chance to exercise independent thought and action" on the job.

Demographic factors. Still another section of a typical QWL survey will solicit demographic information from the respondents so that group differences can be analyzed. The way people perceive their jobs is related to their values and needs, which may vary by age, gender, educational level, and cultural background. Each of these variables is therefore important for understanding the job attitudes that individuals express and should be included in the demographic section of the survey. Other important demographic measures are those defining the individual's place in the organization—including such aspects of organizational membership as tenure, department, or division—and position held.

QWL Surveys: Practical Applications

Planning

The first step in planning a QWL survey is to clearly specify its purpose and how the survey data are to be used. Decisions related to when a QWL survey should be administered, the selection of instruments for the survey, administration procedures, and who is to participate in the survey all depend upon what questions the organization hopes to answer with information from the survey.

QWL surveys can be used profitably to look for causes of problems that have arisen in the workplace. For example, an organization may discover that there has been a sharp decrease in product quality in one department but not in others that produce a similar product. A QWL survey can determine if the job attitudes of workers and their pattern of facet satisfactions also differ among the departments. Such information can form the basis of subsequent organizational development efforts to address the identified problem.

A QWL survey also can provide valuable information for planning and evaluating organizational interventions (e.g., changes in policy affecting benefits, working conditions) or evaluating the impact of such major organizational changes as mergers, restructuring, downsizing, or demographic realignment. Other organizations may routinely assess QWL primarily for the purpose of human resource accounting as suggested by Mirvis and Lawler (1977). Such organizations are likely to be concerned with the relationship between job involvement and satisfaction and the demographic factors involved in organizational membership.

In our own research involving military members, the QWL survey is but one part of a much larger survey that measures perceived quality of life in nonwork domains as well as the quality of life at work. Because one aspect of our research investigates the relationship of individual life domains to the quality of life as a whole, we needed to develop a set of items that could be applied to all the domains.

Survey Content

A QWL survey is distinguished from other standard surveys of employee satisfaction in that it is more comprehensive. A QWL survey should include, at a minimum, the measures outlined in Table 9.1, along with demographic items. That is, it should include measures of overall job satisfaction, facet satisfactions, job characteristics, and job involvement. It might also include a dispositional measure (such as the PANAS or the JAS), thus allowing individual dispositional characteristics to be considered as a moderating variable.

Survey Participants

In our research investigating QWL in the military, we have used a random sample, stratified on the dimensions of hierarchical position in the organization and station location, to assure that participants would be representative of an entire military service. Although few organizational applications will involve a population of similar size, selection of participants should always be determined by the circumstances and the problem(s) being investigated. If a problem (e.g., high turnover rate) is identified with a department or departments of the organization, it may be preferable to administer the survey only within those groups and to include all group members. On the other hand, if one is interested in how QWL may have changed over time as a result of changes in policies or worker demographic factors that affect the entire organization, then the population of interest would be all organizational members. In that case, practical considerations may dictate that a representative sample be used if the organization is large. In smaller organizations where all members can reasonably be included, it is beneficial to do so. Any added administrative costs are likely to be more than offset by increases in statistical power and the impact on morale provided by giving everyone the opportunity to express an opinion.

Survey Administration

Location. A survey about work should be administered at work, and people should be given ample time off from their regular duties to complete the survey. By doing so, the organization signals that it places a great deal of importance on the responses of the employees. Group administration away from individual workstations generally is preferred, helping to assure that individuals can turn their attention to the survey without distractions. Response rates are also maximized with this mode of administration. The individual administering the survey to a group should never be the supervisor of that group because subordinates are likely to perceive such an arrangement as threatening.

Frequency. The military quality of life surveys, including the QWL measures, are to be administered on a 3-year cycle. This time period was chosen because it corresponds to the customary rotation/reassignment cycle in the military. When used to plan and evaluate organizational interventions, the QWL survey will normally be administered at least before and after an intervention is implemented. After the first survey is conducted, the amount of time required to identify, plan, and implement the intervention will of course depend upon the nature of the change to be made. Sufficient time must then be allowed for the change to have an effect before the second survey administration.

Anonymity Versus Identification

Whether respondents are to be identified, either by name or some other method, also will depend upon the subsequent use for which the survey data are intended. If data from the survey are to be combined with information from organizational records or other sources, then it will be necessary to include some form of identification. Respondents can remain anonymous if there is not a specific need for identifying information. Anonymity will increase the likelihood of obtaining honest responses to the more sensitive items, such as satisfaction with supervision.

Why Should QWL Be Surveyed?
Benefits Associated With Improved QWL

Although the number of people who endorse efforts to improve QWL because it is the "right thing to do" is apparently growing, it is more often the traditional issue of the relationship between satisfaction and performance that motivates interest in QWL improvements as one follow-up to QWL surveys. In the following section, some of the QWL benefits for organizations and for individuals are summarized. Periodic QWL surveys are one way organizations may systematically determine the degree to which they are moving to reap these benefits.

Organizational Benefits From QWL

QWL is assumed to affect job effort and performance, organizational identification, job satisfaction, job involvement, and personal alienation. The opportunity to fulfill higher-order needs at work is a primary source of the motivation to work. The more that the job and the organization can gratify the needs of workers, the more effort workers may invest at work, with commensurate improvements in productivity. Satisfaction of needs through organizational membership is associated with assertiveness and self-expression, while the failure to have needs satisfied may lead to alienation (Efraty & Sirgy, 1990).

Productivity and performance. For many years, consultants and researchers assumed that improving QWL would inevitably heighten employee motivation and would thereby improve job performance and productivity. Today, it is recognized that enhancing QWL can improve performance under some, but not all, conditions (Harrison, 1987). It is likely that need satisfaction affects performance mainly through its impact on motivation (Efraty & Sirgy, 1990).[5] If QWL and productivity are causally related, then there is little question that QWL should be a high priority for organizations and that regular surveys should be conducted to assess the level of perceived QWL and the extent to which employee needs are being met.

It is not clear, however, that productivity is the outcome measure that should be of greatest concern to organizations. For many jobs (e.g., police officer or surgeon), productivity is difficult to implement and measure. In addition, pressures to increase productivity can sometimes have unintended negative effects for organizations. For example, increases in job safety and security may raise costs without resulting in bottom line improvements to productivity or revenues. In the long run, it is probably more beneficial for organizations to concentrate on developing a well-trained, loyal work force that is willing and able to adapt to changes than to focus only on productivity.

Absenteeism and turnover. People who arc highly involved in their jobs are less likely to quit their jobs or to be absent (e.g., Farris, 1971; Rabinowitz & Hall, 1977; Siegel & Ruh, 1973). Westley (1979) concluded that alienation and anomie are expressed as withdrawal or a lack of involvement, with the primary symptoms being absenteeism and turnover. Intuitively, it would seem that people who feel that it is all right to be absent do not find their work to be self-enhancing and do not feel any moral obligation to be at the workplace.

Motivation and satisfaction of needs, on the other hand, have consistently been shown to be associated with job involvement and organizational commitment as well as with attendance and low turnover (Harrison, 1987). Attendance also has been found to be related to the degree of congruence between workers' needs and the characteristics of their jobs (Furnham, 1991). Hackman, Pearce, and Wolfe (1978) reported that the extent to which structural job changes (intended to improved QWL) affected absenteeism depended on the strength of the employee's growth needs.

Stress. Occupational stress is emerging as one of the principal social and occupational health concerns of the 1990s. Stress claims accounted for 11% of all worker compensation claims by 1982, with costs exceeding the average cost of all other types of claims according to the National Council on Compensation Insurance (cited in Sauter, 1992). The growing concern with stress-related disorders was recently evidenced by the joint conference of the American Psychological Association and the National Institute for Occupational Safety and Health (NIOSH), where experts in the field developed an agenda for addressing the problems of work and well-being in the 1990s. Much of the work of the conference was devoted to the issue of work design and stress (Keita & Sauter, 1992).

Lack of fit between workers' needs and values and the characteristics of their jobs has been linked with adverse health outcomes. Furnham (1991) reported that a misfit between workers' needs and job characteristics resulted in work frustration and stress. Presumably, a good job-person fit leads to subjective well-being, and a bad fit leads to stress. Karasek (1979) found that redesigning work processes to allow increased decision latitude reduces workers' mental strain without affecting productivity. The opportunity for workers to use their skills and make decisions about work activities was associated with reduced strain at every level of job demand.

Individual Benefits From Improved QWL

Researchers have consistently found positive correlations between measures of quality of life as a whole and QWL (e.g., Campbell, Converse, & Rodgers, 1976), that is, between job and life satisfaction. In addition, positive associations have been found between job satisfaction and mental health (e.g., Furnham & Schaeffer, 1984) and between specific facet satisfactions and mental health. For example, Adelmann (1987) found that both pay and job complexity are significantly related to life satisfaction and morale and that job complexity is inversely related to anxiety.[6]

The relationship between job and life satisfaction also has implications for society as a whole. In his classic study of the relationship between work and nonwork domains, Kornhauser (1965) concluded that routine work is associated with narrow, routine leisure activities that do little to promote self-development, self-expression, or interest in larger social purposes. It also has been suggested that alienated work may cause an individual's frustrations to build until they find release through hostility, punitive family relations, and so on (Seeman, 1967).

While it is important to recognize that the nonwork life of an individual worker may become more or less fulfilling as a result of changes in the workplace (Rice, 1984), the effects of the job on the person and of the person on the job are probably reciprocal throughout the person's work life (Kohn & Schooler, 1978). The main process by which a job affects an individual's personality is thought to be one of simple generalization from the lessons of the job to the person's nonwork life (Kohn & Schooler, 1982). For example, occupational self-direction (the use of initiative, thought, and independent judgment in work) was found by these authors to increase an individual's intellectual flexibility. In turn, intellectual flexibility and self-concept may have important consequences for the individual's place in the organizational hierarchy, determining the opportunity for doing substantively complex and self-directed work.

Conclusions

Although QWL programs have traditionally focused on attainment of outcomes for the individual worker, there are also benefits that accrue to organizations. Improving QWL can contribute directly to reducing turnover and absenteeism, lead to increases in productivity under some conditions, and help create a well-trained loyal work force that is more willing and able to adapt to change (Harrison, 1987). Surveys are the mechanism by which organizations can best monitor the QWL of their employees and determine the job characteristics that are valued by workers. There is also evidence that conducting and reporting the results of QWL surveys can be beneficial to organizations because it enables them to monitor the impact of new management and personnel practices on employees and make modifications where necessary (Mirvis & Lawler, 1984).

At the current time, organizations continue to be measured only by their financial performance and not by the level of QWL they provide to employees (Lawler, 1982). Several corporations have attempted a public accounting of their QWL efforts, however, similar to their yearly financial reports. Such an accounting has been well received by the stockholders and investors of at least one corporation (Mirvis & Lawler, 1977), and there is reason to believe that this practice may spread. Many management theorists believe that it is not only the ethical obligation of organizations to protect the welfare of their employees but also in their self-interest to develop their human resources to increase return on investment and upgrade skills in the labor pool.

Notes

1. For example, Manz and Grothe (1991) demonstrated that the younger cohort of workers they called "vanguard employees" (workers who will be between the ages of 30 and 50 by the year 2000) differed significantly from older workers in terms of their expectations about work. The younger cohort of employees also reported significantly

lower QWL on several different factors than did older comparison groups. Differences between the vanguard workers and the other groups remained significant even after controlling for tenure, hierarchical level, and salary range.

2. The quality of work life experienced by individuals is dependent upon multiple outcomes that they receive or fail to receive from their jobs. The individual compares each outcome that he or she received to some personal standard for the outcome in question, with different outcomes having varying degrees of importance to the individual (Rice, McFarlin, Hunt, & Near, 1985). This relationship is generally linear, with satisfaction increasing as personal standards are met or exceeded. As Rice and his colleagues point out, however, the outcome-standard relationship can take a number of different functional forms, including an inverted U function, in which large discrepancies in either direction result in negative QWL, or an asymptotic function, with either floor or ceiling effects.

3. Westley (1979) defined *alienation* as a condition involving a detachment between work and the self as well as a gap between expectations and fulfillment; *anomie* is the psychological withdrawal from work.

4. Two unresolved questions about facet satisfaction measures are these: (a) How should individual facets be combined to arrive at an overall index of job satisfaction? (b) Which facets should be measured? In their review of the strategies that have been used to combine facet scores, Scarpello and Campbell (1983) described the three most common models: (a) linear compensatory models, in which a high score on one facet can compensate for a low score on another facet; (b) nonlinear conjunctive models, in which a high score on one facet does not compensate for a low score on another; and (c) nonlinear disjunctive models, in which high satisfaction on one facet can outweigh low satisfaction on all other facets. They concluded that the linear model generally performed better than the other two models. The predictive ability of facet measures also can be improved if facets are weighted by their importance to the individual (Rice et al., 1985).

Although the weighting of domain satisfactions by importance does not enhance our ability to predict global life satisfactions from domain satisfactions (Andrews & Withey, 1976; Campbell et al., 1976), Rice and his colleagues (1985) have argued for a weighted sum of *facet satisfactions* within each domain (e.g., work life). They based their use of importance weightings on Locke's (1976) analysis of job satisfaction, reflecting the idea that one can experience extreme levels of affect only when the relevant outcomes are important. According to Locke, the reason that no increment in predictive power can be gained by weighting domain importance is because importance has already been taken into account by individuals in their assessment of the facets of a domain.

5. Hackman, Pearce, and Wolfe (1978) found that the more jobs were enriched by changes in complexity and challenge, the more performance and intrinsic motivation improved, but this was only true for employees high in growth needs. These and other similar results led Furnham (1991) to conclude that it is the degree of fit between the characteristics of the person and his or her job that leads to increases in efficacy.

6. Similarly, Karasek (1979) reported that a combination of low decision latitude and heavy job demands was associated with mental health. Using data from national samples in the United States and Sweden, Karasek also found decision latitude on the job to be inversely related to depression and further found that life dissatisfaction is as strongly related to job characteristics as job dissatisfaction is.

References

Adelmann, P. K. (1987). Occupational complexity, control, and personal income: Their relation to psychological well-being in men and women. *Journal of Applied Psychology, 72,* 529-537.

Andrews, F. M., & Withey, S. B. (1976). *Social indicators of well-being: The development and measurement of perceptual indicators.* New York: Plenum.

Brayfield, A. H., & Rothe, H. F. (1951). An index of job satisfaction. *Journal of Applied Psychology, 35,* 307-311.

Brief, A. P., Burke, M. J., George, J. M., Robinson, B., & Webster, J. (1988). Should negative affectivity remain an unmeasured variable in the study of job stress? *Journal of Applied Psychology, 73,* 193-198.

Campbell, A., Converse, P. E., & Rodgers, W. (1976). *The quality of American life: Perceptions, evaluations, and satisfactions.* New York: Russell Sage.

Efraty, D., & Sirgy, M. J. (1990). The effects of quality of working life (QWL) on employee behavioral responses. *Social Indicators Research, 22,* 31-47.

Farris, G. F. (1971). A predictive study of turnover. *Personnel Psychology, 24,* 311-328.

Fineman, S. (Ed.). (1987). *Unemployment: Personal and social consequences.* London: Tavistock.

Furnham, A. (1991). Work and leisure satisfaction. In F. Strack, M. Argyle, & N. Schwarz (Eds.), *Subjective well-being* (pp. 235-259). New York: Pergamon.

Furnham, A., & Schaeffer, R. (1984). Person-environment fit, job satisfaction, and mental health. *Journal of Occupational Psychology, 57,* 295-307.

George, J. M. (1989). Mood and absence. *Journal of Applied Psychology, 74,* 317-324.

Hackman, J. R., & Lawler, E. E. (1971). Employee reactions to job characteristics. *Journal of Applied Psychology, 55,* 259-286.

Hackman, J. R., & Oldham, G. R. (1975). Development of the job diagnostic survey. *Journal of Applied Psychology, 60,* 259-270.

Hackman, J. R., Pearce, J. L., & Wolfe, J. C. (1978). Effects of changes in job characteristics on work attitudes and behavior: A naturally occurring quasi-experiment. *Organizational Behavior and Human Performance, 21,* 289-304.

Harrison, M. I. (1987). *Diagnosing organizations: Methods, models, and processes.* Newbury Park, CA: Sage.

Herman, J. B., & Hulin, C. L. (1972). Studying organizational attitudes from individual and organizational frames of reference. *Organizational Behavior and Human Performance, 8,* 84-108.

Herzberg, F., Mausner, B., & Snyderman, B. (1959). *The motivation to work.* New York: John Wiley.

Hofstede, G. (1984). The cultural relativity of the quality of life concept. *Academy of Management Review, 9,* 389-398.

Karasek, R. A. (1979). Job demands, decision latitude, and mental strain: Implications for job redesign. *Administrative Sciences Quarterly, 24,* 285-308.

Keita, G. P., & Sauter, S. L. (1992). *Work and well-being: An agenda for the 1990s.* Washington, DC: American Psychological Association.

Kohn, M. L., & Schooler, C. (1978). The reciprocal effects of the substantive complexity of work and intellectual flexibility: A longitudinal assessment. *American Journal of Sociology, 84,* 24-52.

Kohn, M. L., & Schooler, C. (1982). Job conditions and personality: A longitudinal assessment of reciprocal effects. *American Journal of Sociology, 87,* 1257-1286.

Kornhauser, A. W. (1965). *Mental health of the industrial worker.* New York: John Wiley.

Lawler, E. E., III. (1973). *Motivation in work organizations.* Monterey, CA: Brooks/Cole.

Lawler, E. E., III. (1982). Strategies for improving the quality of work life. *American Psychologist, 37,* 486-493.

Levin, I., & Stokes, J. P. (1989). Dispositional approach to job satisfaction: Role of negative affectivity. *Journal of Applied Psychology, 74,* 752-758.

Locke, E. A. (1976). The nature and causes of job satisfaction. In M. D. Dunnette (Ed.), *Handbook of industrial and organizational psychology* (pp. 1279-1349). Chicago: Rand McNally.

Lodahl, T. M., & Kejner, M. (1965). The definition and measurement of job involvement. *Journal of Applied Psychology, 49,* 24-33.

Loscocco, K. A. (1990). Career structures and employee commitment. *Social Science Quarterly, 71,* 53-68.

Loscocco, K. A., & Roschelle, A. R. (1991). Influences on the quality of work and nonwork life: Two decades in review. *Journal of Vocational Behavior, 39,* 182-225.

Manz, C. C., & Grothe, R. (1991). Is the work force vanguard to the 21st century a quality of work life deficient-prone generation? *Journal of Business Research, 23,* 67-82.

Miller, D. C. (1991). *Handbook of research design and social measurement.* Newbury Park, CA: Sage.

Mills, T. (1981). Quality of work life: A clear and present danger. In R. Dorion & L. Brunet (Eds.), *Adapting to a changing world: A reader on quality of working life* (pp. 129-143). Ottawa: Labour Canada.

Mirvis, P. H., & Lawler, E. E., III. (1977). Measuring the financial impact of employee attitudes. *Journal of Applied Psychology, 62,* 1-8.

Mirvis, P. H., & Lawler, E. E., III. (1984). Accounting for the quality of work life. *Journal of Occupational Behaviour, 5,* 197-212.

Mitchell, T. R., & Biglan, A. (1971). Instrumentality theories: Current uses in psychology. *Psychological Bulletin, 76,* 432-454.

Nadler, D. A., & Lawler, E. E., III. (1983, Winter). Quality of work life: Perspectives and directions. *Organizational Dynamics, 11,* 20-30.

Newton, T., & Keenan, T. (1991). Further analyses of the dispositional argument in organizational behavior. *Journal of Applied Psychology, 76,* 781-787.

O'Reilly, C. A. (1977). Personality-job fit: Implications for individual attitudes and performance. *Organizational Behavior and Human Performance, 18,* 36-46.

Quinn, R. P., & Staines, G. L. (1979). *The 1979 quality of employment survey.* Ann Arbor: University of Michigan, Institute for Social Research, Survey Research Center.

Rabinowitz, S., & Hall, D. T. (1977). Organizational research on job involvement. *Psychological Bulletin, 84,* 255-288.

Rice, R. W. (1984). Organizational work and the overall quality of life. In S. Oskamp (Ed.), *Applied social psychology annual 5: Applications in organizational settings* (pp. 155-177). Beverly Hills, CA: Sage.

Rice, R. W., McFarlin, D. B., Hunt, R. G., & Near, J. P. (1985). Organizational work and the perceived quality of life: Toward a conceptual model. *Academy of Management Review, 10,* 296-310.

Salancik, G. R., & Pfeffer, J. (1977). An examination of need satisfaction models of job attitudes. *Administrative Science Quarterly, 22,* 427-456.

Sauter, S. L. (1992). Introduction to the NIOSH proposed national strategy. In G. P. Keita & S. L. Sauter (Eds.), *Work and well-being: An agenda for the 1990s.* Washington, DC: American Psychological Association.

Scarpello, V., & Campbell, J. P. (1983). Job satisfaction: Are all the parts there? *Personnel Psychology, 36,* 577-600.

Schneider, B. S. (1976). *Staffing organizations.* Pacific Palisades, CA: Goodyear.

Seashore, S., Lawler, E., Mirvis, P., & Cammann, C. (Eds.). (1983). *Assessing organizational change.* New York: John Wiley.

Seeman, M. (1967). On the personal consequences of alienation in work. *American Sociological Review, 32,* 273-285.

Sheppard, H. L. (1975). Some indicators of quality of working life: A simplified approach to measurement. In L. E. Davis & A. B. Cherns (Eds.), *The quality of working life: Problems, prospects, and the state of the art* (pp. 119-149). New York: Free Press.

Siegel, A. L., & Ruh, R. A. (1973). Job involvement, participation in decision making, personal background and job behavior. *Organizational Behavior and Human Performance, 9,* 318-327.

Sims, H., Szilagyi, A., & Keller, R. (1976). The measurement of job characteristics. *Academy of Management Journal, 19,* 195-212.

Smith, P. C., Kendall, L. M., & Hulin, C. L. (1969). *The measurement of satisfaction in work and retirement.* Chicago: Rand McNally.

Staw, B. M., Bell, N. E., & Clausen, J. A. (1986). The dispositional approach to job attitudes: A lifetime longitudinal test. *Administrative Science Quarterly, 31,* 56-77.

Staw, B. M., & Ross, J. (1985). Stability in the midst of change: A dispositional approach to job attitudes. *Journal of Applied Psychology, 70,* 469-480.

Strauss, G. (1974). Is there a blue-collar revolt against work? In R. P. Fairfield (Ed.), *Humanizing the workplace* (pp. 19-48). Buffalo, NY: Prometheus.

Watson, D., Clark, L. A., & Tellegen, A. (1988). Development and validation of brief measures of positive and negative affect: The PANAS scales. *Journal of Personality and Social Psychology, 54,* 1063-1070.

Weiss, D. J., Dawis, R. V., England, G. W., & Lofquist, L. H. (1967). *Manual for the Minnesota Satisfaction Questionnaire* (Minnesota Studies in Vocational Rehabilitation, No. 22). Minneapolis: University of Minnesota, Industrial Relations Center.

Westley, W. A. (1979). Problems and solutions in the quality of working life. *Human Relations, 32,* 113-123.

Witt, L. A., Beorkrem, M. N., & Andrews, D. H. (1991). *Positive and negative affect as moderators of the job satisfaction-job attitudes relationship.* Williams Air Force Base, AZ: Armstrong Laboratory.

10

The Military Equal Opportunity Climate Survey

An Example of Surveying in Organizations

DAN LANDIS
MICKEY R. DANSBY
ROBERT H. FALEY

This chapter describes a program of action research (Lewin, 1946) designed to reduce, in one institution—the military—levels of racial and sexual (including sexual harassment) discrimination. The chapter has three aims: (a) to summarize the development of the Military Equal Opportunity Climate Survey (MEOCS), (b) to describe the way the survey is applied in the military setting, and (c) to summarize the most recent psychometric data on the MEOCS. Because we believe, with Lewin (1946), that the best practice comes from good theory (and the other way around), we will spend some time on the conceptual basis of the approach.

AUTHORS' NOTE: Parts of the background section of this chapter are an edited, shortened, and updated version of discussions in Landis (1990) and Landis et al. (1992). This work was partially supported by several summer faculty appointments to the authors from the Defense Equal Opportunity Management Institute. The authors take full responsibility for the opinions and conclusions in this chapter; those writings are not be taken as official or unofficial positions of the U.S. government, the Department of Defense, or any of their agencies.

Conceptual Background

The rationale for the MEOCS is rooted in the study of climate in complex organizations. This area of inquiry was initiated by the publication of the first studies by Lewin and his colleagues (e.g., Lewin, Lippitt, & White, 1939; Lippitt, 1940; Lippitt & White, 1947). Organizational climate research over the years, however, has been termed "fuzzy" (Guion, 1973), "folklore" (Woodman & King, 1978), and a "conceptual morass" (Glick, 1985). As one result of the problems that have plagued organizational climate research, Glick (1985) notes that, recently, the flow of research on organizational climate has been reduced to a trickle.

Glick (1985) suggests that the lack of recent research may be due to conceptual and methodological problems encountered by researchers studying organizational climate. For example, he suggests that many of the problems that plague organizational climate research stem from the inability to resolve whether organizational climate research should focus on the organization or the individual as the unit of theory. Others have suggested that the problems organizational climate researchers encounter are the result of the debate over whether organizational climate should be viewed as a unitary concept (e.g., Schneider, 1975; Zohar, 1980).

These debates aside, the approach described in this chapter focuses on what James and Jones (1974) referred to as the "perceptual measurement-organizational attribute approach" to defining and measuring organizational climate (see also Hellreigel & Slocum, 1974). This differentiates *organizational climate* as it is used here from the term *psychological climate* as defined by James and Jones (1974) and others (e.g., Glick, 1985; Schneider, 1975). The primary difference between the two concepts deals with the source of the variance when individual perceptions of organizational climate are the unit of analysis. *Organizational climate* as defined in this chapter connotes that variance in perceptual scores is related to differences in situations rather than differences in individuals (the latter defines *psychological climate*).

This chapter focuses on one "type" or aspect of organizational climate, what we call here "equal opportunity climate" (EOC). EOC is defined here based on the work of Landis (1990). He describes EOC as "the expectation by an employee that work-related behaviors directed by others toward the person will reflect merit and not one's racial/ethnic group, gender, national origin or membership in any other minority group" (Landis, 1990, p. 29).

This definition takes into account the idea that EOC is conceptualized to possess two specific qualities. First, this definition connotes that EOC is an organizational attribute that can be inferred by employees based on the way their organization deals with equal opportunity (EO) matters (i.e., their perception of the organization's EO environment). Thus EOC refers to the attribute(s) of the organization and not the individual. Second, implicit in this definition is the fact that individuals' perceptions of the EOC within their organization can have serious behavioral consequences for the individual or the organization.

More recent social and political events (the riots in Los Angeles, the passage of the Civil Rights Act of 1991, the confirmation hearings of Clarence Thomas, and so on) suggest that attempts to measure EO are worth considering, if not from a theoretical then from a practical perspective. For example, the Civil Rights Act of 1991 for the first time explicitly recognizes that an "atmosphere of discrimination" (i.e., "negative EOC") can play a determining role in the outcome of many discrimination cases. Thus the ability to measure the discriminatory atmosphere within an organization could prove to be the difference between winning and losing an equal employment opportunity lawsuit. Moreover, even if an employer were to lose, if information on the overall EO climate within the organization were favorable, it might mitigate the extent of the employer's liability (e.g., see *Furnco Construction Corp. v. Waters,* 1978; *Parham v. Southwestern Bell Telephone Co.,* 1970).

Climate and Equal Opportunity

In EO litigation, the presence of a discriminatory climate or "atmosphere of discrimination" is becoming increasingly used as a basis for legal action under Title VII of the Civil Rights Act of 1964, particularly in the area of sexual harassment (Laurent, 1987). The atmosphere of discrimination doctrine is based on an employee's Title VII right to a workplace environment that is neither hostile nor offensive to individuals because of their group membership. According to this doctrine, plaintiffs do not have to establish that a specific discriminatory act had tangible employment-related consequence but only that the debilitating impact of their work environment indirectly affected the conditions of their employment. Many people believe that the atmosphere of discrimination argument will be weakened by the courts as lower judiciaries apply the shifting burden of proof doctrines enunciated in *Wards Cove v. Antonio et al.* (1989) and other decisions. Be that as it may, it is unlikely that the doctrine will cease to exist. Hence it will be to an organization's interest to measure the level of "atmosphere of discrimination" and take whatever action is warranted particularly in light of the tendency of courts to mitigate damages when the organization has demonstrated good faith efforts to eliminate discrimination.

Military Research on Climate and Race/Gender Relations

Studies on race relations. From the promise of President Truman's Executive Order 9981 of 1948 (establishing EO as a fundamental principle in the armed forces of the United States) to the most recent version of the Statement of Human Goals (the EO "mission statement" of the armed forces) issued by the Department of Defense (DoD) on April 17, 1990, equal opportunity and treatment have received emphasis by the various service research organizations. The Army conducted research in the 1970s on both organizational and race relations climate (Brown, Nordlie, & Thomas, 1977; Parker, 1974; Pecorella, 1975; see Day, 1983; Landis, Hope, & Day, 1984, and Thomas, 1988, for a summary). These efforts were an attempt to determine the relationship of EO and treatment of military personnel. But, first, a measure of racial discrimination had to be developed. Because it was recognized that official statistics would be of little use—if for no reason other than that a reporting system did not exist at that time—an alternative strategy was adopted, one that persists today. The approach taken was to develop reasonably good measures of racial attitudes, the reasoning being that such attitudes were the precursors of discriminatory behavior. A major development of these studies was the construction and validation of the Racial Awareness and Perceptions Scale (RAPS), a revised version of the Racial Perceptions Inventory (RPI; Borus, Fiman, Stanton, & Dowd, 1973; Borus, Stanton, Fiman, & Dowd, 1972).[1] This instrument, a set of items in Likert format, concerned beliefs about racial interactions and was used in most of the studies reviewed in this section (Hiett et al., 1978a, 1978b).

The original RAPS consisted of 69 items that, after factor analysis, were shown to cluster into four groupings: perceived discrimination against minorities (PDM), attitudes toward racial integration (ATI), feelings of reverse racism (FRR), and racial climate (RC). Reliabilities (Chronbach's α) were quite good, ranging from .80 (RC) to .95 (PDM).

Later studies (see O'Mara & Tierney, 1978) dropped these figures into the .60 to .80 range. The O'Mara and Tierney study produced an abridged (26-item) version of the RAPS. The reliability information was promising and the RAPS was used in several studies of race relations in the Army and as a criterion for evaluating race relations programs in the service.

Unfortunately, the RAPS did not produce impressive results. The Hiett, McBride, and Fiman (1974) study illustrates the difficulty. This study attempted to relate RAPS scores to the effects of race-relations training as well as to "incidences of discriminatory behaviors." The sample was large (more than 10,000 from all services), with results that were equivocal at best. Of the 42 incidence items, only 4 produced differences between blacks and whites significant at the .01 level. With regard to the effect of training, differences were small and significant only because of the sample size. Nevertheless, the authors still concluded that the RAPS was a valid measure of racial climate (Hiett et al., 1974).

The RAPS and similar instruments focus on racism at the individual level. But, could one define a pattern of organizational indices that would represent "institutional" racism? Nordlie (1977) attempted to approach this problem by measuring changes in institutional racial discrimination in the Army. He found several general patterns: Blacks were underrepresented on outcomes that would be to their advantage (e.g., promotion rates) and overrepresented on those that would be to their disadvantage (e.g., less-than-honorable discharges). Nordlie did not relate these patterns to the RAPS or other such measures. And for very good reason, we can surmise. Undiscussed in this study was the possibility that such indices may be subject to a number of influences, most of which represent institutional survival as opposed to racism. Before such measures could be used to define equal opportunity status, one would have to assure objective assessment over a long enough period of time to eliminate individual impacts on the data.

In a 1972 survey by the Army Research Institute (ARI; Brown et al., 1977), it was reported that there was a notable difference in how the "race problem" was seen by whites and blacks. Whites tended to accept the proposition that the Army is free from racial discrimination while blacks saw the Army as highly discriminatory. This difference was also correlated with grade: Officers and higher enlisted grades of both races tended to see the race problem as less serious than did personnel in the lower enlisted grades. These results were replicated in 1974, for an all-volunteer army population with an increased number of black enlisted personnel (Hiett et al., 1974).

In a longitudinal study of racial climate conducted in a large military unit, O'Mara (1977) reported that the racial climate (based on RAPS scores) appeared to degrade over the 12 months of the study. Unfortunately, no data on possible intervening events were presented, preventing an examination of reasons for the change. Nevertheless, the study is interesting due to its longitudinal design and should be studied as a possible model for future efforts.

Finally, Hiett and Nordlie (1978) concluded that, despite the relative absence of overt interracial violence in the uniformed services, race-related tensions persisted and, in fact, may have been increasing. They reported that, while the frequency of openly hostile types of behavior is low, the overall quality of race relations is somewhere between "good and fair" (based on a 5-point scale). This conclusion was based on a belief that the level of hostile types of behaviors should have led to a higher overall judgment of racial climate. No evidence was reported that would justify this conclusion.

The studies of the 1970s were an important step in the understanding of racial climate in large military organizations. There were problems, however, that may have led to the termination of this line of research. These problems were both internal and external.

Internally, there was a lack of a theoretical structure that would have related RAPS scores to other indices of racial discrimination. Furthermore, it was assumed that the worth of the RAPS would be as a predictor of such indices. It is possible that the authors got things the wrong way around. That is, discriminatory indices are rarely reported events. The reports, further, may have moderate to low reliability. Hence their use as a criterion is problematic, at best. A second problem comes from the measurement strategy adopted: the agree-disagree format of the Likert scale. We will return to this issue later. A last problem, potentially the most serious from an institutional standpoint, was the failure to the see this work in the framework of action research (Lewin, 1946). Thus the stakeholders (e.g., field commanders) were not involved in the conceptualization or use of the measures. All of these problems may have produced marginal results that could not be used to justify continuation of the work in the face of lackluster support for racial integration in the services or in the political arena.

Externally, the studies also ceased to be extended for a number of reasons. The very nature of contract research that is funded on a year-to-year basis prevents long-range efforts from being planned and executed. Hence each succeeding study rarely builds upon the work of previous research in any systematic fashion. Second, the studies came along at a time that saw decreases in overt racial incidents. Some drew the conclusion that the racial tensions of the 1960s were a thing of the past and that research on the topic was no longer of consequence. Reflecting this belief was a congressional mandate in the early 1980s that removed such research from ARI's mission statement. Unfortunately, the flaws in the RAPS program of research contributed to the logic underlying the action of Congress. Yet, more recent research indicates that the interruption of this line of work was premature.

Moving into the late 1980s (a full decade after the studies reviewed above), a recent survey conducted by the Army (*Soldiers Report IV,* 1986) reported that there were race and rank climate differences (although the level of significance was not reported) between minorities and whites and between enlisted personnel and officers. Those differences appeared on such items as "race does not influence whether a soldier will get a fair deal" and "command does not ensure that soldiers have equal opportunity for promotion."

In the most recent study, using a convenience sample of active-duty service personnel, Landis (1990) administered a version of the RAPS as well as a number of other measures. Looking just at the data from Army personnel and comparing the item means with those obtained by Hiett et al. (1978a, 1978b), Landis concluded that little had changed in the intervening decade and a half.

Navy studies. During the same period that the Army was actively researching racial climate, the Navy was also conducting related studies. Bowers (1975) measured organizational climate variables using an instrument called the Survey of Organizations (SOO). In general, he found that scores of the respondents in the Navy were lower on all measures of organizational climate than those for nearly three fourths of civilian respondents. The findings showed more felt discrimination by minorities, particularly blacks. There was also a negative relationship between climate and the amount of felt discrimination; that is, the poorer the climate, the higher the level of felt discrimination.

The SOO led to the development of the Navy's Human Resource Management (HRM) Survey, which, during the late 1970s to the early 1980s, was administered to every operational unit (Rosenfeld, Thomas, Edwards, Thomas, & Thomas, 1991). The HRM's focus was on organizational issues as befits its SOO parentage. But P. J. Thomas and S. Conway (1983)[2] made the point that such measures might be indicative of EO problems and therefore could be used to assess the level of EO climate. This line of thinking led the Navy to establish the HRM as one method of measuring EOC.

Although the HRM survey was widely implemented by the early 1980s, it declined rather rapidly and was replaced by the Command Managed Equal Opportunity Program. The reasons for the change are similar to those given for the death of the RAPS: Commanders felt that it represented "excessive outside control" (Rosenfeld et al., 1991, p. 411).

The most recent attempt to measure EOC in the Navy was carried out by Rosenfeld and his colleagues (Rosenfeld, Culbertson, Booth-Kewley, & Magnusson, 1992): 65 Likert-type items are decomposed into 10 a priori scales. These scales deal with a number of topics (e.g., assignments, training, leadership, discipline) and have reliabilities ranging from .62 to .88. In terms of construct validity, differences between designated groups (e.g., between genders, races, and ranks) appear as expected. These authors concluded that, despite the differences, all "personnel, as a whole, had positive perceptions of EO climate" (p. viii).[3]

Studies from other services. We have been unable to discover programs of equal opportunity research emanating from either the Air Force or the Marine Corps. The reasons for the dearth of research in the Air Force are somewhat of a mystery.

Studies on gender discrimination and harassment. The study of sexual harassment (unwanted and unsolicited behaviors of one gender toward another that have the effect of creating a hostile work environment) has gained particular currency with news reports of highly publicized incidents (e.g., the Tailhook convention of 1991). As salient as these incidents are, we should keep in mind that they represent only one aspect of gender discrimination.

The studies reviewed above (with the exception of Landis, 1990, and Rosenfeld et al., 1992) ignored issues of gender discrimination. Sexual discrimination, however, can be viewed as an aspect of EOC. Such discrimination may be seen as consisting of two separate but overlapping components. One takes the form of more overt sexual harassment as exemplified in the offer of career advancement in exchange for sexual favors. The other component (the perception of women as less competent than men)[4] is much more covert and may possibly be even more damaging to the equal opportunity and treatment of women (see Culbertson & Rosenfeld, this volume, for a more extensive review).

Race and gender effects on climate. There is some evidence that supports the expectation that perceptions of EOC may differ by race and gender. For example, using the Organizational Effectiveness Package (OAP) described by Short (1985), Spicher (1980) found that male and female perceptions of EO treatment differed in the Air Force and were significant on 14 of 23 OAP factors. Men had a more favorable perception than did the women on 11 of the 14 factors. Moreover, officers' perceptions had a higher mean value than enlisted personnel's on all 14 significant factors. In general, the investigation of such effects remains uncharted.

Current measurement strategies in the military. Both the Navy and the Air Force routinely use field surveys designed to measure aspects of service person morale. EO is part of these questionnaires. The Air Force's is part of the Social Actions Staff Assistant Visit (SAV) and consists of 37 questions in a Likert format. A wide set of topics are covered, including drug use, unit leadership, and community environment. Five questions deal with "fair" treatment in the unit. No evidence exists that this survey has been subjected to the usual psychometric tests, and therefore one must be cautious about interpretations. Despite the limitations, this survey is in common use in the Air Force.

The Navy's Equal Opportunity and Sexual Harassment Survey (NEOSH) survey focused specifically on EO and sexual harassment issues (Rosenfeld et al., 1992). This survey is administered biennially, with the first testing in the fall of 1989 and the second in the fall of 1991. This questionnaire contains items covering a variety of EO issues including questions focused specifically on sexual harassment. Most of the items are in Likert format, but some use extensive multiple-response structures. The psychometric properties of the NEOSH seem adequate and it is certainly more well thought out than the SAV.

Summary of military research on climate. In summarizing the findings on climate and racial and sexual discrimination in the military, several points can be made: (a) There were often differences in perceptions of climate between races, between sexes, and between ranks; (b) there has been a primary focus on racial discrimination, particularly discrimination against blacks; and (c) there may be methodological problems deriving from poor conceptual underpinning of the measures used to define climate variables.

While providing a wealth of information regarding climate and race relations in the military, previous efforts at instrument development have some serious drawbacks as measures of EO as defined earlier. The Racial Perceptions Inventory (Borus et al., 1973), the Racial Attitudes and Perceptions Survey (Hiett et al., 1978a, 1978b), the Navy Human

Relations Questionnaire (Stoloff, 1972), and the Enlisted Personnel Questionnaire on Race Relations in the Army (Nordlie & Thomas, 1974) all focused on race relations, mainly between blacks and whites. That focus ignored not only other racial and ethnic minorities but the issues attendant to the integration of women into the armed forces. With these issues now coming to the fore, the domain of interest needs to be expanded to include these other groups. To some extent, this restrictive focus has been alleviated in some of the Navy studies cited earlier. It remained a problem, however, for armed services-wide surveys as late as 1987.

A further issue concerns the instrument format. These instruments asked respondents for their attitudes, feelings, and opinions, often in a Likert scale format, regarding race relations and the climate of their location. None of the measures focused on actual behavioral incidents, and that failing renders the item referent unclear. A further problem is that the time frame referred to in the item was not made clear. The action could have been temporally proximal or distal to the time of survey administration. Moreover, the use of agree-disagree Likert response scales to items may be problematic because, by indicating agreement, the respondent may be saying nothing about the perceived frequency of the behaviors underlying the item. We may really be measuring the individual's affective reaction to *any* kind of discriminatory behavior and not be relating such reaction to the frequency of the actions. In addition, for the most part, the relationships between race-relations climate and organizational outcomes was left unstudied. Clearly, more methodological precision is needed.

The above discussion should not be taken to mean that all previous measures were useless. Many have given valuable information, in particular those developed by the NPRDC group. The measurement strategy assumes, however, that there is a close link between affect and behavior, a position most theorists find problematic (see Triandis, 1976). It would be advantageous to have a measure that was more clearly linked to possible equal opportunity behaviors. Commanders could then use this information to develop targeted programs.

In an effort to address these issues, Landis and his colleagues developed the MEOCS with the assistance of the Defense Equal Opportunity Management Institute[5] (DEOMI; Dansby & Landis, 1991; Fisher, 1988; Landis, 1990; Landis & Fisher, 1987; Landis, Fisher, & Dansby, 1988a, 1988b). Given that the focus of this chapter is on the MEOCS, it will be described in more detail in the next section.

Description of the MEOCS

The current version of the questionnaire consists of five distinct parts. The first part is based on the idea that EOC refers to a person's expectation that certain behaviors have a probability of occurring. Thus, if you anticipate with a high degree of certainty that a minority will be disciplined, whereas a white will not for the same offense, we can conclude that your evaluation of EOC will be negative. This approach is implemented by asking that the respondent estimate the perceived likelihood of each of 50 behaviors occurring during the past 30 days at his or her duty location. The 50 items break down into five independent dimensions, described more fully below.[6]

A second part of the instrument consists of 27 items taken from the RAPS. These items, in a Likert format, have been rewritten to reflect a servicewide referent as well as including gender issues. Initially, these items were included as a way of assessing the relationship of the approach described in the previous paragraph to prior measures. Subsequent theoretical analysis suggests that these items may tap some unique parts of the variance in the indexes of organizational functioning included in the questionnaire.

Three measures of organizational functioning are included. From the battery used by Short (1985), we adapted measures of organizational commitment (12 items), work-group effectiveness (5 items), and job satisfaction (6 items). The rationale for inclusion of such measures was to be able to validate the measure of EOC (i.e., the first section of the questionnaire) against indices of the climate of the organization. All three scales were in a Likert format.

The final section was made of demographic items (19 in all). These items asked about the respondent's experience with discrimination, gender, race/ethnic group, rank, age, and education.

It is beyond the scope of this chapter to give a detailed summary of the research on the MEOCS. That has been given elsewhere (Dansby & Landis, 1991) and the interested reader is referred to that source. A summary of the current data is, however, given in the next section.

A Status Report on the MEOCS Program

The MEOCS was released to the services in the late summer of 1990. From that date to the writing of this chapter (July 1992), the MEOCS has been administered in 169 units with the total number of respondents totaling around 26,000, with another 5,000 in the pipeline. New requests for MEOCS administration are made to the DEOMI at the rate of about 5 per week. Recently, the Commandant of the Marine Corps ordered a Corps-wide administration of the instrument.[7] The demographic breakdown of the total data base is shown in Table 10.1.

Approximately 62% of the sample comes from the Navy, reflecting the earlier adoption of the instrument by that service; 67% of the sample is white, a lower fraction than in the total services; and 16% is female, a figure some 6% above the DoD fraction. These departures from the DoD population are probably due to the oversampling of minority groups and women in the early administrations of the MEOCS. In addition, commanders who have diverse units may be more interested in the MEOCS data than those with more homogeneous groups.

A normative study was fielded in the summer of 1992. In this effort, a random sample of 20,000 (stratified on gender, race, and rank) from the Army and Navy was selected. The purpose of this study is to set Army and Navy norms for each of the MEOCS factors. Using these data, commanders will be able to assess the relationship of their unit to the relevant distribution for their service. These comparisons should be available in early 1993. Currently, the only comparisons that can be made are with the total MEOCS data base, a sample possibly biased by the unit-volunteer nature of the process and oversampling of minorities in early administrations.

Psychometric Properties of the MEOCS

Structure. The MEOCS has been subjected to repeated principal components analyses. These analyses have, fortunately, converged to a common solution. The behavioral perception portion of the survey (50 items) contains five orthogonal factors: sexual harassment and discrimination (10 items), differential command behaviors (10 items), positive command behaviors (10 items), racist/sexist behaviors (10 items), and reverse discrimination behaviors (10 items). The attitude (modified RAPS) section (27 items) has four orthogonal factors: discrimination against minorities (9 items), agreement with reverse discrimination (7 items), racial separation (4 items), and belief in integration (4 items). Each of the organizational indices was found to have a unifactor structure.

Reliability. Table 10.2 presents the interitem consistency (Chronbach's α) for each section of the questionnaire. In addition, the effect of experience in the military (lower enlisted versus higher ranks) is shown.

Table 10.1 Demographic Characteristics of MEOCS Sample (as of July 31, 1992)

	Officers					Warrant Officers					Enlisted					
	White	Black	His-panic	Asian	American Indian	White	Black	His-panic	Asian	American Indian	White	Black	His-panic	Asian	American Indian	Total
Air Force:																
Males	162	8	8	9	13	4	4	4	10	11	332	68	36	24	15	708
Females	18	4	0	8	7	0	2	1	5	2	58	18	2	6	1	132
Army:																
Males	531	83	37	23	10	112	21	21	15	14	1,707	641	276	123	83	3,697
Females	58	12	2	9	4	6	7	1	19	10	256	251	35	31	21	722
Navy:																
Males	1,683	91	67	72	26	86	40	18	15	8	6,483	1,851	678	785	250	12,153
Females	520	53	17	29	10	2	8	2	3	0	1,429	491	139	73	39	2,815
Marines:																
Males	498	40	22	7	10	46	15	4	9	4	1,452	402	214	44	50	2,817
Females	41	4	0	5	7	6	4	1	2	0	150	56	23	7	8	314
Coast Guard:																
Males	153	3	5	5	3	48	9	3	7	5	492	62	41	21	19	876
Females	9	0	0	1	3	1	2	0	0	0	55	13	2	3	1	90
Totals	3,673	298	158	168	93	311	112	55	85	54	12,414	3,853	1,446	1,117	487	24,324

Table 10.2 Reliability of MEOCS Factors

| | | Chronbach's α | |
Dimension	Total Sample	E1-3	E4-E9
Behaviors:			
sexual discrimination and harassment	.89	.87	.89
differential command behaviors	.90	.89	.90
positive command	.86	.82	.85
racist/sexist	.85	.82	.85
reverse discrimination	.79	.76	.79
Attitudes:			
discrimination against minorities	.91	.89	.91
agreement with reverse discrimination	.75	.72	.75
agreement with racial separatism	.82	.80	.81
belief in integration	.60	.50	.58
Organizational climate:			
commitment	.83	.78	.82
work-group effectiveness	.87	.84	.87
job satisfaction	.81	.77	.81

SOURCE: Data are from Landis, Faley, and Dansby (1992).

We can note two conclusions. First, length of time in the military does not affect the reliability of the judgments. The variation is on the order of .04%, suggesting that such judgments are formed rapidly as one enters the military. Second, all of the factors, save one, meet acceptable levels of reliability. An earlier study (Landis & Fisher, 1987) demonstrated adequate test-retest reliability on a sample of students at the DEOMI.

Range of scores. Table 10.3 presents mean scores for the behavioral factors by service, sex, and race. In general, the scores are as expected. That is, women estimate that sexual harassment/discrimination behaviors are more likely than do men; blacks judge that differential command behaviors are more likely than do whites; and whites of any group see positive behaviors more often than do minorities or women. We can also note, with Rosenfeld et al. (1992), that the means are shifted toward the positive end of the scale. Whether this justifies a finding that the respondents see equal opportunity in the military in a generally positive light will have to wait for further studies.

Mean scores on the equal opportunity attitude portion of the MEOCS are given in Table 10.4. Low scores on discrimination against minorities

Table 10.3 Mean Equal Opportunity Climate Behaviors by Service, Sex, and Race

Service/Sex/Race	SHB	DCB	PCB	RSB	RDB	N
			Dimension			
Air Force:						
Male						
Black	3.41	3.51[a]	2.57	3.33	3.82	80
White	3.95	4.51	2.02	3.89[a]	4.13	498
Hispanic	3.40	3.73	2.45	3.44	3.86	49
Female						
Black	3.21[a]	3.51[a]	2.38	3.32[a]	3.92[a]	24
White	3.43	4.41	2.00	3.85	4.16	76
Hispanic[b]						
Army:						
Male						
Black	3.69	3.76	2.75	3.46	4.07	745
White	4.01[a]	4.47	2.15	3.69	4.00	2345
Hispanic	3.84	4.05	3.63[a]	3.47	3.96	334
Female						
Black	3.45	3.66	2.76	3.52	4.09	270
White	3.53	4.33	2.10	3.62	4.06	320
Hispanic	3.35	3.82	2.50	3.33	4.00	38
Navy:						
Male						
Black	3.61	3.84	2.57	3.37	4.09	1981
White	4.00	4.56[a]	2.01	3.78	4.15	8249
Hispanic	3.78	4.16	2.40	3.37	4.07	763
Female						
Black	3.53	3.81	2.58	3.55	4.29[a]	552
White	3.58	4.50	1.99	3.77	4.21	1950
Hispanic	3.72	4.24	2.30	3.70	4.14	158
Marines:						
Male						
Black	3.57	3.72	2.62	3.34	4.00	457
White	3.83	4.49	2.01	3.58	3.99	1995
Hispanic	3.70	4.09	2.39	3.33	3.97	240
Female						
Black	3.44	3.88	2.60	3.52	4.16	64
White	3.38	4.56[a]	1.96[a]	3.55	4.25	197
Hispanic	3.37	3.84	2.29	3.35	3.98	24

NOTE: SHB = sexual discrimination/harassment, DCB = differential command behaviors, PCB = positive command behaviors, RSB = racist/sexist behaviors, RDB = reverse discrimination behaviors.
a. Extreme scores in each column.
b. Too few responses.

Table 10.4 Mean Equal Opportunity Attitude by Service, Sex, and Race

Service/Sex/Race	Dimension			
	DM	*RD*	*SA*	*BI*
Air Force:				
Male				
Black	2.99	3.61	3.99	2.59
White	4.19	3.52	4.36	2.27
Hispanic	3.24	3.53	3.94[a]	2.65
Female				
Black	2.98	3.93[a]	4.07	2.72
White	3.78	3.82	4.44[a]	2.28
Hispanic[b]				
Army:				
Male				
Black	2.91	3.60	4.10	2.68
White	3.63	3.54	4.43	2.42
Hispanic	3.32	3.43	3.99	2.58
Female				
Black	2.75	3.75	4.27	3.02[a]
White	4.12	3.23	4.16	2.36
Hispanic	2.95	3.53	4.31	2.84
Navy:				
Male				
Black	2.98	3.67	4.12	2.64
White	4.20[a]	3.30	4.29	2.26[a]
Hispanic	3.41	3.53	4.12	2.50
Female				
Black	2.81	3.89	4.39	2.83
White	3.73	3.58	4.52	2.44
Hispanic	3.47	3.68	4.37	2.57
Marines:				
Male				
Black	2.85	3.66	4.10	2.75
White	4.11	3.13[a]	4.11	2.34
Hispanic	3.38	3.39	4.05	2.62
Female				
Black	2.71[a]	3.75	4.24	2.92
White	3.64	3.43	4.43	2.54
Hispanic	3.11	3.66	4.11	2.60

NOTE: DM = discrimination against minorities, RD = reverse discrimination, SA = separatism, BI = belief in integration.
a. Extreme scores in each column.
b. Too few responses.

(DM), reverse discrimination (RD), and racial separatism (SA) indicate that respondents agree with negative attitude statements (e.g., "More severe punishments are given out to minority as compared to majority offenders for the same types of offenses."). Such scores indicate negative feelings about equal opportunity in the service. Low scores, on the other hand, for the belief in integration (BI) variable indicate positive attributions about the service. Again, we note that minority individuals have considerably more negative attitudes than majority persons. Comparing these scores with those obtained by Rosenfeld et al. (1992) indicates more negative attitudes from our respondents. Of course, although the response dimension was the same in the two studies, the items were different. It may be that the MEOCS elicits more negative affect because of its item domain than does the instrument used by Rosenfeld et al. (1992). In any case, it would seem that any conclusion about the state of equal opportunity climate in the military, or any of its parts, is premature.

Table 10.5 gives the organizational indices mean values by service, sex, and race. In general, again, minorities have lower commitment and perceived work-group effectiveness as well lower levels of satisfaction. The differences on these variables between the groups, however, are less than appear on the other parts of the MEOCS.

The MEOCS Approach:
Organizational Assessment and Intervention

For some years now, organization development (OD) consultants have used surveys (along with other techniques) as a basis for organizational assessment and change. Bowers and Franklin (1975) describe the basic process of survey-guided development. Hausser, Pecorella, and Wissler (1977) summarize the main goal of survey-guided development, which is "to facilitate interventions or changes in organizational functioning that will lead to increased organizational effectiveness by providing accurate and useful information about how the organization actually functions, how it might ideally function, and how to make the actual functioning more like the ideal functioning" (p. 5).[8]

Practical implementation of the MEOCS assessment program is loosely based on these classical approaches to organizational assessment and intervention; however, some modifications are required because of the sheer enormity of the task and the limited resources available to conduct

Table 10.5 Mean Organizational Indexes by Service, Sex, and Race

Service/Sex/Race	Commitment	Index Effectiveness	Satisfaction
Air Force:			
Male			
Black	2.62	2.03	3.72
White	2.41	1.91	3.78
Hispanic	2.66	2.39[a]	3.51[a]
Female			
Black	2.58	2.00	3.74
White	2.29[a]	1.72[a]	3.92
Hispanic[b]			
Army:			
Male			
Black	2.77	2.14	3.63
White	2.65	2.04	3.66
Hispanic	2.75	2.31	3.56
Female			
Black	3.02[a]	2.32	3.55
White	2.75	1.99	3.65
Hispanic	2.99	2.03	3.66
Navy:			
Male			
Black	2.78	2.15	3.73
White	2.52	1.86	3.88
Hispanic	2.67	2.11	3.80
Female			
Black	2.84	2.12	3.79
White	2.57	1.89	3.84
Hispanic	2.61	2.05	3.93[a]
Marines:			
Male			
Black	2.59	2.10	3.61
White	2.39	1.89	3.74
Hispanic	2.48	2.20	3.65
Female			
Black	2.77	1.89	3.72
White	2.39	1.81	3.79
Hispanic	2.45	2.10	3.81

NOTE: Low scores on commitment and effectiveness indicate positive ratings; low scores on satisfaction indicate negative ratings.
a. Extreme scores in each column.
b. Too few responses.

the MEOCS program. The approach is presented based on a six-step model:

1. Contact
2. Contract
3. Data gathering
4. Data analysis
5. Feedback of information
6. Follow-up

Before discussing these six stages, some preliminary background is in order.

Background

As discussed previously, the MEOCS measures a number of EO and organizational factors that are of interest to military leaders. From its inception, the MEOCS was designed to be a voluntary, confidential survey, with feedback returned exclusively to the requesting commander. These features make the survey an ideal tool for a commander who desires a self-assessment of his or her unit prior to proactive intervention to improve the productivity of the unit and quality of life for its members. Because the MEOCS is administered only at the commander's request, he or she has a sense of control and responsibility for the program. This may not be true of typical military assessment (inspection) programs, which are generally of the top-down variety. Confidentiality lessens fear of the misuse of information (for political manipulation and so on; see Zawachi & Warrick, 1976) that often accompanies data gathering in the public sector. Commanders are assured that they alone receive MEOCS results; they alone decide with whom the results are shared. Such control and "ownership" is critical to the success of the MEOCS as a tool for constructive change (Bowers & Franklin, 1975). The MEOCS is offered free of charge to all military commanders in the DoD and the U.S. Coast Guard. Potential clients therefore number in the thousands.

Operation of the program is simple and direct. Upon learning about the MEOCS, a commander sends a letter of request to the DEOMI. Three consultants within the Directorate of Liaison and External Training process the request and perform all subsequent actions. The consultants determine which version of the survey (based on service, gender composition, and other unit demographic factors) is appropriate and send the requesting commander a camera-ready copy, along with answer sheets and instructions on proper administration. A unit project officer reproduces the survey booklets, administers the survey according to DEOMI's guidelines, and returns the completed answer sheets. Answer sheets are scanned into a raw data file, which is subsequently analyzed using a commercial statistical analysis program. (The data are also added to a cumulative data base maintained at the DEOMI.) A series of computer programs developed by the second author collect and format output from the statistical program and automatically generate a feedback package, which is returned to the commander. The system is known as the Automated MEOCS Analysis System (AMAS) and allows a complete feedback package to be constructed (starting with the scored data) in about an hour.

After the results are returned to the unit, follow-up actions are the commander's responsibility and option. Most commands have equal opportunity program advisers who may be directed to establish an action plan. The DEOMI also provides consultation and training teams at the commander's request.[9]

With the general process in mind, we now address the six stages identified previously.

Contact

Initial contact with the commander is essential to the program's success. The MEOCS program must rely on advertisement and personal recommendations by satisfied "customers" to prompt initial contact. Unlike traditional OD programs, where interactions with the client are normally face-to-face after the initial contact (Schein, 1969), the MEOCS approach relies on correspondence and telephone communication. Because the commander's contact is voluntary, acceptance of the process and the likelihood of constructive action are enhanced. This supports the general OD philosophy of helping the client help him- or herself (Schein, 1969) using a collaborative approach (Harvey & Brown, 1988). It is difficult, however, to assess the level of commitment ("ownership"; Bowers & Franklin, 1975) by the commander without face-to-face contact. Perhaps the commander's involvement is due to pressure from those higher in the chain of command; if so, much energy may be wasted in attempts to discount the validity of the process or the results (Harvey & Brown, 1988). Constructive action as a result of the survey would be unlikely under these conditions.

The DEOMI attempts to ensure at least some level of commitment from the client by requiring that the unit commander request the survey rather than accepting requests from staff officers or others who may have an "ax to grind." Identifying the commander as the client also provides assurance that the client is powerful enough to influence others (E. Schein, 1969; V. Schein, 1985; Harvey & Brown, 1988). This assurance is particularly important where EO issues are involved (Sargent, 1985).

If the client does not provide the information in the letter requesting the MEOCS, the DEOMI obtains certain demographic and organizational information during the contact stage. For example, some units are too small to employ the MEOCS effectively; some combat units have no women in them and require a special version of the survey. In general, the DEOMI restricts the MEOCS to units of at least 200 persons. Instructions are given for sampling. For small units, the total populations is surveyed; for large units (e.g., more than 1,000), a 10% random sample (using the last digit of the social security number as a selector) is used. Once the preliminary contact is made, the DEOMI proceeds to the contracting stage.

Contract

Efforts during the contracting stage are focused on the psychological contract (Harvey & Brown, 1988): What are the mutual expectations of the commander and the DEOMI? It is imperative that the commander understand what the survey will and will not provide, what the unit's responsibilities are, how much time the process will take, and what the product (feedback) will be like. Though there is no charge for the survey, unit resources are required: the project officer's time, respondents' time, reproduction and administrative costs, costs associated with feeding back the results to unit members, resources used in follow-up activities, and so on. The DEOMI provides the commander with a detailed overview before the process begins.

Experience has revealed some common misunderstandings in the contracting stage. Some commanders believe that the MEOCS provides counts of EO incidents. (It measures perceptions—attitudes—of unit members.) Others believe they will be able to request special analysis of their data. This latter point needs some explication.

Though some unique analyses may be provided on a case-by-case basis, the large volume of surveys—more than 400 requests in the first 6 months of 1992—normally precludes special request processing. Instead, the standard feedback package includes analyses that were most commonly requested during the first 50 administrations of the MEOCS. These data include means of all factors, comparisons with the total MEOCS data base, and significance of differences between gender, racial, rank, and experience with discrimination groups. Commanders sometimes request analyses of specific items; in the initial stages of the program, these requests were often satisfied. That is no longer true, however. Commanders sometimes, also, add items to the survey and request that the DEOMI provide analysis. These requests are usually rejected because of the unknown psychometric properties of these "homegrown" items. The adding of these items is discouraged because of the possible impact on the other portions of the questionnaire.

Still other commanders believe the DEOMI will correct any problems identified in the survey. (This is a command responsibility.[10]) Whatever the misconceptions, they must be corrected early if the customer (commander) is to be satisfied with the product (MEOCS results).

Data Gathering

The unit project officer is responsible for data gathering and is critical to the success of the project. The DEOMI instructions to the project officer stress confidentiality (e.g., use of envelopes for survey return), timeliness, and administrative procedures. The DEOMI must depend on the unit project officer to properly administer the survey. Project officers are urged to contact the DEOMI by telephone if they have any questions or concerns.

The commander's support of the project facilitates cooperation and good response rates from the respondents. Each survey is accompanied by a letter from the commander (based on a DEOMI model) emphasizing the importance of the survey and soliciting the candid opinions and cooperation of respondents. Respondents are advised that taking the survey is voluntary and no adverse action will be taken against nonparticipants. The large volume of surveys processed does not permit analysis of individual comments; therefore they are not solicited.

Once the data are gathered, the response sheets are mailed to the DEOMI for analysis.

Data Analysis

Data analysis is automated and involves three steps. First, survey answer sheets are scanned into a data file. This raw data file is checked for obvious errors (e.g., data that were uninterpretable by the scanner due to stray marks on the scan sheet, responses outside the range of the survey). Where possible, these errors are corrected; otherwise, they are coded as missing data.

The second step is to analyze the data file using a standard statistical package. Reports are generated providing extensive descriptive statistics on the factor scores: numbers of valid responses, means, standard deviations, modes, percentages of respondents above and below the neutral points on the scales, minimums, and maximums. Counts, means, standard deviations, minimums, and maximums are also provided for each individual item. Frequency distributions with histograms are generated for demographic and selected other items, where appropriate. A number of relevant subgroups are compared: majority and minority members, men and women, officers and enlisted personnel, junior enlisted and senior enlisted, junior officers and senior officers, those who have experienced discrimination and those who haven't, and those who have filed a formal complaint versus those who haven't; t tests are conducted between all subgroups.

The third step is to create the data-based reports that become part of the feedback package. The output from the statistical package is processed using a computer program that was designed by the second author to remove extraneous material and produce tables suitable for return to the requesting commander. A second program produces an automated executive summary that contains introductory explanations, frequency reports on the number of respondents by subgroup, comparisons of the overall unit factor score means with the DEOMI data base means for all services and the appropriate service, and combined graphic (bar graphs) and numerical representations for the overall comparisons and major subgroup comparisons. Verbal anchors (e.g., for sexual harassment and discrimination, the verbal anchor might be as follows: "Your unit's score implies: Small chance of occurring") are used to describe the unit's overall results. Subgroup comparisons that are statistically significant are annotated "Statistically Reliable Difference." The DEOMI is currently conducting studies to establish service norms based on probability samples. These norms will be compared with the data base averages and will replace the data base averages in the statistical comparisons. Once the basic reports have been generated, the feedback package is assembled.

Feedback

The feedback package includes the executive summary containing a general description of the MEOCS factors and specific results for the unit, background and technical information on the survey, detailed statistical results, and recommended actions and resources. The executive summary is designed to give busy commanders an immediate grasp of the results without being weighed down by ancillary issues.

The feedback package is based on a "layering" approach. The executive summary contains key results in a simple, direct format. Most commanders will find all the information that they require in the executive summary. More detailed explanations of the philosophy and meaning of the survey and its factors are attached as tabs. Possible actions (where problems are indicated) and resources are also included as tabs. The detailed statistical tables are included for those who have an interest in this level of analysis. All EO advisers (EOAs), who most often help the commander interpret the results, are trained at the DEOMI in the interpretation of MEOCS feedback.

It is essential that the feedback be understandable, meaningful, and useful to the commander. Keeping it simple and layering the package enhances understanding. The data base subgroup comparisons make the information more meaningful and useful by pointing out possible areas for development. As Bowers and Franklin (1975) suggest, "Diagnostic data are most valuable when they are compared to a standard" (p. 71). The package recommends the commander pursue issues highlighted by the survey results in three ways. First, the results should be considered only one source of information; they should be validated through other approaches (interviews, team meetings, unit records, and so on). The trained EOA is likely to be assigned primary responsibility for follow-up. Second, the results should be briefed and discussed with the unit members. Feedback to those who provided the data has a number of beneficial results, such as assuring them that their views have been considered and garnering support for any follow-up activities. Third, actions should be planned to address validated problems. The EO usually spearheads the action planning, perhaps based on activities and resources recommended in the feedback package or employing a mobile training team from the DEOMI.

As Schein (1969) points out, the consultant's role is to help the organization help itself. Providing objective feedback from the survey is a tool toward that end, but the unit commander and his or her staff are clearly responsible for any further plans or actions.

Follow-Up

In a typical MEOCS administration, the commander will use the survey results and other data gathered in the unit to plan interventions designed to improve the EO and organizational climate. The DEOMI feedback package provides a model and suggestions for this activity. In some cases, the commander may take no action at all. This is within the commander's prerogative. To enhance acceptance and chances for constructive change, all follow-up activities should be viewed as unit initiated. Resistance to change is increased when the change is seen as "imposed" by some external agent; likewise, participation of unit members in the planning increases acceptance (Harvey & Brown, 1988).

The DEOMI recommends that the commander request another administration of the MEOCS about 6 to 8 months after the initial survey. The purpose is to assess the results of interventions and adjust the action plan appropriately.

Conclusions

This chapter has outlined a new approach to the measurement and use of EOC in the military organization. Our approach is based on the notion that EOC depends on anticipated, rather than real, actions. Those actions are behaviors that are applied differentially as a function of the recipient's race or gender. Traditional Likert-type scales measure, we believe, the respondent's affective reaction to either behavior or attitude statements. Such reaction may be, it is true, related to the level of anticipated behaviors, but there is not a compelling theoretical reason that they should be closely tied. The nomological net that sees EOC as one of potentially a very large set of climates allows investigations of the relationships among those aspects of the organization. For example, Landis, Faley, and Dansby (1992) have demonstrated that EOC variables account for 61% of the variance in commitment scores. Cross-validating this finding using the data from the normative sample will add significantly to our knowledge about the antecedents of commitment to an organization.

The measurement models used to develop the MEOCS have been, and are being, applied to other settings. SOD (Survey of Organizational Diversity) is used in an industrial situation while the UEOCS (University Equal Opportunity Climate Survey) can be applied in an higher education setting.[11] Other versions are under development.

From the standpoint of action research, unless an organizational survey provides timely, meaningful, and useful results to those who are responsible for organizational change, it will have little impact (positive or negative) on the organization. The DoD's MEOCS process is designed to provide such results. The effects of doing nothing may be tragic for the military and any other organization.

Notes

1. The RPI was, actually, a revised version of the Campbell and Schulman (1968) survey of racial attitudes in urban areas.

2. This study was interesting for another reason: It may have been the first to include Navy-based minorities other than African Americans. Thus the sample included whites, African Americans, Hispanics, and Filipinos as well as women.

3. This conclusion assumes that the underlying metric in the Likert format reflects the psychological anchoring in the EO climate domain. And, further, it assumes that any bias in the selection of the "zero" point is negligible between groups. As Boucher and Osgood (1969) demonstrated in a discussion of the "Pollyanna hypothesis," however, such an assumption is rarely justified. Their recommendation is that ratings of items be standardized within each group across all items, an approach used in a study of 31 language groups by Osgood and his colleagues (Osgood, May, & Miron, 1975). Osgood et al. (1975) describe the rationale as follows: "A composite score of 1.0 on one factor in one culture [may] not indicate exactly the same intensity as a score of 1.0 in another. This could be for . . . two reasons: (1) Human cultures may display generalized biases toward one or the other poles of common dimensions of qualifying; these are 'constant' errors. . . . To provide an alternative way of comparing cultures, we have standardized the composite scores. . . . This standardization has the effect of transforming the origin of the space for each culture to the centroid of its own concept points" (p. 245). This is an approach rarely taken in attitude research (including our own) because the assumption is that all groups within a larger culture have the same amount of bias. As we develop larger and larger data sets, such an approach might be well worth considering. In such a case, our conclusions might turn out to be overstated.

4. Both of these components are assumed to lead to a hostile work environment that is differentially applied on the basis of gender. Hence these behaviors fall under the prohibitions of Title VII of the 1964 Civil Rights Act.

5. The DEOMI is a training facility tasked to provide instruction in EO issues to EO advisers from all armed services and the Coast Guard. Prior to 1987, its research efforts were minimal and focused entirely on internal program evaluation. In 1987, however, the Defense Equal Opportunity Council specifically tasked the DEOMI to become a center for research into EO issues.

6. Strictly speaking, it is this part that reflects the unique part of the MEOCS and perhaps should use that name. Through usage, however, *MEOCS* has come to refer to the total questionnaire. Rather than fight a losing battle, we have adopted the common way of citing the instrument.

7. Actually, administration of the survey on a mandatory basis is not recommended by the DEOMI, on the basis that it violates the sense of ownership that a voluntary administration would engender. The information needed by the commandant can be achieved by doing a stratified random sample of the Corps as part of a normative study.

8. The goals of Hausser et al. (1977) have been applied to the equal opportunity setting by Neely and Luthans (1978). French (1985) traces the growth of the survey feedback approach, beginning with the seminal work of Rensis Likert at the Survey Research Center (founded in 1946) at the University of Michigan. French identifies survey research and feedback methodology as one of the three roots of systematic OD activities. A classic intervention model is outlined by Schein (1969) and involves seven steps: (a) initial contact with the client organization; (b) defining the relationship, formal contract, and psychological contract; (c) selecting a setting and a method of work; (d) data gathering and diagnosis; (e) intervention; (f) reducing involvement; and (f) termination (Schein, 1969, p. 78).

Other researchers and practitioners have developed similar models. For example, Lippitt and Lippitt (1978) discuss six phases: contact and entry, formulating a contract and establishing a helping relationship, problem identification and diagnostic analysis, goal setting and planning, taking action and cycling feedback, and contract completion (continuity, support, and termination). Nadler (1977) simplifies the process into five steps: planning to collect data, collecting data, analyzing data, feeding back data, and following up. A similar approach was used at the (no longer extant) Air Force Leadership and Management Development Center, where survey-guided intervention was a keystone in the Air Force's voluntary OD program. The Navy also relied heavily on survey feedback in their OD program (known as Human Resources Management), which was implemented across the Navy (Umstot, 1980).

9. The individual command is responsible for the costs (e.g., travel and housing). The DEOMI bears the personnel costs.

10. As indicated earlier, the DEOMI will provide consultation on possible strategies for ameliorating any problems identified by the MEOCS. The implementation of these recommendations, however, is totally a command responsibility.

11. For information on applications of the MEOCS model to nonmilitary settings, contact Dan Landis, D. K. Research and Consultation Group, Rt. 3, Box 60, Oxford, MS 38655.

References

Borus, J. F., Fiman, B., Stanton, M. D., & Dowd, A. F. (1973). The racial perceptions inventory. *Archives of General Psychiatry, 29,* 270-275.

Borus, J. F., Stanton, M. D., Fiman, B., & Dowd, A. (1972). *Racial perceptions in the Army: An approach. American Journal of Psychiatry, 128*(11), 1369-1374.

Boucher, J., & Osgood, C. E. (1969). The Pollyanna hypothesis. *Journal of Verbal Learning and Behavior, 8,* 1-8.

Bowers, D. G. (1975). *Navy manpower: Values, practices, and human resource requirements.* Ann Arbor: University of Michigan, Institute for Social Research.

Bowers, D. G., & Franklin, J. L. (1975). *Survey-guided development: Data-based organizational change.* Ann Arbor: University of Michigan, Institute for Social Research.

Brown, D. K., Nordlie, P. G., & Thomas, J. A. (1977). *Changes in black and white perceptions of the Army's race relations/equal opportunity programs: 1972-1974* (Technical report TR-77-B3). Alexandria, VA: U.S. Army Research Institute for the Behavioral and Social Sciences.

Campbell, A., & Schulman, H. (1968). Racial attitudes in fifteen American cities. In *Supplemental Studies for the National Advisory Commission on Civil Disorders.* Washington, DC: Government Printing Office.

Dansby, M. R., & Landis, D. (1991). Measuring equal opportunity in the military environment. *International Journal of Intercultural Relations, 15,* 399-406.

Day, H. D. (1983). Race relations training in the military. In D. Landis & R. Brislin (Eds.), *Handbook of intercultural training* (Vol. 2, pp. 241-289). Elmsford, NY: Pergamon.

Faley, R. H. (1982). Sexual harassment: Critical review of legal cases with general principles and preventive strategies. *Personnel Psychology, 35,* 583-600.

Fisher, G. (1988). *Equal opportunity climate: Development and initial validation of an assessment instrument.* Unpublished doctoral dissertation, Department of Psychology, University of Mississippi.

French, W. L. (1985). The emergence and early history of organization development with references to influences upon and interactions among some of the key actors. In D. D. Warrick (Ed.), *Contemporary organization development.* Glenview, IL: Scott, Foresman.

Furnco Construction Corp v. Waters, 17 FEP Cases 1062 (1978).

Glick, W. H. (1985). Conceptualizing and measuring organizational and psychological climate: Pitfalls in multilevel research. *Academy of Management Review, 10*(3), 601-616.

Guion, R. M. (1973). A note on organizational climate. *Organizational Behavior and Human Performance, 9,* 120-125.

Harvey, D. F., & Brown, D. R. (1988). *An experiential approach to organization development.* Englewood Cliffs, NJ: Prentice-Hall.

Hausser, D. L., Pecorella, P. A., & Wissler, A. L. (1977). *Survey-guided development II: A manual for consultants.* La Jolla, CA: University Associates.

Hellreigel, D., & Slocum, J., Jr. (1974). Organizational climate: Measures, research and contingencies. *Academy of Management Journal, 17,* 255-280.

Hiett, R., McBride, R., & Fiman, B. (1974). *Measuring the impact of race relations programs in the military* (Technical Paper HSR-RR-74/5-TR). Alexandria, VA: U.S. Army Institute for the Behavioral and Social Sciences.

Hiett, R., McBride, R., Fiman, B., Thomas, J., O'Mara, F., & Sevilla, E. (1978a). *The racial attitudes and perceptions survey (RAPS)* (ARI Technical Paper 338 AD A 064 263). Alexandria, VA: U.S. Army Research Institute for the Behavioral and Social Sciences.

Hiett, R., McBride, R., Fiman, B., Thomas, J., O'Mara, F., & Sevilla, E. (1978b). *The utility of the Racial Attitudes and Perceptions Survey (RAPS) for assessing the impact of race relations training in the military* (ARI Technical Paper 339 AD A062 246). Alexandria, VA: U.S. Army Research Institute for the Behavioral and Social Sciences.

Hiett, R. L., & Nordlie, P. G. (1978). *An analysis of the unit race relations training program in the U.S. Army.* Alexandria, VA: U.S. Army Research Institute.

James, L. R., & Jones, A. P. (1974). Organizational climate: A review of theory and practice. *Psychological Bulletin, 81,* 1096-1112.

Landis, D. (January, 1990). *Military Equal Opportunity Climate Survey: Reliability, construct validity and preliminary field test.* Oxford: University of Mississippi, Center for Applied Research and Evaluation.

Landis, D., Faley, R., & Dansby, M. (1992). *The effect of equal opportunity climate on commitment to a career in the service: A latent variables analysis.* Patrick Air Force Base, FL: Directorate of Research, Defense Equal Opportunity Management Institute.

Landis, D., & Fisher, G. (1987). *Construction and preliminary validation of an instrument to measure equal opportunity climate* (Contract No. F49620-85-C-0013). Patrick AFB, FL: Air Force Office of Scientific Research.

Landis, D., Fisher, G., & Dansby, M. R. (1988a, May). *Equal opportunity climate development and measurement of a concept* (Charles M. Solley, Jr., Festschrift). Paper presented at the Department of Psychology, Wayne State University, Detroit.

Landis, D., Fisher, G., & Dansby, M. R. (1988b, April). Construction and preliminary validation of an equal opportunity climate assessment instrument. In *Proceedings of Psychology in the DoD Symposium* (Technical report 88-1). Colorado Springs: U.S. Air Force Academy.

Landis, D., Hope, R. A., & Day, H. R. (1984). Training for desegregation in the military. In N. Miller & M. Brewer (Eds.), *Groups in contact: The psychology of desegregation.* New York: Academic Press.

Laurent, A. (1987, June 8). Hostile environment gives twist to sex bias case. *Navy Times.*

Lewin, K. (1946). Action research and minority problems. *Journal of Social Issues, 4,* 34-46.

Lewin, K., Lippitt, L., & White, R. K. (1939). Patterns of aggressive behavior in experimentally created social climates. *Journal of Social Psychology, 10,* 271-299.

Lippitt, G., & Lippitt, R. (1978). *The consulting process in action.* San Diego, CA: University Associates.

Lippitt, R. (1940). *An analysis of group reactions to three types of experimentally created social climates.* Unpublished doctoral thesis, University of Iowa, Iowa City.

Lippitt, R., & White, R. (1947). An experimental study of leadership and group life. In T. Newcomb & E. Hartley (Eds.), *Readings in social psychology.* New York: Holt.

Nadler, D. A. (1977). *Feedback and organization development: Using data-based methods.* Reading, MA: Addison-Wesley.

Neely, G., & Luthans, F. (1978). Using survey feedback to achieve enlightened AA/EO. *Personnel, 55*(3), 18-23.

Nordlie, P. G. (1977). *Measuring changes in institutional racial discrimination in the Army.* McLean, VA: Human Sciences Research, Inc.

Nordlie, P. G., & Thomas, J. A. (1974). *Black and white perceptions of the Army's equal opportunity and treatment programs* (ARI Technical Paper 252). Alexandria, VA: U.S. Army Research Institute for the Behavioral and Social Sciences.

O'Mara, F. (1977). *A longitudinal study of racial climate in an infantry division* (Research memorandum 77-24). Alexandria, VA: U.S. Army Research Institute for the Behavioral and Social Sciences.

O'Mara, F., & Tierney, W. (1978). *RAPS-2: An abridged version of the Racial Attitudes and Perceptions Survey* (ARI technical paper 340). Alexandria, VA: U.S. Army Institute for the Behavioral and Social Sciences.

Osgood, C. E., May, W., & Miron, M. (1975). *Cross-cultural universals of affective meaning.* Urbana: University of Illinois Press.

Parham v. Southwestern Bell Telephone Co., 2 FEP Cases 1017 (1970).

Parker, W. S. (1974). *Differences in organizational practice and preferences in the Navy by race.* Ann Arbor: University of Michigan, Institute for Social Research.

Pecorella, P. A. (1975). *Predictors of race discrimination in the Navy.* Ann Arbor: University of Michigan, Institute for Social Research.

Rosenfeld, P., Culbertson, A. L., Booth-Kewley, S., & Magnusson, P. (1992). *Assessment of equal opportunity climate: Results of the 1989 Navy-wide survey* (Technical report TR-92-14). San Diego, CA: Navy Personnel Research and Development Center.

Rosenfeld, P., Thomas, M. D., Edwards, J. E., Thomas, P. J., & Thomas, E. D. (1991). Navy research into race, ethnicity, and gender issues: A historical review. *International Journal of Intercultural Relations, 15,* 407-426.

Sargent, A. G. (1985). Affirmative action: A guide to systems change for managers. In D. D. Warrick (Ed.), *Contemporary organization development.* Glenview, IL: Scott, Foresman.

Schein, E. H. (1969). *Process consultation: Its role in organization development.* Reading, MA: Addison-Wesley.

Schein, V. E. (1985). Organizational realities: The politics of change. In D. D. Warrick (Ed.), *Contemporary organization development.* Glenview, IL: Scott, Foresman.

Schneider, B. (1975). Organizational climates: An essay. *Personnel Psychology, 28,* 447-479.

Short, L. O. (1985). *The United States Air Force Organizational Assessment Package.* Maxwell Air Force Base, AL: Leadership and Management Development Center, Air University.

Soldiers Report IV. (1986). Washington, DC: Department of the Army, Directorate of Human Resource Development.

Spicher, C. R. (1980). *Equal opportunity and treatment: Perceptions of United States Air Force military men and women.* Maxwell Air Force Base, AL: Air Command and Staff College.

Stoloff, P. H. (1972). *Use of Navy Human Relations Questionnaire with U.S. Army personnel* (CNA memorandum 1879-2). Baltimore, MD: Institute of Naval Studies: Center for Naval Analysis.

Thomas, J. A. (1988, September). *Race relations research in the U.S. Army in the 1970's.* Washington, DC: U.S. Army Research Institute for the Behavioral and Social Sciences.

Thomas, P. J., & Conway, S. (1983, January). *Racial/ethnic and gender differences in responses to the human resource management survey of personnel assigned to the Atlantic and Pacific fleets* (NPRDC spec. report 83-10). San Diego, CA: Navy Personnel Research and Development Center.

Triandis, H. C. (1976). *Interpersonal behavior.* Urbana: University of Illinois Press.

Umstot, D. D. (1980). Organization development technology in the military: A surprising merger? *Academy of Management Review, 5*(2), 189-201.

Wards Cove Packing Company, Inc., et al., v. Frank Antonio et al. 490 U.S. —, 104 L. Ed. 2d 733, 109 S.Ct. — (No. 87-1387; 1989).

Woodman, R. W., & King, D. C. (1978). Organizational climate: Science or folklore? *Academy of Management Review, 3,* 816-826.

Zawachi, R. A., & Warrick, D. D. (1976). *Organizational development: Managing change in the public sector.* Chicago: International Personnel Management Association.

Zohar, D. (1980). Safety climate in industrial organizations: Theoretical and applied implications. *Journal of applied Psychology, 64,* 96-102.

11

Identifying Security Risks in Organizations

Development and Use of a Security Exit Survey Instrument

ROBERT A. GIACALONE
STEPHEN B. KNOUSE

An exit survey is a questionnaire, interview, or discussion conducted during one of the last working days between a representative of an organization and a person whose employment with that organization has ended. As a management tool, an exit survey can play a major role in reducing an organization's voluntary turnover rate and uncovering problems that may be unrelated to turnover (Garretson & Teel, 1982).

Although personnel departments have traditionally used the exit interview as a tool to reduce costly employee turnover, exit interviews can be an effective means of gathering general data about employees' impressions and experiences with the organization. Exit surveys are also good public relations tools (Lefkowitz & Katz, 1969). The traditional topics covered during exit interviews are varied and may include the reason for departure; ratings of the job, supervision, working conditions, advancement opportunities, training, and pay; and things the employee liked best (and least) about the job.

Empirical Research on Exit Interviews and Exit Questionnaires

There has been relatively little empirical research on the psychometric properties of exit interviews and questionnaires. Lefkowitz and Katz (1969) compared exit interview data with a follow-up questionnaire for voluntary resignees of a garment factory. They found no significant correlations between the reasons given for termination between the two instruments. Indeed, they found that 59% of the subjects reported different reasons for terminations on the two instruments. They concluded that the exit interview was hampered by low reliability due to the attitude of voluntary resignees, the training of the interviewer, and the subjectivity of the instrument.

Hinrichs (1975) compared exit interviews conducted by company management, follow-up questionnaires, and exit interviews conducted by independent consultants of voluntary resignees from a large manufacturing company. For a 3-year period, he found that data obtained from exit interviews conducted by management did not correlate significantly with the questionnaires for eight reasons for termination (advancement, pay, freedom of action, job location, nature of work, working conditions, personal reasons, and resume education). When comparing the exit interviews conducted by management with those conducted by the consultant, Hinrichs found that 44% of the interviewees gave very different reasons for leaving on the two instruments. Further, he found significantly more negative comments in the consultant interviews compared with the management interviews.

Zarandona and Camuso (1985) compared exit interviews given at the time of separation with an independent telephone survey taken 18 months later. They found that the stated reason for separation had changed over the 18-month period. For example, salary and benefits were cited significantly less as the reason for leaving on the second survey, while supervision was cited significantly more frequently. Zarandona and Camuso concluded that, because respondents had no reason to be untruthful on the second survey, respondents must have distorted their answers in the original exit interview at the time of separation.

Information Distortion in the Exit Interview

These three studies show evidence of information distortion, particularly in an exit interview conducted by management at the time of separation. Hinrichs (1975) suggested that exiting employees did not want to discuss uncomfortable material because they might want a letter of recommendation from management later. In addition, the management interviewer lacked training in interviewing and was probably personally involved in reasons surrounding the employees' decision to leave. This may have resulted in defensiveness and selective perception in what the employee was saying.

Other researchers have identified additional reasons for information distortion. The exiting employee may fear retribution from the management interviewer (Jablonsky, 1975) or fear that negative information from the manager may reach the new employer (Zarandona & Camuso, 1985). Moreover, the exiting employee may perceive the interview as too personal (Drost, O'Brien, & Marsh, 1987) or believe that the managers conducting the exit interview do not care (Jablonsky, 1975) or believe that the interviewee has nothing to gain from the process— that is, the interview process is not worth the effort (Garretson & Teel, 1982). Further, the interviewee may believe that the management interviewer may exact retribution on remaining fellow employees based on information from the interview (Giacalone, Knouse, & Ashworth, 1991).

Consequently, several researchers have recommended a *standardized exit survey* over the more problematic exit interview (Hilb, 1978; Hinrichs, 1975; Lefkowitz & Katz, 1969). For example, within the Department of Defense (DoD), standardized exit surveys have been used extensively (see Giacalone & Rosenfeld, 1990; Martindale, 1988). The application of exit surveys within the DoD has, however, been the same as one would expect to find within the traditional human resources department of any organization. This application stresses the use of an exit survey to determine the reasons for personnel turnover and as a tool for gathering information for policy change and organizational development (see Giacalone & Rosenfeld, 1990, for an example). To date, however, the exit survey has not been systematically applied to security issues.

The Exit Survey and Security

Prevention of security problems, financial or otherwise, is a complicated process that requires the same rigor that one might use in trying to solve other behavioral problems. Suspicion of potential criminal behavior, however, often leads officials to try to remedy such problems by quickly planning, developing, and implementing crime prevention programs. Experts (Frisbie, 1982; Littlejohn, 1988) have noted that these steps are, in fact, the latter phases of crime prevention. The first phase, *crime analysis,* should precede all plans and implementation until data gathering provides an overall assessment of risk.

An exit interview is an excellent method for gathering data to provide an overall assessment of crime risk (see Lapides, 1979). By skillful use of pointed questions, the exit interview can provide insight into the respondents' knowledge of crime frequency as well as the places where such crimes occurred. More important, such information can provide useful information for security auditors. The auditors can then determine how and when the crime occurred and, ultimately, who committed the crime. Essentially, information gleaned through the exit interview can supply most of the data that crime experts wish to have (see Frisbie, 1982; Hemphill, 1976; Hollinger & Clark, 1983; Lapides, 1979; Taylor, 1986).[1]

We propose that organizations would do well to produce a prototype security exit survey instrument (SESI) that would be used in much the same way as would traditional exit surveys. The creation of such an SESI would require testing the effectiveness of that instrument and determining the extent to which the instrument is subject to response distortion. It is understood that no single SESI would be applicable to all units, plants, divisions, or departments within an organization. Thus the process that we will describe is intended to be a prototype SESI. The general procedures for developing and testing other SESIs would be tailored to the needs of specific plants, subunits, departments, or divisions of an organization.

Implications of Using SESIs

The implications for using SESIs in organizations are numerous. First, an SESI would provide significant information regarding prevalence of crimes and security breaches as well as locations and procedures that make an organization susceptible to such problems. This information allows organizational planning to focus more specifically on troublesome areas that the security exit survey has identified.

On a more basic level, the use of an SESI signals an overt interest in security matters to staff. Such signals will both make security issues more salient in the future (and thus provide more and better data) and alert potential violators to the organization's commitment to the apprehension of such offenders.

Finally, an SESI may serve as the initial step in developing an information system that allows the organization to monitor trends and major changes over time. Much as the monitoring of exit data in nonsecurity matters fosters a focus on shifting employee concerns, auditing security exit survey data over time can provide insight into the changing patterns of security problems and changing susceptibility to security violations. The monitoring of such changing trends will, in and of itself, provide indications of those locations, procedures, and events that security must scrutinize more closely in the future.

Creating an SESI

The creation of an SESI should be done in five phases. In the first phase, primary information/category gathering takes place. In the second phase, structured interviews and nominal group exercises should provide the categories that will later be used in the actual SESI. In the third phase, the SESI is constructed. In the fourth phase, the SESI is tested for both effectiveness (in terms of useful information) and response distortion. Finally, in the last phase, the SESI is implemented.

Phase 1: Category/Information Gathering

Individuals who will create an SESI should begin by familiarizing themselves with the literature on organization-related instances of security breaches. While this review may encompass research in business, public administration, military science, or psychological literature that focuses on security breaches, these individuals must decide what *facet* of security they are interested in. Individuals creating security exit surveys that focus on theft should seek out literature in that area, while those focusing on industrial espionage might find literature on that area. It must be stressed that the goal of this first phase is to identify issues that deal with the relevant organizational security concerns rather than acquiring a more general overview of the security area.

Phase 2: Interviews and the
Nominal Group Techniques (NGT)

The first phase should be followed by structured, open-ended interviews that are based on information gathered in the first phase. These interviews will focus on what crimes or potential crimes have occurred or might occur in the organization as well as what locations and/or procedures make the organization susceptible to security risks. If possible, interviews should be conducted on an individual basis to minimize social pressure and maximize interview input. To minimize any evaluation apprehension, interviewees should be informed that their responses will be confidential and that these responses will be pooled rather than considered individually.

To support and further elaborate on the interviews and information derived from the first phase, large groups of personnel should be asked to engage in a modified Nominal Group Technique (NGT) exercise. NGT is an information-gathering and decision-making process that tries to maximize the handling-information advantages to be derived from both individual and group interviews. To enhance creativity during the *idea generation step,* individuals work ideas alone and thereby avoid the pressure of the group. This step is followed by the *idea-evaluation phase* during which groups discuss generated ideas (Gustafson, Shulka, Delbecq, & Walster, 1973; Van de Ven & Delbecq, 1974).

For example, individuals could be asked individually to silently write down a list of known or potential financial crimes that they have seen or heard of in their organization. In addition, these individuals would be asked to describe potential locations or procedures that make the organization susceptible to security problems. All individuals would then take turns presenting the ideas that they have written. These ideas are summarized by the NGT leader on flip charts (as they are presented by the individual participants) as discrete statements of crime types, locations, and procedures. To avoid intimidation of participants, the discussion should only focus on clarifying the exact meaning of the issues raised rather than evaluating their merit or veracity. Finally, using a Likert scale, participants should be asked to vote for those issues that they think are most likely security issues. In those cases where the sensitivity of the issues is high, it is likely that no one will want to discuss what they know. In this case, the open discussion of issues may have to be eliminated, and the information written down should be collected anonymously.

Phase 3: Construction of an SESI

In Phase 3, the information from the Phase 2 interviews and NGTs must be carefully reviewed and content analyzed. A list of known or possible crime problems and the potential locations or procedures that

Table 11.1 Sample Stealing Survey: Circumstances

Based on your experience in this organization, rate the extent to which each of the following procedures, actions, or events make it easy to steal. Use the scale below.

a. Make it very easy
b. Make it easy
c. Do not affect it
d. Make it difficult
e. Make it very difficult

1. Fire drills
2. Bomb drills
3. Failure to make people sign for equipment
4. Lack of shop inventories
5. Disinterest by security personnel
6. Easy after-hours access
7. Lack of a security badge system
8. Unsecured equipment
9. Lack of personnel or supervision
10. Lack of accountability
11. No random bag checks
12. Multiple points of entry
13. Inadequate storage facilities
14. Letting people from different divisions' shops use each other's equipment
15. Improper watch standards
16. Unsecured exits
17. No alarms on doors
18. Unattended areas
19. Easy key access

---

make the organization susceptible to security risks (from the second phase) should be developed from this review and content analysis. That list, with appended Likert-type rating scales, would then be transformed into an SESI. The portion of the SESI that pertains to suspect locations and procedures should ask respondents to rate how easy it would be to engage in various types of security breaches. Tables 11.1-11.3 show an example of what such a survey might look like.

The survey should then be pretested on members of the personnel, a representative group of regular employees, and staff from the security department. The pretest of the SESI would be concerned with item clarity, redundancy, sensitivity, and information accuracy. Although this pretest need not be complicated, it must assure that these issues are addressed.

Table 11.2 Sample Stealing Survey: Items

Based on your experience with this organization, how easy would it be to steal each of the following items? Use the scale below.

        a. Very difficult
        b. Difficult
        c. Unsure
        d. Easy
        e. Very easy

1. Repair parts
2. Test equipment
3. Vending machine money
4. Food
5. Metals/wire
6. Software
7. Office supplies
8. Computers
9. Small parts on the production line
10. Printers
11. Paper towels, cleaning supplies
12. Personal property
13. Power tools
14. Hand tools
15. Cables
16. Machine accessories
17. Optical instruments
18. Video equipment (VCR/TV)
19. Audio equipment
20. Telephones
21. Publications and tech manuals
22. Paints

Item clarity can be tested by administering the SESI to a pilot group of respondents and then asking them to mark those questions that are unclear in meaning. These respondents should then be probed for the reasons the items were unclear, and adjustments should be made to address the concerns raised. At the same time, respondents should be asked to mark those items that appear to ask to same question. Careful attention should be given to eliminating those questions in which there is obvious agreement among respondents as to *item redundancy*.

Item sensitivity should be measured by giving the pilot group a second SESI whose questions do not require them to address security

Table 11.3 Sample Stealing Survey: Locations

Based on your experience in this organizations, how easy would it be to steal from each of the following places/locations? Use the scale below.

a. Very difficult
b. Difficult
c. Unsure
d. Easy
e. Very easy

  1. Parking lots
  2. Locker rooms
  3. Metals shop
  5. Wood shop
  6. Loading docks
  7. Transportation office
  8. Welding division
  9. Electric shop
 10. Sheet metal shop
 11. External storage areas
 12. Rewind shop
 13. Executive offices
 14. Electronics shop
 15. Supply receiving
 16. Mail room
 17. Machine shop

---

issues but to explore the extent to which responses to each of the items in the SESI might make them look bad. Essentially, the potential for social desirability response bias should be tested.

Finally, *information accuracy* should be tested by showing the SESI to an individual (or group) who is (are) knowledgeable in the location in which the SESI would be administered. These individuals could identify those items in the SESI that do not accurately describe the environment within which the SESI will be administered. Such items could be rephrased or eliminated.

Phase 4: Test Phase

In the fourth phase, a test of the new SESI should be undertaken. A random sample of employees would be surveyed with the SESI. In this phase, a simple trial of the instrument is not the only goal. The SESI needs to be tested for reliability, response distortion, and variation in the format of the instrument.

Measures of Reliability

Although reliability measures are the crucial first step for evaluating the effectiveness of any measurement instrument, reliability measures for exit interviews are rarely reported (Hinrichs, 1975). Because reliability is a multidimensional concept, it is recommended that multiple measures be used (Campbell, 1976). Reliability of the security dimensions in the instrument can be assessed with procedures such as Cronbach's coefficient alpha. In addition, consistency of the instrument over time can be assessed by test-retest reliability.

Response Distortion

Response distortion is a major problem affecting the validity of the exit interview. We propose a number of checks on response distortion, including an impression management test, tests for social desirability, comparisons of exiting employees with nonexiting employees, and comparisons of a separate SESI with an SESI embedded in a nonsecurity exit survey.

Response distortion: Impression management test. The problem of response distortion is based on a respondent's attempt to create a good impression in the eyes of the survey administrator or the organization. Such attempts are collectively known as *impression management*—an attempt by an individual to control images others have of him or her (see Giacalone, 1985; Goffman, 1959; Schlenker, 1980). Impression management is particularly prevalent in social situations where status differences are present (see Schlenker, 1980). For example, an individual's relationship with his or her supervisor can influence the departing employee's willingness to discuss issues in the exit interview (Knouse & Giacalone, 1992). Based on this perspective, we advocate administration of the survey in a way that would reduce or eliminate the respondent's desire to appear in any particular socially desirable way.

One specific issue is anonymity in responding. Individuals tend to believe that impression management techniques are less effective when their identity is not known to their audience. Consequently, impression managers are less likely to distort responses when their input into surveys is anonymous (see Giacalone & Rosenfeld, 1986, 1989; Schlenker, 1980). To test for impression management effects, respondents can be given either the SESI, which requests the standard identification of name, social security number, and other personnel data (a condition conducive to impression management), or a variation of the SESI on which they would not place identifying information on the survey (a condition not conducive to impression management). A comparison of the two conditions would show whether the SESI is susceptible to impression management concerns.

While such a test of impression management may appear academic in nature, it has significant practical implications. If, after testing for impression management, it is shown that respondents provide more favorable responses when identified, future surveys must be given under anonymous conditions to mitigate bias. If no such effect is shown, however, practitioners should consider administering an identified survey so that responses may be tied to the individual and can therefore be used to determine trends. For example, identification of the respondent can help in the creation of a data base in which the organization can monitor and compare the responses given by exiting personnel in all departments. Similarly, identification of the respondent allows for comparison of responses by job, length of stay, geographic location, and so on. Such comparisons may provide further insight into critical security problems. Of course, in all instances, the practitioner should ensure that the responses are confidential.

Response distortion test: Social desirability. Another perspective focuses on individual tendencies to respond in socially desirable ways. Respondents who are high in the *need for social desirability* (see Crowne & Marlowe, 1964) will distort their responses in line with what they perceive to be the most socially appropriate responses in a given situation. Respondents who are high in *fear of negative evaluation* (Watson & Friend, 1969) distort their responses because of a generalized fear that others will see them in a negative light. Based on this perspective, researchers would advocate administration of the SESI along with these personality scales to a pretest group prior to implementing the actual (official) administration of the SESI. Such a pretest could provide indications as to whether all or part of the SESI is subject to personality-related response distortions.

The administration of an SESI along with a pretest administration of either concern for negative evaluation (Watson & Friend, 1969) or social desirability measures (e.g., Crowne & Marlowe, 1964) provides a rigorous measure of such social desirability response biases. Here, too, it may be important to determine whether information regarding particular types of offenses and/or suspected nonsecure locations and procedures are distorted by a respondent's level of these traits. The accuracy of responses to those issues that are highly correlated with these social desirability measures would be questionable.

Comparing Exiting Versus Nonexiting Personnel

A fundamental premise underlying SESIs is that an exiting employee is more likely to provide information regarding organizational problems than nonexiting employees (see Drost et al., 1987; Giacalone & Duhon, 1991). At the time of exiting, an employee is less intimidated by the potential repercussions of the information provided.

To ascertain whether an SESI is, in fact, an effective way of gathering information regarding sensitive security issues, a separate group of personnel *who are not exiting the organization* should be given the same exit survey. The nonexiting group's responses will provide comparison information regarding whether an SESI given during the exiting process provides better information regarding wrongdoing. If the SESI is effective, exiting personnel could provide more quality information than those who are not exiting. This conclusion depends, however, on two assumptions. The first assumption is that poor communication channels exist within the organization. Such poor communication would lessen the chances that nonexiting employees would reveal sensitive information. Second, there must be enough exiting personnel to provide statistical power to make the results useful.

Comparing a Distinct SESI With an Embedded SESI

The literature on general exit surveying has long been concerned with the potential problem of distorted responding (Giacalone & Rosenfeld, 1990; Hinrichs, 1975), especially when an exit survey focuses on a sensitive issue. While research shows that such distortion is probably not premeditated (Giacalone & Duhon, 1991), it may be that the salience of the issue evokes an automatic self-presentational or impression management response (Schlenker, 1980).

To see whether more information can be obtained from respondents, one group of exiting employees should be given the SESI, a survey whose purpose is clearly salient. Another group should be given the *same* survey embedded in a more generic exit survey such as those used by the military (see Giacalone & Rosenfeld, 1990). A comparison of the responses from the two groups could steer future efforts in the direction of a discrete SESI or one that is already part of the exit process.

Because the comparison of exiting and nonexiting employees may appear to be an expensive process that is economically unfeasible, the practical implications must be considered. A comparison of exiting and nonexiting personnel need be performed only when the survey is first created and then on successive revisions of the survey. If differences exist, this comparison provides justification for giving the survey to exiting personnel at the time of separation. Thus what appears to be a long-term expense is rather manageable if done so infrequently. If no differences are found between exiting and nonexiting personnel, the exit survey can become a "security survey" and therefore be given at any time. Hence the process of comparing exiting and nonexiting personnel offers the organization one form of verification that the process does indeed yield different results.

Phase 5: Implementation

Format of the SESI. Analysis of Phase 4 test data will determine several characteristics of the final SESI: to what degree confidentiality of respondent data is needed, whether any personality data need to be collected in conjunction with the SESI, and whether the SESI should be a separate instrument or embedded in established exit interview procedures. In addition, a baseline for comparing exiting with nonexiting personnel is available. Obviously, the extent to which organizations collect expensive and time-consuming corollary data, such as personality measures and data on nonexiting personnel, will depend on the security needs and resources of the organization.

Exit Interviews, Follow-Ups, and Longitudinal Data Collection

The Exit Interview

Some organizations may choose to use an interview format rather than a questionnaire format to conduct security exit surveys. The SESI administrator would need to be aware that the exit interview literature is divided about who is best for conducting an exit interview (Giacalone et al., 1991: Hinrichs, 1971, 1975; Zarandona & Camuso, 1985). Internal organizational members would have more knowledge of the organization, but they might be constrained by political ties or commitment to the organization. Also, exit interviews by internal members might elicit more impression management and social desirability responding because external interviewers (i.e., expert consultants) may be more objective and knowledgeable about a variety of security problems. Because they are outsiders without internal ties, however, they may not understand nuances of organizational operations.

The choice of internal or external interviewers will depend on several factors, such as the nature, complexity, and severity of security problems. Internal interviewers may be more appropriate for more routine, less complex, less severe problems. External interviewers may be better for unique, complex, severe problems.

Follow-Up

It is important to obtain the forwarding addresses of exiting persons to conduct follow-up surveys, if necessary. When the persons have become physically separated from the organization for a period of time, they have the opportunity to reflect back on their views (Giacalone et al., 1991). Such viewpoints may provide an addendum to the data they provided at the time of separation. In addition, these data may be used to evaluate instrument reliability and response distortion.

Longitudinal Data Collection

Because longitudinal data are important in any personnel activity, it is necessary to retain SESI data and personnel records of exiting persons along with organizational crime data for several years. These data will provide both longitudinal trends in security problems and explanatory variables for anomalies in these trends. Special programs, such as Martindale Software's EXITQ, can manage the compiling and analysis of these data (Martindale, 1988).

Created by the U.S. Army Yuma Proving Ground, EXITQ is a commercially available computer-administered questionnaire that runs on IBM compatible personal computers. The user can create a customized exit questionnaire from a list of 200 master questions including branching questions (the answer to one question leads to other questions being presented). In addition, the user can alter questions with a built-in word processor. The exiting employee is led through the questions by the program and can change answers as he or she proceeds. The employee's responses can be merged with both a parallel computer questionnaire completed by the employee's supervisor and the organization's personnel data base on the employee. The program can also produce analysis reports on questionnaire answers broken down by demographic variables, such as gender, age, race, marital status, pay, and length of employment, and can analyze response categories by separations within specified periods of time.

Among the major advantages of EXITQ are the overall positive reaction of exiting employees who have used it as well as greater consistency in their perceptions about the organization (Martindale, 1988; Meyer, 1991).

Conclusions and Practical Implications

The extensive steps in gathering information, interviewing, survey construction, testing, and administration are designed to enhance reliability and validity in the SESI. At the same time, these steps are expensive and time consuming. One could argue that poor security measures result in high costs and require extensive time for corrective actions. Thus the large savings from an effective security instrument, such as the SESI, should justify its high cost.

Realistically, however, many organizations, particularly smaller firms, do not have the extensive financial and human resources to construct and implement the SESI. Moreover, they do not have the relatively large number of continuously exiting employees needed to provide the data base for constructing the SESI. Therefore the SESI may be more appropriate for large organizations. Considering the huge numbers of exiting employees projected for several large U.S. corporations, such as the 74,000 layoffs projected for General Motors in the next 5 years ("The Board Revolt," 1992), and considering the extensive downsizing of certain federal government organizations, including the U.S. military, large organizations may be in a unique position to justify the SESI. They may have a sufficient number of exiting employees and resources gained through restructuring to implement the SESI to improve the working environment of the organization's remaining employees.

Note

1. In actuality, the properly structured and developed exit survey can provide *all* of this information, although this would require the creation of a *computerized system,* developed for a broader range of organizations, and over a much longer period of time.

References

The board revolt. (April 22, 1992). *Business Week, 3262,* 31-33.

Campbell, J. P. (1976). Psychometric theory. In M. D. Dunnette (Ed.), *Handbook of industrial and organizational psychology* (pp. 185-222). Chicago: Rand McNally.

Crowne, D. P., & Marlowe, D. (1964). *The approval motive: Studies in evaluative dependence.* New York: John Wiley.

Drost, D. A., O'Brien, F. P., & Marsh, S. (1987, February). Exit interviews: Master the possibilities. *Personnel Administrator, 32*(2), 104-110.

Frisbie, D. (1982). Crime analysis in crime prevention planning. In L. J. Fennelly (Ed.), *Handbook of loss prevention and crime prevention* (pp. 110-116). Boston: Butterworths.

Garretson, P., & Teel, K. S. (1982). The exit interview: Effective tool or meaningless gesture? *Personnel, 4,* 70-77.

Giacalone, R. A. (1985). On slipping when you thought you had put your best foot forward: Self-promotion, self-destruction, and entitlements. *Group and Organizational Studies, 10,* 61-80.

Giacalone, R. A., & Duhon, D. (1991). Assessing intended employee behavior in exit interviews. *Journal of Psychology: Applied and Interdisciplinary, 125,* 83-90.

Giacalone, R. A., Knouse, S. B., & Ashworth, D. N. (1991). Impression management and exit interview distortion. In R. A. Giacalone & P. Rosenfeld (Eds.), *Applied impression management: How image-making affects managerial decisions* (pp. 97-110). Newbury Park, CA: Sage.

Giacalone, R. A., & Rosenfeld, P. (1986). Self-presentation and self-promotion in an organizational setting. *Journal of Social Psychology, 126,* 321-326.

Giacalone, R. A., & Rosenfeld, P. (1989). *Impression management in the organization.* Hillsdale, NJ: Lawrence Erlbaum.

Giacalone, R. A., & Rosenfeld, P. (1990). *Family separation and petty regulations as dissatisfiers on the Navy separation questionnaires* (NPRDC TN-90-13). San Diego, CA: Navy Personnel Research and Development Center.

Goffman, E. (1959). *The presentation of self in everyday life.* Garden City, NY: Doubleday.

Gustafson, D. H., Shulka, R. K., Delbecq, A., & Walster, W. G. (1973). A comparative study of differences in subjective likelihood estimates made by individuals, interacting groups, Delphi groups, and nominal groups. *Organizational Behavior and Human Performance, 9,* 280-291.

Hemphill, C. F., Jr. (1976). *Management's role in loss prevention.* New York: AMACOM.

Hilb, M. (1978). The standardized exit interview. *Personnel Journal, 6,* 327-329.

Hinrichs, J. R. (1971). Employees coming and going. *Personnel, 48,* 30-35.

Hinrichs, J. R. (1975). Measurement of reasons for resignation of professionals: Questionnaire versus company and consultant exit interviews. *Journal of Applied Psychology, 60,* 530-532.

Hollinger, R. C., & Clark, J. P. (1983). *Theft by employees*. Lexington, MA: Lexington.

Jablonsky, W. A. (1975). How useful are exit interviews? *Supervisory Management, 20*(5), 8-14.

Knouse, S. B., & Giacalone, R. A. (1992). Discussion willingness in the exit interview. *Canadian Journal of Administrative Sciences, 9*, 24-29.

Lapides, G. A. (1979, May). Exit interviews as a loss prevention technique. *Security Management, 25*, 20-25.

Lefkowitz, J., & Katz, M. L. (1969). Validity of exit interviews. *Personnel Psychology, 22*, 445-455.

Littlejohn, R. F. (1988). Security studies: Accent on collaboration. *Security Management, 32*, 69-71.

Martindale, L. D. (1988). Automating the analysis of employee turnover. *Personnel, 65*, 19-21.

Meyer, G. (1991). New program conducts exit interviews. *HR Magazine, 36*(1), 27-32.

Schlenker, B. R. (1980). *Impression management*. Monterey, CA: Brooks/Cole.

Taylor, R. R. (1986). A positive guide to theft deterrence. *Personnel Journal, 65*, 36-40.

Van de Ven, A. H., & Delbecq, A. L. (1974). The effectiveness of nominal, Delphi, and interacting group decision making processes. *Academy of Management Journal, 17*, 605-621.

Watson, D., & Friend, R. (1969). Measurement of socio-evaluative anxiety. *Journal of Consulting and Clinical Psychology, 33*, 448-457.

Zarandona, J. L., & Camuso, M. A. (1985, March). A study of exit interviews: Does the last word count? *Personnel*, pp. 47-48.

Author Index

257

Subject Index

accuracy, 61
administration modes, 5
  computer, 73-97, 254-255
  computer-assisted telephone interviews
    (CATI), 79-80, 114
  electronic mail (e-mail), 112
  face-to-face interviews, 77-78
  fax, 115
  paper, 76-77
  scannable, 80-82
  telephone interviews, 78-80, 112, 114
Anita Hill-Clarence Thomas Hearings, 164,
  183-184
anonymity, 8, 18, 19, 20, 32, 95, 111, 113,
  170, 201-202
Army Research Institute (ARI), 214, 216
automation, 92

benchmarking, 122, 130, 133

Civil Rights Act of 1991, 212
cognitive bias, 181
confidentiality, 123-124, 129, 130-131, 228

consortiums, 4, 122-140
consultants, 5, 7, 139-140, 182-183
costs, 4, 9, 11, 16, 19, 73, 75, 82-83, 86,
  106, 127-129, 130, 136
crime analysis, 243

data, 84
  analysis, 21-23, 115-118
  coding, 19-20
  entry, 18-21, 75
  gathering missing, 20-21, 75, 90
  verification, 19
data analysis, 232
Defense Equal Opportunity Management
  Institute (DEOMI), 219
demographics, 7-8, 24, 171. *See also* respondent characteristics
Department of Defense Survey of Sex Roles,
  168
dimensionality, 11-12, 20, 22, 27

Equal Employment Opportunity Commission (EEOC), 171-172, 184

About the Authors

Robert L. Armacost is Assistant Professor in the Department of Industrial Engineering and Management Systems at the University of Central Florida. He earned a D.Sc. degree in operations research from George Washington University. His current research interests include the application of mathematical programming and decision models to operational problems. He has published in such journals as *Operations Research, Mathematical Programming, Decision Sciences, Journal of Business Research, European Journal of Operational Research*, and the *Journal of Business Ethics*. He is a member of ORSA, TIMS, MPS, DSI, AOM, Omega Rho, and Sigma Xi.

Stephanie Booth-Kewley (Ph.D., University of California, Riverside) is a Personnel Research Psychologist at the Navy Personnel Research and Development Center (NPRDC) in San Diego. Her current research interests are personality, survey methodology, and gender and ethnic issues. She has published articles in *Psychological Bulletin, American Psychologist*, and the *Journal of Applied Psychology*. An article she cowrote for the journal *Psychological Bulletin* (1987, Vol. 101) was the ninth most cited article in psychology during the period from 1986 through 1990 according to a study done by the Institute for Scientific Information.

Amy L. Culbertson (M.S., University of Wisconsin) is a Personnel Research Psychologist at the Navy Personnel Research and Development Center in San Diego. She served as coinvestigator on a Navy-wide project studying sexual harassment among active-duty personnel. She is also involved in research and evaluation related to the implementation of Total Quality Leadership (TQL) in the Navy. In addition to publishing on the topic of sexual harassment, she has recently cowritten a guide describing innovative personnel management systems implemented in a Navy TQL organization.

Mickey R. Dansby received his Ph.D. in social psychology from the University of Florida in 1979. He has served on the faculties of the United States Air Force Academy, Florida Institute of Technology, and Rollins College. He is past Director of Research and Analysis for the Air Force Leadership and Management Development Center and also served as Director of Research for the Defense Equal Opportunity Management Institute. He has written a number of articles and technical papers on survey research and other social psychology topics.

Richard A. Dunnington is a consultant who specializes in the development of survey systems within organizations. He coordinated the development of the IBM survey system for 25 years as manager of personnel research and later strategic personnel research. He was co-founder of the Mayflower Group, a consortium of companies who conduct organizational surveys on a regular basis. He has been a research consultant for the Mayflower Group and is currently a Fellow of the Human Resources Policy Institute, School of Management, Boston University. Since his retirement from IBM in 1982, he has worked with a number of companies including GTE, Johnson & Johnson, Exxon, Esso Chemical Canada, Schering-Plough Corporation, Duke Power, Philip Morris International, and Philadelphia Electric Company.

Solomon Dutka is Chief Executive Officer, Audits & Surveys, Fellow of the American Sub-Commission on Statistical Sampling, a member of the U.S. Census Advisory Committee, and Fellow of the American Association for the Advancement of Science. He is past President of the Market Research Council of New York and recipient of its 1984 Hall of Fame Award. He is Adjunct Professor of Statistics, New York University Graduate School of Business Administration, and has written many articles and books on the application of statistical methods to survey research.

Jack E. Edwards (Ph.D., Ohio University) is a Personnel Research Psychologist at the Navy Personnel Research and Development Center, where he has been involved in projects examining attitude measurement, officer selection, military discipline, and combat leadership. He was previously a tenured Associate Professor of Psychology at Illinois Institute of Technology. He continues to teach as Adjunct Professor at San Diego State University, California State University at San Marcos, and the California School of Professional Psychology. His research has appeared in the *Journal of Applied Psychology, Personnel Psychology, Applied Psychological Measurement,* and the *Hispanic Journal of Behavioral Sciences.*

Robert H. Faley is Associate Professor of Management at Kent State University. Before coming to the School of Business at Kent State, he was Assistant Professor at the Krannert Graduate School of Management at Purdue University. His areas of interest include employee selection and appraisal, human resource information systems, and the organizational ramifications of federal regulations, especially in the area of equal employment opportunity. He is coauthor, with Rich Arvey, of *Fairness in Selecting Employees.*

Lester R. Frankel is Senior Vice President, Audits & Surveys, Fellow and past President of the American Statistical Association, Lt. (jg) USNR Medical Statistics, Chairman, Subcommittee on Uniform Minimum Data Sets, National Committee on Vital and Health Statistics, and has served on National Research Council Panels on Decennial Census Plans (1970) and Survey Measurement of Subjective Phenomena. He is a member of the Publications Committee of the International Statistical Institute and received the Man of the Year Award (1975) from the American Association of Public Opinion Research.

Robert A. Giacalone is a tenured Associate Professor of Management Systems at the E. Claiborne Robins School of Business, University of Richmond. He has been a consultant in both the private and the public sectors and is a frequently requested speaker on a variety of management topics. He is coeditor of two books, *Impression Management in the Organization* (Lawrence Erlbaum, 1989) and *Applied Impression Management: How Image Making Affects Managerial Decisions* (Sage, 1991), and has served as Guest Editor of a special issue on Behavioral Aspects of Business Ethics in the *Journal of Business Ethics.* He has also written more than

40 articles on ethics, employee sabotage, exit interviewing, and politics in organizational life. Most recently, Sage Publications named him Series Editor for the new Sage Series in Business Ethics. Along with Paul Rosenfeld and Catherine A. Riordan, he is busily working on his third book dealing with impression management in organization.

Jamshid C. Hosseini is Assistant Professor of Management Science at Marquette University. He obtained his Ph.D. in systems science/management science from Portland State University. His research interests are in the application of multivariate techniques as well as general systems methodology tools to organizational problems. He has recent publications in *Decision Sciences, Journal of Business Research, Journal of Managerial Issues, Business Horizons, Business Ethics Quarterly, Advances in Consumer Research, Developments in Marketing Science*, and *Proceedings* of AMA, SGSR, and DSI. He is the 1992-1993 President Elect for the American Statistical Association, Milwaukee Chapter. He is a member of ASA, DSI, TIMS, and AMS.

Elyse W. Kerce (Ph.D., Claremont Graduate School) is a Personnel Research Psychologist at the Navy Personnel Research and Development Center in San Diego. She is currently principal investigator on Department of Navy Quality of Life research programs that use comprehensive surveys to assess the quality of military life for members and their families. She is also principal investigator on a project designed to assess the effectiveness of retraining programs for the rehabilitation of military members confined for disciplinary offenses.

Stephen B. Knouse (Ph.D., The Ohio State University) is Professor of Management at the University of Southwestern Louisiana. He has previously taught at Pennsylvania State University at Erie and has been a Senior Faculty Researcher in equal opportunity and in Total Quality Management at the Defense Equal Opportunity Management Institute and at the Navy Personnel Research and Development Center. His research interests are in Total Quality Management, minority work issues, and impression management in organizations. His publications have appeared in a number of journals including *Personnel, Personnel Psychology*, and the *Journal of Business Ethics*. He has edited a special issue on equal opportunity research in the military for the *International Journal of Intercultural Relations*. He is also the senior editor of *Hispanics in the Workplace* (Sage, 1992).

Dan Landis (Ph.D., general-theoretical psychology, Wayne State University, 1963) is Professor of Psychology and Director of the Center for Applied Research and Evaluation, University of Mississippi, and President of D. K. Research and Consultation Group. He is past Dean of the College of Liberal Arts at the University of Mississippi, Chair of Psychology at Indiana University-Purdue University at Indianapolis, and founder of the Center for Social Development at the University City Science Center in Philadelphia. He is the author/coauthor of more than 100 books, articles, technical reports, and presentations in areas such as perception, statistics, racial discrimination, sexual behavior and attitudes, and cross-cultural psychology and training. He is the founding and continuing editor of the *International Journal of Intercultural Relations,* the coeditor/author of *Ethnic Conflict* (Sage, 1985), and the coeditor/author of *Handbook of Intercultural Training* (a three-volume work published by Pergamon Press).

Mark A. LoVerde is Manager of Human Resources Research and Process Development at Ameritech Services, Inc., and is currently Ameritech's representative to the Telecommunications Employee Survey Consortium. He has also held a position as a market researcher for a midsized software company and has been an external consultant on employee attitude surveys for several companies. He has a master's degree in industrial and organizational psychology from the Illinois Institute of Technology, where he is working on his Ph.D. Previous publications include a chapter on employment testing and the ADA (with Gary Morris) as well as articles on statistical power and performance appraisal.

Gary W. Morris is Director of Workforce Utilization at Ameritech Services, Inc., in Hoffman Estates, Illinois. Among other things, he is responsible for overseeing Ameritech's employee opinion survey program and providing staff support to its operating entities. He is also responsible for maintaining Ameritech's affiliation with the Telecommunication Employee Survey consortium, serving as its Chairman from 1990 to 1992. Prior to joining Ameritech, he worked in human resource planning at United Airlines and, prior to that, was Assistant Professor of Psychology at Illinois Institute of Technology. He has a Ph.D. in quantitative psychology from Ohio State University and a master's degree in experimental psychology from the University of Texas at El Paso.

Paul Rosenfeld (Ph.D., State University of New York at Albany) is a Personnel Research Psychologist at the Navy Personnel Research and Development Center (NPRDC) in San Diego. He is currently principal investigator on the Navy Equal Opportunity/Sexual Harassment Survey Project, which assesses equal opportunity climate and the occurrence of sexual harassment among active-duty Navy personnel. In addition to his work with the Navy, he is also Adjunct Professor at the California School of Professional Psychology. He formerly was Assistant Professor of Psychology at Pennsylvania State University, Erie. He has previously cowritten a social psychology textbook (with his mentor James T. Tedeschi and Svenn Lindkold) and coedited (with lifelong friend and colleague Bob Giacalone) two books relating to impression management in organizational settings. He is also coeditor (with Steve Knouse and Amy Culbertson) of a book, *Hispanics in the Workplace* (Sage, 1992). He is currently coediting (with Bob Giacalone and Catherine A. Riordan) a special issue of the *American Behavioral Scientist* dealing with impression management and diversity.

Marie D. Thomas (Ph.D., Fordham University) is a Personnel Research Psychologist at the Navy Personnel Research and Development Center. She was previously a tenured Associate Professor of Psychology at the College of Mount St. Vincent in New York City. She continues to teach as Adjunct Professor at San Diego State University and California State University at San Marcos. Her research interests include gender and ethnicity issues and the role of women in the Navy. She has cowritten numerous publications on these topics.

Patricia J. Thomas directs the Office of Women and Multicultural Research at the Navy Personnel Research and Development Center in San Diego. She earned her M.S. degree from San Diego State University and has worked for the Navy for almost 30 years as Research Psychologist. Since 1975, the focus of her research has been women in the Navy and she is widely recognized as a leading authority on issues related to Navy women. Previously, she was a consultant to the Spanish Ministry of Defense as plans were formulated to accept women into the military. She served on the Department of Defense Commission on Reserve Affairs, the 1990-1991 Navy Women's Study Group, and currently is Technical Consultant to the Secretary of the Navy's Standing Committee on Military and Civilian Women.